WHAT IF AMERICA WERE A CHRISTIAN NATION AGAIN?

★ ★ ★ ★ ★

D. JAMES KENNEDY
WITH JERRY NEWCOMBE

Publishers Since 1798

THOMAS NELSON PUBLISHERS®
Nashville

A Division of Thomas Nelson, Inc.
www.ThomasNelson.com

Published in Nashville, Tennessee, by Thomas Nelson, Inc.

All Scripture quotations are from THE NEW KING JAMES VERSION unless otherwise designated. Copyright © 1982 by Thomas Nelson, Inc. Used by permission. All rights reserved.

Scriptures marked KJV are from the King James Version of the Bible.

Scripture quotations marked NIV are taken from *The Holy Bible: New International Version*®. Copyright © 1973, 1978, 1984 by International Bible Society. Used by permission of Zondervan Publishing House. All rights reserved.

Library of Congress Cataloging-in-Publication Data

Library of Congress Control Number: 2003110937
ISBN 0-7852-7042-6

Printed in the United States of America
5 6 — 07 06 05 04

This book is dedicated to Tom Rogeberg, Executive Vice President of Coral Ridge Ministries Media, Inc., who is doing a wonderful job directing our television, radio, print, Internet, and affiliated ministries in order to restore America to a Christian nation again.

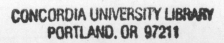

CONTENTS

PART THREE
Where Our Nation Could Be Headed:
A New Birth of Freedom

PART ONE

★ ★ ★ ★ ★

Where We Came From:
America's Godly Heritage

★ ★ ★ ★ ★

INTRODUCTION

"The wicked shall be turned into hell,
And all the nations that forget God."
—Psalm 9:17

L ITTLE DID JEREMIAH DENTON JR., AN AMERICAN
pilot who was captured in Vietnam in 1965, realize he would
return to a virtually different country. He served his country in isolation and torture at the "Hanoi Hilton" for almost eight years.
Cut off from the rest of the world and the news back home, how
could he know how much the American landscape was changing?
He was released in 1973 and experienced more than the usual culture shock on his return.

Consider the differences between the United States of 1965 and
that of 1973. During those eight years the floodgates of pornography
were opened. Abortion became legal and was becoming widespread.
Many marriages floundered, and the divorce rate skyrocketed.
Millions were beginning to live in sin, only they resented anyone calling it that. The "gay" movement was just getting started and march-
ing down the streets. They were just a couple years behind the
women's liberation movement, which had also taken to the streets.

Television producers were pushing the envelope at every turn.
(I have to admit, we have become so jaded that the risqué or questionable programs of the 1970s seem rated G compared to some of

today's fare.) And in the movie theater, anything went. In fact, the year of Denton's imprisonment, the Academy Award winner was *The Sound of Music.* A few years later, that honor was bestowed on *Midnight Cowboy,* the first X-rated movie to win such a prestigious prize. In some cases, X-rated movies had gone from back-alley, out-of-the-way hellholes populated by dirty old men in their raincoats, to mainstream movie theaters.

Here is what Jeremiah Denton said about that:

> When I came home and was driven from NAS, Norfolk to the hospital at Portsmouth and saw all these signs—X-rated movies, massage parlors, these dumpy-looking places—and I asked [my wife] Jane, "What are those?" And then saw the magazines on the magazine racks in the Naval Hospital, I was shocked. I couldn't believe that my country, a country which had succeeded in getting one nation under God placed back in the Pledge had gotten to this place . . . [for example,] Sodom and Gomorrah, homosexuality, the practice of it being viewed as a lifestyle choice, as if it's sugar or cream in your coffee. I have nothing against people who have abnormal sexual inclinations. But I have everything against regarding that as normal.[1]

In 1980, Jeremiah ran for the United States Senate and won. He became a powerful advocate for positive values. He promoted abstinence programs and pro-family legislation. But he lost his bid for reelection in 1986. Apparently, even the state of Alabama was not ready for a full return to the Judeo-Christian values that had helped create the United States of America.

FROM *LEAVE IT TO BEAVER* TO *BEAVIS AND BUTTHEAD*

In less than forty years, our culture has gone from the strong family values of a society with a Christian consensus to a society that glorifies violence, illicit sex, and rebellion. We have severed ourselves from the roots of what made us great in the first place. We have gone from *Leave It to Beaver* to *Beavis and Butthead* in some thirty to forty years.

During the Civil War, in his classic Gettysburg Address, President Lincoln said that this nation needed "a new birth of freedom."[2] Today, we are engaged in another type of civil war, and we are again in need of a new birth of freedom.

OUR NATION'S ROOTS

All nations that have ever existed have been founded upon some theistic or antitheistic principle—whether the Hinduism of India, the Confucianism of China, the Mohammedanism of Saudi Arabia, or the atheism of modern China and the former Soviet Union. If we know our history, we know that America was a nation founded upon Christ and His Word. But that foundation is crumbling in our time.

Today some in our country are busily tearing apart that foundation. They would gnash their teeth at the idea that this is a Christian nation and will not be satisfied until they have removed every vestige of our Christian heritage from not only the minds, but also the monuments of this country.

What made us great in the first place is our rich Christian heritage. It's time to reclaim it. In this book, I set out to document the incontrovertible facts that America began as a Christian nation; that background comprises Part One, "America's Godly Heritage." In Part Two, "The Culture Clash," I will examine several of the issues that are tearing us apart as a country. Finally in Part Three, "A New Birth of Freedom," I will discuss how we can get back on track before it's too late.

Please note that in no way am I advocating a theocracy. Nor are any reputable members of the so-called religious right. Not one of them. There was only one true theocracy in the history of the world, and that was ancient Israel. All I am advocating is a return, as much as possible, to the faith of our nation's founders. I am calling for full religious liberty once again so the gospel can go forth unhindered and uncensored. I am calling for an end to the secular witch hunt against "any sneaky vestiges of religion left in public places."[3]

ONE NATION UNDER GOD

It's time we rediscovered what it means to be "one nation under God," as President Abraham Lincoln said in the Gettysburg Address. It's time we understand the full meaning of our national motto, "In God we trust." It's time we stop the "state-sanctioned atheism" that has been stripping the public square of plaques of the Ten Commandments or statues of Christ or anything else that offends secular sensibilities. The great misunderstanding of "the separation of church and state" (words not found in our Constitution) is closer in spirit and letter of the law to the old Soviet Union than it is to the spirit, letter of the law, actions, and writings of the founders of this country. That includes even the least religious among them, such as Thomas Jefferson and Ben Franklin.

Here's my challenge for you to consider at the outset. Suppose someone now were to leave our country for eight years, as Jeremiah Denton did. When he returned, would he find it better, worse, or about the same?

May God grant that America become a truly Christian nation once again, so that the answer would be "better." And may our nation experience a new birth of freedom.

★ ★ ★ ★ ★

ONE

GOD'S PROVIDENTIAL HAND ON AMERICA

"Extol Him who rides on the clouds."
—PSALM 68:4

HAVE YOU EVER WONDERED ABOUT THE EYE ON THE back of the dollar bill? What is that all about? And there's a foreign saying with it: *Annuit Coeptis*. What does that mean? It's simply Latin for "He has favored our undertakings." *He* being? God. The eye represents the eye of God, of Providence, and refers to the role of Providence in the founding of America.[1]

But America has amnesia. We have forgotten the true founder of this great land: He who "plants His footsteps in the sea and rides upon the storm."[2] The Scripture declares, "Let God arise, let His enemies be scattered; let those also who hate Him flee before Him" (Ps. 68:1), and "Sing to God, sing praises to His name; extol Him who rides on the clouds, by His name YAH, and rejoice before Him" (Ps. 68:4). The founders of this country had multiple reasons to believe that God was scattering their enemies.

God is sovereign over the universe, over history, over the nations, over all His creation. "For He commands and raises the stormy wind, which lifts up the waves of the sea" (Ps. 107:25). I believe that if we study the history of America (even centuries before its settling and founding), we can see the hand of God at work. But we have not remembered the invisible hand of that One who brought us to Plymouth Rock and established our nation of religious freedom.

THE GREATEST HERO

We would do well to remember the greatest hero who ever fought for the freedom of America, that One who has fought to establish this Christian land, where God may be worshiped in spirit and truth, the gospel may be proclaimed freely, and Christ may be adored and His kingdom advanced.[3]

That was the reason the Pilgrims and Puritans came to this nation: to advance the gospel and kingdom of our Lord, Jesus Christ.[4] This statement typifies what we find in America's founding documents, e.g., the colonial charters, compacts, covenants, and codes of law.

GOD'S ACTIONS IN THE BIBLE

Over and over in the Bible we read about God's sovereign acts as the ultimate ruler of the nations. He raises up and tears down whom He will so that His redemptive purposes may be accomplished. For example, He provided a land flowing with milk and honey for His people. But to acquire this land, they had to conquer the Canaanites, with His help. The wickedness of the Canaanites was so intense that it was like a cancer to humankind early on in the history of nations. God was using His people to remove this cancer from humanity (see Deut. 9:5).

The sovereign God declares about Himself, through Isaiah the prophet:

I am the LORD, and there is no other;
There is no God besides Me.
I will gird you, though you have not known Me,

That they may know from the rising of the sun to its setting
That there is none besides Me.
I am the LORD, and there is no other . . . (Isa. 45:5–6).

And so, to achieve His sovereign purposes, God gave His people victory over His enemies, especially in circumstances that were *humanly impossible*. We see this again and again in the Bible:

- At God's instructions, the Israelites marched seven times around Jericho and the priests blew trumpets. The seventh time, as the people shouted, the walls fell down, and the Hebrews were able to conquer their enemy (Josh. 5 and 6).

- God worked repeated miracles so that the Hebrews could conquer the Canaanites and claim the land of Israel as their own. The entire book of Joshua tells this story.

- Jumping ahead to centuries later, the Syrian army was determined to take the prophet Elisha captive and bring him back to Syria. So, under cover of darkness, the Syrian soldiers surrounded the prophet's home in Dothan. Humanly speaking, there was no way out. But come morning, Elisha didn't fear, and his servant couldn't understand why he was so calm. The prophet asked the Lord to open the servant's eyes that he might see the supernatural help awaiting Elisha's command. "And behold, the mountain was full of horses and chariots of fire all around Elisha" (2 Kings 6:17). God in His sovereignty won the battle that day, which ended on a peaceful note.

- One night, thousands upon thousands of Assyrian troops surrounded Judah, poised to strike the next day. King Hezekiah had no recourse but prayer. In the middle of the night, an angel of the Lord struck the Assyrians and slew 185,000 of them. That ended the threat (2 Kings 19).

Often in the Bible we see some king who rose up in his own strength—or so it would seem—only to find out that God was acting behind the scenes. God raised this man up, even, for instance, if it was to wreak vengeance on God's own rebellious people. (God is no respecter of persons. When the Canaanites were irredeemably wicked, He used the Israelites to judge them. Later, when the Israelites were hopelessly evil, He used the Assyrians and the Babylonians to judge them.)

The ancient Hebrew prophet Habakkuk puzzled over one episode like this. How could a holy and perfect God use sinful men, the Assyrians, to punish a sinful people, the Israelites, especially in light of the fact that the former were more sinful than the latter? God answered Habakkuk that the Assyrians likewise would face their judgment. For now, though, God was using the Assyrians for His sovereign purposes, to punish His wayward people—judgment always begins at the household of God.

We see God's sovereign hand throughout the Bible. In His presence, Isaiah reminds us, the nations are like dust on a scale (Is. 40:15). Is it too much to believe that God is also sovereign over history? I don't think so. As Helmut Thielecke once put it (writing in the 1960s), "When the drama of history is over, Jesus Christ will stand alone upon the stage. All the great figures of history—Pharaoh, Alexander the Great, Charlemagne, Churchill, Stalin, . . . Mao Tse-Tung—will realize they have been bit actors in a drama produced by another."[5] I believe God has acted sovereignly in history, and if we know the right clues to look for, we can discern His hand.

GOD'S ACTIONS IN AMERICA

The early Americans felt that God helped them repeatedly. Without His help, they could not have settled their colonies or even survived in the difficult conditions in this initially hostile land. They certainly could not have defeated the greatest military power in the world with a ragtag army of farmers who were simply trying to protect their homeland. But they, too, had read the Bible stories of Joshua, Hezekiah, and Elisha. Was it unreasonable for them to assume that the sovereign Lord was aiding their cause?

In 1778 George Washington wrote a letter to a fellow patriot, Thomas Nelson Jr., in which he marveled at how much the Lord was helping the American cause: "The hand of Providence has been so conspicuous in all this [the colonies' victories in the American War for Independence], that he must be worse than an infidel that lacks faith, and more than wicked, that has not gratitude enough to acknowledge his obligations."[6] In other words, God has helped us so much that anyone who can't see that and can't thank Him must be worse than an unbeliever.

Like George Washington, I believe that God established this land of America, a nation in His providence, a nation unique in the history of the world. Did you know that America was the first nation in the history of this planet that had freedom of religion? Many people today don't realize this. They think it was just a commonplace sort of thing. Religious tyranny prevailed all over the globe. Gradually some nations rose to religious tolerance, such as England (long after their mistreatment of the Pilgrims, Puritans, Quakers, and the like), but under mere religious tolerance. The state still discriminated against those believers who dissented against the prevailing state church. In fact, if one was a religious dissenter in a country practicing religious tolerance, there were often limits on one's political and economic citizenship rights. Only in America was full religious freedom granted for the very first time.

I believe that God set our continent apart—separating it by two oceans—not to be discovered until around the time of the Reformation. Here God established a certain sort of nation, a nation that was founded by the Pilgrims and the Puritans and others who came with evangelical Christianity. Here the Bible was believed and the gospel was preached. It was an evangelical nation. As late as 1775, 98 percent of the people were of this basic religious persuasion.[7]

How did this come to be? Humanly speaking, we could have easily been something else. But if God, in His providence, ordained that this is what this nation should be, then all down through the ages, in fact from all eternity, God intended that it would be so. He guided our path and led us to this end.

In the words of William Cowper, the hymn writer: "God moves in a mysterious way, His wonders to perform. He plants His footsteps on the sea, and rides upon the storm."[8] So come with me back through the centuries, and let us ride with God upon the winds, the sea, and the storm. Let us see and acknowledge His invisible hand—the One who led us to this place, where we could begin as an evangelical Christian nation, the nation that even now does more to send the gospel to the four corners of the world than any nation in history. A nation where Christ is adored and His Word is believed by tens of millions.

North America could have been a Spanish nation.

THE SPANISH ATTEMPTS

Consider the career of Columbus himself and how that could have affected the future of this nation. Columbus, we are told, was the discoverer of America. If that is the case, then why was America not colonized by the Portuguese or the Spanish, as were Central America, the Caribbean, and South America?

Columbus's ship, historians tell us, was headed directly toward the Carolinas. But during the long voyage, the frightened, restless crew threatened mutiny. They planned to throw the admiral overboard and return to Europe. Suddenly, the cry went up that land had been sighted to the southwest. Columbus's log tells us that they headed toward that land, but what they had seen was merely a cloud on the horizon. Still the mutiny was averted.

Several days later, however, the men were once again ready to overthrow the admiral. Oddly enough, a flock of birds flew over the ship, heading southwest. A second correction was made, which diverted the ship from heading toward north Florida; thus, Columbus landed at San Salvador (in the Bahamas). For all of his faults, Columbus was motivated by the Lord to make his historic, death-defying voyage. Nonetheless, the colonies the Spanish settled turned out extremely different from those settled by the Pilgrims and Puritans from England. And to think, if it had not been for the flight of some birds, America would probably have the same culture and religion as that of South and Central America today.

Were the cloud and those feathered creatures just a coincidence, or the hand of God? I believe that just as God used a talking donkey to set Balaam straight (Num. 22:21–31), so He used a cloud and a flight of birds to change Columbus's destination.

THE "INVINCIBLE" ARMADA

A century later, the Spaniards tried to conquer and punish Great Britain—which could have directly changed the future of America. In 1588 (thirty-two years before the Pilgrims sailed), the greatest armada that had ever been seen in the history of the world flowed out of Spain's rivers into the ocean. The "Invincible Armada," the Spanish Armada, determined once and for all to crush and destroy the English. This was an attempt by Catholic Spain to bring Protestant England back under the primacy of the pope. But not far from Lisbon, a storm destroyed a number of Spanish ships. In this weakened condition, the Spaniards met the British, were routed, and tried to flee the northern route past Scotland, where a succession of storms totally destroyed the "invincible" armada. England was left as the mistress of the seas. Therefore, Anglo-Saxons and Celtics rather than the Spaniards became the dominant force in Europe and in America.

The hand of God? Or mere coincidence?

THE FRENCH ATTEMPTS

On the other hand, this nation could have been French and could have carried the type of government and religion that the French would have brought with it. Again, the providential hand of God intervened.

In 1606, fourteen years before the Pilgrims landed at Plymouth, the French made an effort to colonize New England. Under the leadership of Pierre DeMonts, they made three attempts. On the first two, their ships were driven from the coast by strong winds, while on the third attempt, the ships were destroyed on the treacherous shoals of Cape Cod, and DeMonts was killed.

Later, after the English had colonized New England, the French made another attempt to colonize the New World—this time they would have to destroy the British who already had multiple Puritan settlements there. In 1746, the French swept down from Nova Scotia under the leadership of the Duke D'Anville, with forty men-of-war and thousands of French troops, determined to completely wipe out the English colonists and make New England a French possession.

Receiving intelligence of this coming attack, Reverend Mr. Prince in the Old South Church at Boston stood up before the congregation and called for a day of fasting and prayer so God would intervene. As he prayed, the shutters of the church suddenly began to rattle, startling the whole congregation. He stopped praying and realized that a strong wind had begun to blow. So he returned to even more earnest prayer. Gradually the wind picked up until it became a raging gale. The Duke D'Anville was not only routed, his fleet was destroyed. Thousands of troops were drowned, and the duke and his leading general committed suicide.

Jumping ahead a century, in the great battle of Waterloo in 1815, the pronouncement of judgment against Napoleon was to come to pass. When asked whose side God was on, Napoleon responded, "God is on the side of the final reserve," a pragmatic response. In other words, whichever army held a force in reserve and would be able to bring it forward at the critical moment would be the victor, and that, he concluded, was the side God was on.

At the battle of Waterloo, as the British and French were engaged in this great conflict that would decide the future of Europe and subsequently of America, Marshal Marquis de Grouchy had the final reserve. But, as he was bringing it forward to join Napoleon in routing the British, God opened the fountains of heaven and poured out a rain that turned the earth to mud, so the forces of de Grouchy and his artillery were not able to arrive in time. The issue was already divinely settled by the time his forces came upon the scene.

As with all of these events, I believe it was God at work. He is the One who plants His footsteps upon the sea and rides upon the storm. Someone once quipped that a coincidence is a miracle in which God chooses to remain anonymous.

THE PILGRIMS' LAND

Consider God's providential hand during the colonial period. The *Mayflower* itself was a wine cargo boat. The wine had penetrated much of the interior of the ship, which prevented many diseases from afflicting the Pilgrims and strangers on that historic voyage in 1620. Death was common on such voyages, yet only one man died on the voyage over, a profane, Pilgrim-hating crew member.

Furthermore, at the Pilgrims' coming, these shores bristled with tomahawks, arrows, and hostile natives all along the east coast, as the Spanish had discovered when they tried to settle in Florida. One of the fiercest of those tribes dwelt near Plymouth and most surely would have slaughtered those Pilgrims in the first few days of their arrival. However, three years before they arrived, a pestilence destroyed virtually all of the Indians, leaving nothing but the corn they had stored up for winter, the same corn that saved the Pilgrims from utter extinction during that first winter.

There is probably no place else on the east coast of America where they could have survived. You may know that the Pilgrims tried to leave and go farther south but again, the winds drove them back. These same winds were under the direction of the invisible hand of the Almighty, who conducts the affairs of men.

Another providential event occurred in 1609, before the Pilgrims came. Samuel de Champlain, the French general from Quebec, attacked the Iroquois Indians, killing a number of them. With the blast of his harquebus, he had forever alienated the Iroquois, making them implacable foes of the French and allies of the English during the French and Indian wars. These wars could have, again, destroyed the English settlements, Puritan and all, and established the French in this country, as well as Canada.

The Puritans were spiritual cousins of the Pilgrims, who followed them in migrating to this land in the 1630s and quickly outnumbered them. They did their best to apply biblical principles to civil government and thus laid an important foundation for this country. The great leader of the Puritans was John Winthrop, who articulated their vision in 1630 in this now-famous line: "We must consider that we shall be as a City upon a Hill, the eyes of all people are upon us."[9] To this day, presidents, politicians, commentators, pastors, and authors cite this classic line from the early days of America. In a sense, it helped create the template for a uniquely free and Christian America.

Providence also protected the father of our nation through many difficult battles.

PROVIDENCE AND GEORGE WASHINGTON

Time and again, before and during the War for Independence, God seemed to act on America's behalf. For example, He repeatedly spared the life of the military general who led us to victory, George Washington. Once, in 1755, during the French and Indian Wars, when he was in his early twenties, Washington survived a massacre of sorts in a battle outside Pittsburgh by the banks of the Monongahela River. An Indian who lay in concealment leaped up and fired at Washington when he was only three or four paces away. Yet the Indian missed the general. Another Indian shot fifteen bullets at Washington and missed him fifteen times. During this same encounter Washington had two horses shot out from under him. He had four bullet holes in his coat.

After he survived this incredible battle, when all the other British and American officers were killed, Colonel Washington wrote his brother, "Death was leveling my companions on every side of me; but, by the all-powerful dispensations of Providence, I have been protected."[10] David Barton has written a book about this battle and the way God spared Washington's life; it's appropriately entitled, *The Bulletproof George Washington*.[11] He was never once wounded in all the years that he served his country.

Jumping ahead to the American Revolution, one time, outside Philadelphia, Major Patrick Ferguson of the British Army and his troops hid in the woods, waiting to ambush American soldiers. As Ferguson, who was on horseback, scanned the site, a man with a tall hat rode toward him. The two men eyed each other briefly, but the horseman with the tall hat simply turned aside and trotted away. Major Ferguson leveled his gun between the shoulder blades of the retreating figure and said he could easily have put four or five bullets in this man's back. But he hated to shoot a man in the back. Later he learned the identity of that figure: George Washington.

And then came the famous incident at Brooklyn Heights in 1776, when the British Army surrounded Washington's army on land while the British fleet lay offshore. There was no way of escape; the following morning they would be destroyed. Washington determined to try to slip his army away during the night on every rowboat and sloop that he could muster. His officers told him they would be seen from the British frigates and destroyed, but Washington resolved to go ahead. As they started to embark, a fog rolled in from the sea, totally concealing them. When the fog lifted in the morning, the British were astounded to find that the American Army had completely disappeared.

Even more amazing is the fact that a woman in Brooklyn who was a British sympathizer discovered Washington's plan and hastily sent her servant to reveal it to the British. But by the providence of God, the servant rushed into the Hessian lines. These Hessians, German mercenaries hired by the British, could not understand one word the servant spoke. They kept him until the morning when they had an interpreter who told them, too late, what Washington was going to do—and by this time had already done.

Later Washington's army was trapped in Trenton. The ground was muddy from rain and the artillery could not be moved. Seeing the helpless condition of the American army and the lateness of the hour, the British determined to rest overnight, believing the Americans incapable of escape. But during the night, the wind changed and blew from the north and the temperature plummeted. The wet ground froze solid as concrete, and Washington, taking the advantage, led his artillery away down a side road. By dawn he had escaped.

And then, of course, there was Yorktown in 1781. Many people do not realize that when Cornwallis discovered he was trapped at Yorktown with no place to go, he decided to emulate what Washington had done. Consequently, during that final night, he determined to make his escape, and he began to slip away in boats under cover of darkness. But when a good portion of his army was afloat in small boats, a sudden storm came up and swamped them, leaving Cornwallis in utter despair. The following morning, he and his British troops came out between twin lines of Americans to the slow beat of drums, carrying the white flag of surrender. For indeed, He who planteth His feet upon the sea and rideth upon the storm had determined that it was neither to be Britain's state church nor her monarchy that would govern America. Rather, America would be a free nation, and it would be that Puritan and evangelical form of Christianity that would give birth to our nation.

Was this the hand of God, or merely coincidence? Again, Washington himself said that an American who was ungrateful to God in light of all of His providential acts on behalf of our country was "worse than an infidel."[12]

A HURRICANE HELPS

Even a hurricane was used by God to shape our institutions. In the Leeward Islands, before the time of the Revolution, a great hurricane blasted those islands, as many had before. A fifteen-year-old boy witnessed this particular storm's fury on the island of Nevus and wrote a magnificently stated, graphic account. He sent his account to a newspaper, where it was printed and picked up by others. Here is one sentence: "The roaring of the sea and wind— fiery meteors flying about in the air—the prodigious glare of almost perpetual lightning—the crash of the falling houses—and the ear-piercing shrieks of the distressed, were sufficient to strike astonishment into Angels."[13] Overnight, this teenage boy discovered that he was a celebrity in the West Indies. His precociousness observed, he was sent to Boston and New York for schooling, and thus Alexander Hamilton, whose brilliance helped forge the documents and institutions of this nation, struck a match to light the American flame for independence. But it was first ignited by Him who rides upon the storm.

★ ★ ★ ★ ★

TWO

The Pilgrim Adventure

"Blessed are those who are persecuted
for righteousness' sake,
For theirs is the kingdom of heaven."
—JESUS CHRIST, MATTHEW 5:10

E VERY NOVEMBER, WE TAKE TIME OFF TO BE WITH family and loved ones and enjoy food, fellowship, and more food. This special American festival of Thanksgiving is an annual, culture-wide, built-in reminder of our unique Christian heritage.

And we all know that Thanksgiving was first celebrated by the Pilgrims, those hardy and brave men and women who came to these shores so long ago and founded this nation for us. We owe them such a debt of gratitude.

But who exactly were they?

Why did they come?

What do they have to say to us today?

Unfortunately, our public schools have usually expurgated from our history books any of the religious or spiritual significance of their coming. In fact, incredible as it may seem, one textbook, in discussing the first Thanksgiving celebration, has the Pilgrims giving thanks to the Indians, not to God!

So the average young person growing up today knows virtually nothing about the real founding of this country. Who were the Pilgrims? Or should I say, *what* were the Pilgrims? They were a congregation of dedicated Christians. Note that: *a congregation.*

They wanted to live their lives in peace and serve the Lord, but they also desired to be intermediaries ("stepping stones," as they worded it) for the promotion of the gospel into all the world.[1]

A CHURCH-RELOCATION PROJECT

It's hard for many to believe, but America essentially began as a church-relocation project. To understand that church and why they relocated, we have to go back to the seventeenth century. About the year 1600 and a little before, great foment was taking place in the Church of England. Though the church had cut its ties with Rome through Henry VIII in the early 1500s, there was little change in church teaching and practice. But there was a tremendous movement called the Puritan Movement, which began, of course, with Martin Luther, and more specifically with John Calvin, the reformer of Geneva. Their teaching had begun to influence many throughout Europe. In fact, many people had fled from England and Scotland to Geneva as refugees, and had later returned to purify the church and its doctrine, teaching, life, government, and customs.

But they met with a great deal of opposition from the established church in England. So a smaller group, known as the Separatists, decided to separate from the church. We know them today as the Pilgrims. "Pilgrims," of course, meant that they were wanderers—wanderers across many thousands of miles of this planet. They derived their name from 1 Peter 2:11: "Beloved, I beg you as sojourners and *pilgrims* . . ." [emphasis mine]. And in that sense, all true Christians are pilgrims because our real home is in heaven.

This secret congregation began in eastern England in the counties of Lincolnshire, Yorkshire, and Nottinghamshire, particularly in the sleepy town of Scrooby. In 1606 a group of these Separatists made a covenant with God and with each other to walk according to all the light God had given them—or would yet give them—out of His Word, according to the best of their ability, regardless of persecution or suffering.

The most famous of the Pilgrims, William Bradford, joined the secret group in Scrooby as a twelve-year-old boy. Bradford was an orphan, and Elder William Brewster practically adopted him.

Despite his young age, Bradford had delved into the Word of God, and he was so deep in his studies that every Sunday he walked twelve miles to church and twelve miles back home again in order to hear what he described as the illuminating ministry of Richard Clyfton. This was the beginning of William Bradford's prayerful, watchful, careful walk with the Lord. In spite of the fact that many people urged him to stay away from the Puritans and the Separatists, he would not be dissuaded from this. Eventually, in America, William Bradford became their second governor and was reelected to that post year after year. He also wrote one of the first books ever penned on American soil, *Of Plymouth Plantation*, a firsthand account that chronicles the whole Pilgrim saga.

A young man named John Robinson came to assist Richard Clyfton as the minister of this church, and shortly thereafter he replaced him when Clyfton left to go to Amsterdam. Robinson had graduated from Cambridge University Divinity School and had been ordained as a minister in the Church of England. This remarkable young man became known as "the Pilgrim's pastor." He loved his congregation, and they loved him.

It is said that he was a brilliant young man who loved to examine issues thoroughly until he knew every aspect of them. Well schooled in Greek, Hebrew, Latin, and theology, Robinson kept peace with others. A man of irenic disposition, he was affable and sociable. He was also a Puritan determined to live according to the Word of God, but he met so much opposition that he finally decided he would withdraw from the church and join the Separatists at Scrooby.

Robinson met Richard Clyfton, interestingly enough, in Elder

William Brewster's manor home. Some years before, Brewster's father had come to take care of the manor house of the Archbishop of York, who was absent. Brewster lived there as a regent to collect ecclesiastical taxes and fees from the local population. Ironically, the Pilgrims first began to meet in the manor house of that Anglican archbishop.

During the first few years of this Scrooby congregation, the Pilgrims would hide out and move from place to place. Their homes were watched, and they were thrown in jail. William Bradford points out that the whole Pilgrim story begins with persecution, and so he opens *Of Plymouth Plantation* on this note: "It is well known unto the godly . . . how ever since the first breaking out of the light of the gospel in our honorable nation of England, Satan hath raised, maintained and continued [wars and oppositions] against the saints."[2]

There was little freedom for nonconformists in the time of Elizabeth, so when James I came to the throne, the Separatists hoped that things would get better. Instead they got worse. He felt that the only way he could control the church was through the bishops, and if he lost the power of the church, it would subvert his reign. His motto was "No Bishop, no King."[3]

James I declared of religious nonconformists (Puritans, Pilgrims, Presbyterians), "I will make them conform, or I will harry them out of the land or do worse."[4] One of the groups that he "harried out of the land" of England was this little underground church at Scrooby.

At Scrooby they had a precious treasure: the Bible in their own language—the Geneva Bible. This was against the law at this time for the Church of England, just as it had been for the Church of Rome. The late Dr. Robert Bartlett, a direct Pilgrim descendent, Pilgrim expert, and author of *The Pilgrim Way*, observes, "It was against the law to have any kind of a religious meeting—secret, separate from the Church of England or even to read the Bible in public. Those were criminal offenses. So all these meetings were held secretly by these seekers who wanted to improve the Church of England."[5]

It's so amazing to think that millions alive today know the name of King James solely because of the classic, high-quality Bible translation that bears his name. Yet his push for that 1611 translation was essentially an anti-Puritan measure.

King James I set out to translate the Scriptures in order to replace an influential version he disdained, the Geneva Bible, which came out in 1560 and was widespread for two generations. The Pilgrims and Puritans loved this Bible. Robert Linder points out, "Its Calvinistic annotations greatly irritated James I of England, but delighted and instructed his increasingly Puritan subjects."[6] It wasn't really the text or the translation of the Scriptures that bothered the king. It was the footnotes—the "Calvinistic annotations" on the sides and at the bottom. Commentaries on passages such as "We ought to obey God rather than men" (Acts 5:29) were enough to raise any monarch's eyebrows.

As the Puritans and the Pilgrims read the Word of God, they realized that things were not right in the church or in the land. The whole movement that brought these people to America began when people began to study the holy Scriptures for themselves. So this is a nation that was born of the Bible, even as *Newsweek* said some years ago. "Historians are now coming to realize that the Bible, even more than the Constitution, founded this nation of America."[7]

HARRIED OUT OF THE LAND

Finally, Robinson and his people decided they could do nothing else but leave England so they could worship according to the Word of God and the dictates of their consciences. The Netherlands was their chosen place of refuge.

This was not an easy step to take. Bradford writes, "Being thus constrained to leave their native soil and country, their lands and livings, and all their friends and familiar acquaintance . . . it was by many thought an adventure almost desperate; a case intolerable and a misery worse than death."[8]

Here they were, determined to go to Holland, a place of religious liberty, to which others had gone before. They made arrangements with an English captain to take them there. However, as they got in the long boats to go out to the ship, they were robbed of their money and possessions, brought back to the magistrates, and thrown into prison. The ship's captain had betrayed them. Thus, although King James threatened to harry nonconformists *out* of the land, the Pilgrims found that their departure was not welcomed either.

After being imprisoned for some time, they were finally released, and after many other difficulties, they arranged with a Dutch captain to take them to Amsterdam. And so, piece by piece, group by group, they finally were back together in Amsterdam, where there were also some other English congregations.

THEIR TIME IN HOLLAND

The Pilgrims' time in Holland was sweet at first. They could finally worship Christ freely. Bradford says of it, "Being thus settled (after many difficulties) they continued many years in a comfortable condition, enjoying much sweet and delightful society and spiritual comfort together in the ways of God."[9]

They initially settled in Amsterdam for a year, but discovered that many of the English-speaking congregations in that city were overly argumentative. Being a man of peace, John Robinson, in concert with his congregation, decided they should move away from the endless controversies, so they went to the interior city of Leyden for eleven more years.

The Pilgrims were in Holland a total of twelve years, and it was during those years that Robinson formed and developed this people into what would be in a sense the founding fathers and mothers of our country.

After their years in Leyden, the Pilgrims realized they had to move on again. The Dutch people at that time were very worldly, and there was a great deal of impiety and ungodliness among them. The Sabbath was grossly profaned. The children of the Pilgrims were growing up, and some were marrying Dutch people; the congregation was afraid that it would disappear over time. So they decided to move to a new land where they could worship and live according to the teachings of the Scripture.

Bradford writes, "After they had lived in this city about some eleven or twelve years . . . and sundry of them were taken away by death . . . and they saw and found by experience the hardness of the place and country . . . yea, some preferred and chose the prisons in England rather than this liberty in Holland with these afflictions."[10]

The Journey to America

The Pilgrims faced a dilemma. They knew they could neither stay in Holland nor return to England. Instead, they chose to go to the New World. Reports of the first permanent English settlement in America—Jamestown—were beginning to be heard in the Old World. Although Jamestown certainly had its share of problems, this idea was attractive to the Pilgrims because they could worship in peace and rear their children in the faith.

They determined that they could not all go to America at once. In 1620, only a minority was willing and able to make the long trip across the Atlantic. So as eager as Pastor Robinson was to go, he decided to stay with the majority, which included wives, children, and the elderly, until the day when he could join them in America.

Robinson wrote a letter to the Pilgrims who were leaving, in which he reminded them to imitate the pattern of self-government that they had followed as a congregation for years: "Lastly, whereas you are to become a body politic, using amongst yourselves civil government, and are not furnished with any persons of special eminence above the rest, to be chosen by you into office of government. Let your wisdom and godliness appear, not only in choosing such persons as do entirely love, and will diligently promote the common good, but also in yielding unto them all due honor and obedience in their lawful administrations."[11] Note the democratic principles they put into practice as they sought to live according to the precepts of the Bible.

THE VOYAGE OF THE MAYFLOWER

The *Mayflower*'s voyage was pleasant at first, and then horrific. Bradford writes, "After they had enjoyed fair winds and weather for a season, they were encountered many times with cross winds and met with fierce storms with which the ship was [wickedly] shaken."[12]

After sixty-six days through this howling, fierce, and vast wilderness of sea, they made it to Cape Cod. They had hoped to arrive there in late summer, but many delays brought them to the Cape during the dead of winter, a very dreary time. When they attempted to sail south, they were completely hindered by the dangerous shoals along the coast, which they interpreted as the hand of God, guiding them to stay there. So they landed on the Provincetown tip and tried to set up some sort of protection against the snow, wind, and cold. There were no Howard Johnson Motor Lodges to stop in!

William Bradford wrote, "Being thus arrived in a good harbor, and brought safe to land, they fell upon their knees and blessed the God of heaven who had brought them over the vast and furious ocean, and delivered them from all the perils and miseries thereof, again to set their feet on the firm and stable earth."[13]

THE MAYFLOWER COMPACT

At this point, the Pilgrims were forced to improvise. Before they left England, they had received official permission—ironically enough from King James, as mediated by a friend of theirs in high places—to establish a colony in the northern parts of Virginia, near and around present-day New York City. But now here they were, several miles from there, having no way in the harsh winter to get where they were supposed to be. So they decided to create a charter for self-government for all the men to sign. One hundred sixty-seven years later this charter—the Mayflower Compact—became the cornerstone of the United States Constitution. This classic document, a political restatement of their spiritual covenant made fourteen years earlier, begins by recognizing the hand of God who had been leading them all along:

> In the name of God, Amen. We whose names are underwritten, the loyal subjects of our dread sovereign lord, King James . . . Having undertaken for the glory of God, and advancement of the Christian faith, and the honor of our king and country, a voyage to plant the first colony in the northern parts of Virginia; do by these present, solemnly and mutually in the presence of God and one of another, covenant and combine ourselves together into a civil body politic, for our better ordering and preservation, and furtherance of the ends aforesaid.[14]

In *A History of the English-Speaking Peoples*, Winston Churchill calls the Mayflower Compact "one of the remarkable documents in history."[15] Paul Johnson, author of *A History of the American People*, points out that the Mayflower Compact was "the single most important formative event in early American history, which would ultimately have an important bearing on the crisis of the American Republic."[16] The great nineteenth-century historian George Bancroft writes, "In the cabin of the *Mayflower* humanity recovered its rights, and instituted government on the basis of 'equal laws' enacted by all the people for 'the general good.'"[17] Even today, pundits refer to the "body politic," echoing this charter.

After making history in the captain's quarters of the ship, the Pilgrims turned to more mundane matters—trying to find a place to settle down. They explored up and down the Cape Cod coast and finally settled on Plymouth, where they found a clearing.

During that first winter of 1620–21, they had to stay aboard the ship; it was too difficult to build homes in the freezing wilderness. Three or four of them died just about every day. Some of the crew members who were dying of contagious diseases were abandoned by their former drinking buddies. Only the Pilgrims helped them. This touched the hard hearts of some of the crew. "Oh!" one of them cried to the Pilgrims, "you, I now see, show your love like Christians indeed one to another, but we let one another lie and die like dogs."[18]

Fortunately the winter did not last long. The first mild day of spring came March 3, but by this time half of the Pilgrims were dead. If it had been a long winter, they might all have died, and America would have had an altogether different history.

It was amazing that the Pilgrims landed where they did. Being blown off course turned out to be beneficial to their survival. For example, the few Indians they encountered were not as significant a threat as they could have been. As mentioned previously, a plague had struck the area about three years before the Pilgrims came, killing about 95 percent of the Indians. The Pilgrims came to land that was already cleared for them by those no longer living. And one of the Native Americans who did survive, Squanto, spoke English and helped them successfully settle there. Furthermore, he was an intermediary to forge a long-lasting peace treaty with surrounding tribes.

In the spring, the *Mayflower* sailed back to England with not one Pilgrim aboard. No one was abandoning the mission or breaking the covenant, despite the inauspicious start. The Pilgrims also managed to get through the second year. Eventually, over the course of several years, many members of the Pilgrim church from

Leyden came to join them in their new land. Unfortunately, Pastor John Robinson never saw the New World. In 1625 he suddenly took ill and died in just a couple of days. So Elder William Brewster, who had been sent on the first ship to America to be the acting pastor, continued to lead the congregation.

The Pilgrims showed great devotion to Christ every Sabbath. They had morning services at eight, nine, ten, and eleven o'clock. A one-hour sermon was preached at each service—except everyone stayed for the *entire* four hours. First Brewster would preach for an hour, and then some member of the congregation would preach for an hour, and another one for another hour, and of course, there were prayers and the singing of songs as well (usually the Psalms).

They met again in the afternoon, where they had another four hours of worship. So, each Sabbath day, the Pilgrims worshiped God in eight hours of services, a true indication of their dedication.

In *Of Plymouth Plantation,* William Bradford summarizes the whole Pilgrim adventure, giving God all the glory:

> Thus out of small beginnings greater things have been produced by His hand that made all things of nothing, and gives being to all things that are; and, as one small candle may light a thousand, so the light here kindled hath shone unto many, yea in some sort to our whole nation; let the glorious name of Jehovah have all the praise.[19]

★ ★ ★ ★ ★

THREE

"Our Lives, Our Fortunes, Our Sacred Honor"

"Where the Spirit of the Lord is,
there is liberty."
—2 Corinthians 3:17

In 1776, fifty-six men—representing three million people—signed perhaps the most revolutionary document in history: the Declaration of Independence. If the fledgling colonies *succeeded* in defending themselves from the most powerful nation on earth, it was worth the risk. If they *failed*, these fifty-six men were signing their death warrants.

In fact, a little-known historical fact is that the copies with all the signers' names were not immediately made public. While these men signed the document in August of 1776 (having adopted it on the fourth of July), for the first six months or so the only *publicly displayed* versions had two signatures: John Hancock, president of the Continental Congress, which issued the Declaration, and Charles Thomson, the secretary of that august body. That's because the British Crown deemed this action treasonous and punishable by death.

What prompted the Congress to eventually allow public displays of all the names? In December 1776, Washington achieved a brilliant victory in the Battle of Trenton, even though the odds were completely against him. While Trenton wasn't an important, strategic gain, it was a tremendous boost to the war effort. It convinced Congress that the colonists could actually win this thing. So beginning in January 1777, fully signed copies of the Declaration began to be posted throughout the colonies.

The level of the signers' commitment and their willingness to sacrifice to secure liberty under God's law is evident in the final words of their declaration: "And for the support of this declaration, with a firm reliance on the protection of divine providence, we mutually pledge to each other our lives, our fortunes, and our sacred honor."[1]

CHRISTIANITY AND THE DECLARATION OF INDEPENDENCE

Note that the framers were placing everything on the line and trusting God for the results. The late Dr. M. E. Bradford of the University of Dallas researched the founding fathers, including the Christian commitments of the signers of the Declaration of Independence. He concluded that of the fifty-six men who signed the nation's birth certificate, clearly fifty, maybe fifty-two, were Trinitarian Christians.[2]

David Barton points out that of the fifty-six men, definitely twenty-four, possibly twenty-seven, had seminary degrees. This was not an assembly of atheists, agnostics, and Deists, as we're so often told today.

Paul Johnson says, "As we have seen, America had been founded primarily for religious purposes, and the Great Awakening had been the original dynamic of the continental movement for independence. The Americans were overwhelmingly churchgoing, much more so than the English, whose rule they rejected. There is no question that the Declaration of Independence was, to those who signed it, a religious as well as a secular act."[3]

Listen to a sampling of the signers' own words about Christianity, the Bible, and God.

- *Samuel Adams, the father of the American Revolution:* "The right to freedom being the gift of God Almighty . . . the rights of the colonists as Christians . . . may best be understood by reading and carefully studying the institutions of The Great Law Giver and the Head of the Christian Church, which are to be found clearly written and promulgated in the New Testament."[4]

- *John Adams also of Massachusetts, second cousin to Samuel and our nation's second president:* "The Bible is the best book in the world. It contains more of my little philosophy than all the libraries I have seen; and such parts of it as I cannot reconcile to my little philosophy, I postpone for future investigation."[5]

- *Thomas Jefferson of Virginia, chief author of the Declaration of Independence:* "The God who gave us life, gave us liberty at the same time."[6]

- *William Livingston of New York:* "The land we possess is the gift of Heaven to our fathers, and Divine Providence seems to have decreed it to our latest posterity."[7]

- *Dr. Benjamin Rush of Pennsylvania:* "I know there is an objection among many people to teaching children doctrines of any kind, because they are liable to be controverted. But let us not be wiser than our Maker. If moral precepts alone could have reformed mankind, the mission of the Son of God into all the world would have been unnecessary. The perfect morality of the Gospel rests upon the doctrine which, though often controverted, has never been refuted: I mean the vicarious life and death of the Son of God."[8]

And on it goes. Even the few nonbelievers who signed the Declaration had a Christian world-and-life view, including Benjamin Franklin.

The Divine Source of Our Rights

Furthermore, virtually every one of them knew the Scriptures and was positively influenced by them. Even the ones who weren't necessarily born-again Christians saw clearly that our rights come from God, not the state. What the state giveth the state can taketh away. Not so with the view of these men. Since our rights come from God, it is the duty of the state to acknowledge that fact and not infringe upon them.

Note how the Declaration of Independence mentions God four times:

- "the Laws of Nature and Nature's God . . ."

- "all men are created equal, that they are endowed by their Creator with certain unalienable rights . . ."

- "appealing to the Supreme Judge of the World for the Rectitude of our Intentions"

- "with a firm Reliance on the Protection of Divine Providence . . ."[9]

Today people sometimes say that "nature's God" refers to some god other than the God of the Bible. That's incorrect. The entire phrase "the Laws of Nature and Nature's God" comes directly from Sir William Blackstone's *Commentaries on the Laws of England*. Jefferson had a copy of this classic, four-volume work, which clarifies that natural law comes from God (in nature) and that revealed law also comes from God (in revelation, in the Holy Scriptures).[10]

EXHAUSTING ALL OPTIONS BEFORE DECLARING INDEPENDENCE

The founders did not lightly enter into this agreement to declare independence. This came after months and even years of trying to work out differences.

NO TAXATION WITHOUT REPRESENTATION

For the last half-century or so, American schools have taught that the causes of the American Revolution were economic in nature—"no taxation without representation." The economic component certainly played a part in the war, but it was not the most important factor. Much more important than the tax increases (which was Britain's way to finance the costly French and Indian Wars of 1754–63) was the representation part. "No taxation *without representation.*" The colonists would have paid the tax increases, begrudgingly, if they had had some say in the matter.

RELIGIOUS COMPONENTS

Religious factors played a part in this conflict as well. The American colonists were largely religious refugees, mostly Calvinists who had fled persecution from England in the previous century. (In addition, hundreds of thousands of Presbyterians fled Scotland and Ireland and settled in America in the first half of the eighteenth century.)

British historian Paul Johnson points out, "And it is important to remember that America, as a whole, was a religious breakaway from Anglicanism . . . . Anglican arrogance in the early 17th century came home to roost in the 1770s."[11]

Dr. M. E. Bradford observed that Great Britain had plans to impose the Anglican Church on all of America, thus abrogating all the sacrifices of the colonists' forefathers and mothers.[12] This was unthinkable to the colonists, even many of the Anglicans.

Meanwhile, the Great Awakening, a great spiritual revival that swept up and down the Atlantic Coast in the 1740s and beyond, helped unify the disparate colonies and get them to communicate with each other for the first time. This spiritual movement began with Jonathan Edwards, one-time president of Princeton, and culminated with traveling evangelist George Whitefield, perhaps the first man to go into each of the thirteen colonies.

Benjamin Franklin, who disagreed with Whitefield's religious views, was impressed with his ability to sway such large crowds. As Franklin noted in his *Autobiography* about the impact of Whitefield, "It was wonderful to see the change soon made in the manners of our inhabitants."[13]

And the American colonies soon began to see their common plight: what Great Britain did to one colony affected the other colonies. In particular, what King George did against Boston and Massachusetts would not go unchallenged by the other colonies.

THE MASSACHUSETTS BAY CHARTER

In 1774, partly in response to the Boston Tea Party, Great Britain revoked the charter of Massachusetts, which had been hotly contested in the previous century. This charter guaranteed religious freedom and other civil liberties. Now all this was in jeopardy. Historian George Bancroft writes, "Without previous notice to Massachusetts and without a hearing, it took away rights and liberties which the people had enjoyed from the foundation of the colony, except in the evil days of James II, and which had been renewed in the charter from William and Mary."[14]

THE REVOKING OF THE CHARTER

King George III was in effect declaring that charter invalid. He was outlawing the townhouse meetings. Educated men and women used to self-rule don't take too kindly to their freedoms being arbitrarily taken away.

New England moved quicker to independence than the rest of the colonies, because of the feisty Puritan spirit. Two years before the Declaration, the people of Middlesex met at Concord in 1774 and declared, "Our fathers left us a fair inheritance, purchased by blood and treasure; this we are resolved to transmit equally fair to our children; no danger shall affright, no difficulties intimidate us; and if, in support of our rights, we are called to encounter even death, we are yet undaunted; sensible that he can never die too soon who lays down his life in support of the laws and liberties of his country."[15]

Similarly, in 1774, the Massachusetts Provincial Congress resolved that "Resistance to tyranny becomes the Christian and social duty of each individual . . . Continue steadfast, and with a proper sense of your dependence on God, nobly defend those rights which heaven gave, and no man ought to take from us."[16]

BOSTON—THE LIGHTNING ROD OF THE REVOLUTION

The patriots of Boston, the Sons of Liberty, recognized their unique role as the center of the conflict. Spurred on by Christian patriot Samuel Adams, the "father of the Revolution," they saw this as a spiritual struggle between good and evil. The committee of Boston sent a letter to all the other towns in the area: "Being stationed by Providence in the front rank of the conflict, we trust we shall not be left by heaven to do anything derogatory to our common liberties, unworthy of the fame of our ancestors, or inconsistent with our former professions."[17]

What the king was doing arbitrarily to Boston—in revoking the colony's charter and in shutting down its port—he could do to the rest of the colonies. So the rest of them rallied behind their fellow colonists. Virginia attorney Thomson Mason said that the injustices done to Boston seemed to be "little less than a declaration of war."[18] Virginian George Washington declared, "Unhappy it is to reflect that a brother's sword has been sheathed in a brother's breast, and that the once happy and peaceful plains of America are either to be drenched with blood or inhabited by slaves. Sad alternative! But can a virtuous man hesitate in his choice?"[19]

Prior to signing the Declaration, blood had been spilled in Boston, Lexington, Concord, and near Charleston, South Carolina. The British threat to submission by force was everywhere. Only after careful and deliberate evaluation did the founders decide to consider independence.

FAITHFUL TO THE CAUSE, REGARDLESS OF RESULTS

The fifty-six men who signed the Declaration put their convictions above their convenience. Samuel Adams said that even if the results turned out disastrously, they would still be doing the right thing. As they were signing the Declaration of Independence, Adams said to Benjamin Rush, "If it were revealed to me that nine hundred Americans out of every thousand will perish in a war for liberty, I would vote for that war rather than see my country enslaved. The survivors of such a war, though few, would propagate a nation of free men."[20]

With few exceptions, these members of the 1776 Continental Congress were prosperous men. They were bold, but they were not reckless adventurers. They had much to lose in this venture— above all, their lives. Benjamin Franklin said, "We must all hang together or assuredly we shall all hang separately."[21] Indeed, King George III had promised a hangman's noose for anyone guilty of treason, and now these fifty-six men became officially marked targets. *The American's Own Book*, published in 1853, stated, "The patriots who signed that document, did it, almost literally, with ropes about their necks, it being generally supposed that they would, if unsuccessful, be hung as rebels."[22] John Hancock, the president of this Congress, made his signature extremely large so the king could read it without spectacles.

Their faith in the Lord served to cement their convictions that they were doing the right thing. And it sustained them during the horrible war, during which they paid a high price for signing the Declaration. As they said in the final sentence of our nation's birth certificate:

> And for the support of this declaration, with a firm reliance on the protection of divine providence, we mutually pledge to each other . . .
>   • our lives,
>   • our fortunes, and
>   • our sacred honor.[23]

For the rest of the chapter I'd like to consider each of these phrases, as we see the enormous price our founders paid to make this declaration.[24]

"Our Lives"

At least five of the Declaration signers died during the war because of their pledge. John Morton of Pennsylvania was the first of the signers to die. A former loyalist and a very sensitive man, Morton reportedly died of a broken heart because so many loyalist neighbors, friends, and even relatives shunned him for signing the Declaration. But to his dying day, he had no doubts that what he had done was right.

The British laid waste much of the homeland of Thomas Lynch Jr. of South Carolina, so he and his family sought temporary refuge in France. Tragically, they perished at sea.

During the war, Button Gwinnett of Georgia died in a duel with a loyalist enemy. Dueling has since been banned—by the actions of the Church.[25] We also lost one of our most gifted founding fathers, Alexander Hamilton, because of a duel. But that was much later.

Philip Livingston of New York died of overwork while serving Congress in 1778. Of course, we know much more in our day about how stress can be a killer. Livingston died for a good cause.

A worse fate awaited Judge Richard Stockton of New Jersey and his family, who were hunted down by the British and captured. While Congress managed to secure an early release for Stockton, he had been terribly mistreated in prison—a common problem in that war. Soon after his release, his health broke, and he died before the war ended. In his will Stockton declared his desire that his children would "subscribe to the entire belief of the great leading doctrine of the Christian religion."[26]

"Our Fortunes"

These men were to suffer more in this realm than in any of the other pledges they made at the end of the Declaration (their lives, their fortunes, and their sacred honor). Because these fifty-six men were so marked by the British, their land, farms, and houses were *special* targets of the British torch.

At least twelve of the signers had their homes plundered, and many of their houses were destroyed by fire. Of course, the men who signed the Declaration were by no means the only Americans who lost their property. But the British went out of their way to target these "treasonous" men.

Rev. John Witherspoon learned that the British burned down the beloved library of the College of New Jersey. Dr. Witherspoon was president of that Presbyterian college, which is today called Princeton.

Several of the signers temporarily lost their livelihoods because of the war, as the British or the hired Hessian mercenaries destroyed their farms and mills and scorched their farmlands.

Out of all the signers, perhaps Thomas Nelson Jr. of Virginia paid the most dramatic price, in property. In 1781, Nelson was forced to evacuate his stately house in Yorktown. When he learned that Cornwallis was using it as headquarters, Nelson insisted that *his own home* be destroyed by cannon, lest it be used to the advantage of the enemy. Earlier Nelson had raised two million dollars for the cause of independence by putting his property up for collateral. He was thus bankrupted by the war and died eight years later.

"OUR SACRED HONOR"

Although some of the signers were offered bribes to recant, they didn't. Though some faced hostile opposition from loyalist neighbors and friends, they didn't back down. And though some of their families were forced to suffer because of their stance, none of the signers of the Declaration of Independence violated their sacred honor. Not one of them betrayed the cause of liberty.

Dr. Benjamin Rush, one of the signers, was an avid Bible reader and a key promoter of the American Sunday School Union. Rush once showed the ultimate source of the strength of these men to prevail in such difficult circumstances: "A Christian cannot fail of being useful to the republic, for his religion teaches him that no man 'liveth to himself.'"[27]

Back then, one's word was binding. One's honor meant a great deal, and was even worth fighting for.

Through the whole ordeal, many of the signers paid a high price, and all were willing to pay it. They were willing to sacrifice their own lives and comfort so that they and future generations could enjoy religious, political, and economic freedom—so that these United States could become one nation, under God.

WASHINGTON'S RESPONSE UPON RECEIVING THE DECLARATION

While the men in Congress were busy declaring our independence, George Washington was out on the battlefield fighting for the same thing. Bill Federer, author of *America's God and Country*, notes the general's reaction upon receiving a reproduction of the document: "On July 9, 1776, upon receiving a copy of the Declaration of Independence from the Continental Congress, General George Washington issued the orders from his headquarters in New York authorizing the Continental Army to appoint and pay chaplains in every regiment."[28] Washington declared that these chaplains were there "to see that all inferior officers and soldiers pay them a suitable respect and attend carefully upon religious exercises." Why? "The blessing and protection of Heaven are at all times necessary but especially so in times of public distress and danger . . ."[29]

Our nation was founded upon the principles of the Bible and a reliance upon almighty God. As George Washington said in his first inaugural address, "[I]t would be peculiarly improper to omit in this first official act my fervent supplications to that Almighty Being who rules over the universe, who presides in the councils of nations, and whose providential aids can supply every human defect."[30]

Sadly, we have now turned our backs on the God of our founding fathers. George Washington warned that "reason and experience both forbid us to expect that national morality can prevail in exclusion of religious principles."[31] Yet modern America has chosen to exclude religious principles.

★ ★ ★ ★ ★

FOUR

THE REAL THOMAS JEFFERSON

"Render therefore to Caesar the things that are Caesar's;
and to God the things that are God's."
—JESUS CHRIST, MATTHEW 22:21

W E KNOW THAT GEORGE WASHINGTON, JOHN JAY, Alexander Hamilton, and James Madison were all professing Christians. The Bible instructed their worldview. In fact, most of the founding fathers of this country were believers in Jesus. For example, in his multivolume series, *The Shaping of America*, historian Page Smith points out, "Many, as we have seen, served their country as politicians and diplomats, especially the latter, and when they retired *gave their attention to the advancement of Christianity* through the encouragement of missionary activity."[1]

But when we come to Thomas Jefferson, it's quite a different story, as we all know. He has been called an atheist, an infidel, one who was hostile to religion, a Deist, a skeptic. He rarely attended church, expunged the miracles from a Bible, and produced the "Jefferson's Bible," which had no miracles in it.

Jefferson originated the "separation of church and state" doctrine to keep religion out of government, out of the schools, out of the public life of America. He is the guru of separation, the darling of the liberal left, the leader of the effort to eradicate Christianity from America. Yes, we all know Thomas Jefferson, the patron saint of the ACLU and People for the American Way, don't we?

Or do we?

No, I don't think we do.

MAY I INTRODUCE . . . THE *Real* THOMAS JEFFERSON?

I have just described to you a fictional character who is about as real as Santa Claus or the Easter Bunny. He is the creation of the secular elite, our secular educational system, the media, and of liberal judges.

Instead, I would like to introduce you to someone that I am quite confident 99 percent of you don't know: President Thomas Jefferson. After I introduced this man to members of the Coral Ridge Presbyterian Church one Sunday morning, many people told me they had never met this man before.

Now, lest some cynic reading this book decide that I am inventing a character of my own, let me state that what I bring to you here comes from the writings of people like

- Dr. James H. Hudson, curator and chief of the Manuscript Division of American History in the Library of Congress, the largest collection of human wisdom found anywhere in the world—twenty-two million volumes. He has at his hand and under his care more authentic manuscripts from the founding of this country than any other person on the planet. Yes, quite an authority.

- Paul Johnson, eminent historian who has written much on the history of Western culture, including his *A History of the American People*.[2]

- William Federer, author of *America's God and Government*.[3]

- David Barton, one of the most knowledgeable men in the country today on the Christian history of America.[4]

- Mark A. Beliles, chairman of the board of the Providence Foundation, who wrote an excellent essay entitled "Jefferson's Religious Life" in his updating of the so-called "Jefferson Bible."[5]

Yet few Americans know the man these prominent historians portray. I remember several years ago on the National Day of Prayer, the mayor of Ft. Lauderdale opened a community room for citizens who wished to gather there and pray. The president of the Florida ACLU wrote a guest editorial in the newspaper, expressing horror that such a thing as that could be done: "Why, doesn't our mayor know anything about Thomas Jefferson? Has he never heard of the separation of church and state? Does he not know that Jefferson would be appalled by the unconscionable deed that he is performing by letting Christians come into a public building and pray?"

I'm afraid that our ACLU officer doesn't know Thomas Jefferson either.

The "separation of church and state" has never been and is not now a part of the Constitution of the United States. It is, indeed, a myth that has been imported into that Constitution by others. Besides, as we'll see later, when the Constitution and the First Amendment were written, Jefferson was thousands of miles away in France. So he should not be viewed as the authority on what the writers meant.

JEFFERSON'S BACKGROUND

Thomas Jefferson was the chief author of the Declaration of Independence (1776), served as secretary of state (1785–89), and as president (1801–09). He was born in Virginia in an Episcopal family, or Anglican, as they were known then. He attended church regularly all of his life and was an active member of the Anglican Church. He also attended Presbyterian, Methodist, and Baptist churches and was particularly thrilled when all four of those denominations held services together in a courthouse.

Some might say that when Jefferson grew up, he learned better. Not so. He followed the Anglican faith in its orthodoxy all his life. He went to a Christian school and was taught by Christian pastors. As a grown man, he served on the vestry of the Anglican Church, which was the equivalent of being an elder in the Presbyterian Church. Not only that, he supported the church financially. His own financial records attest to this. Author Mark Beliles points out that he gave money to pastors, "churches, Bible societies, and Christian schools and colleges."[6]

And then, as we all know, Jefferson went to France in 1785 as secretary of state. The godless French Revolution (1789) was fomenting and soon a river of blood flowed throughout the country as the French people decided to get rid of virtually all vestiges of Christianity—even use of the terms B.C. and A.D.—so they could start all over again. Unbelief and skepticism reigned. The revolutionaries even abolished the seven-day week because of its Jewish-Christian roots and its concept of a Sabbath. Instead, they created a ten-day week.[7] About a decade later, Napoleon undid all these changes to the calendar.

BLOWS TO HIS FAITH

While Jefferson was in France, his wife, whom he adored, died, leaving him with his two-year-old daughter. Then both his mother and his best friend also died. Ordinarily, he would have gone to the congregation of the church where he served and found solace and consolation from them, and his pastor would have helped him work through his grief. There was no such church in Paris.

And so Jefferson's faith received a tremendous blow, and from that point on he began to question certain tenets of the faith, including the Trinity. However, I should point out that it wasn't until 1813 (some years after he left office and even longer after he wrote the Declaration of Independence) that he ever stated that disbelief, even in private letters. By 1813 he had adopted essentially a Unitarian view, rejecting the deity of Christ. By the way, the Unitarians at that time were *vastly* different from now; they were biblical in their orientation. In fact, Jefferson was a Bible scholar. He read the Bible daily. As George Washington read it an hour every morning and an hour every night, with prayer, so Jefferson read the Bible in English, Greek, Latin, and French.

What About the "Jefferson Bible"?

Similarly, the so-called "Jefferson Bible" is a myth. There never was a Jefferson Bible per se. Jefferson did cut out the miracles from the Gospels (not a recommended approach) in order to produce a book on ethics—the ethics and morals of Jesus Christ for the purpose of evangelizing and educating the American Indians. Jefferson remarked, "Of all the systems of morality, ancient or modern, which have come under my observation, none appear to me so pure as that of Jesus."[8] Thus, the so-called "Jefferson Bible" was really a tool to introduce the teachings of Jesus to Indians.[9]

In fact, the Indians were a great concern of his. While president, Jefferson approved government money for building a church for the Indians and for the support of a missionary. He also gave his own money to help reach the Indians. He believed that this simplified statement of the ethics of Jesus Christ (the so-called "Jefferson Bible") would help to civilize and educate these people. Specifically, President Thomas Jefferson recommended that Congress ratify a treaty with the Kaskaskia Tribe of Indians, which they did on December 3, 1803. Included in Jefferson's recommended treaty was the annual support of a Catholic missionary priest of $100 to be paid out of the federal treasury. The treaty stated:

And whereas the greater part of the said tribe have been baptized and received into the Catholic Church, to which they are much attached, the United States will give annually, for seven years, one hundred dollars toward the support of a priest of that religion, who will engage to perform for said tribe the duties of his office, and also to instruct as many of their children as possible, in the rudiments of literature, and the United States will further give the sum of three hundred dollars, to assist the said tribe in the erection of a church.[10]

Author William J. Federer adds that this wasn't the only such treaty: "Later in 1806 and 1807, two other similar treaties were made with the Wynadotte and Cherokee tribes."[11] If Jefferson believed in the separation of church and state, then he repeatedly violated this doctrine.

Jefferson never called his Gospels-minus-the-miracles (the teachings and ethics of Jesus) a "Bible." Instead he called it a system of ethics, the greatest the world has ever known. Therefore he only included the teachings of Christ about ethics and morals to present them to the Indians.

HOW ABOUT THE "SEPARATION OF CHURCH AND STATE"?

Today we are told that Jefferson intended the strict separation of church and state. But like so much of the historical record surrounding Jefferson, this has been turned upside down and made to be the very opposite of what Jefferson intended. Late in 1801, while he was president, he received a letter from the Association of Baptists in Danbury, Connecticut, who were concerned about the threat of the newly formed federal government. This "leviathan," they feared, could become a great danger to their Christian faith and to their churches.

First of all, Jefferson was out of the country when the Constitution was written (1787) and when the Bill of Rights was proposed and passed (1789), and had virtually nothing to do with the drafting of these documents. On the first day of the year 1802, Jefferson wrote back to the Danbury Baptists. In this letter, he said that he was greatly impressed that the American people, through the First Amendment had, in effect, erected a "wall of separation between the church and the state," so the Baptists didn't need to fear that the federal government was going to intrude upon their religion or in any way disturb their faith.

Because of the significance of this letter, I have reproduced its entire contents in the endnotes. Note that this letter ends with Jefferson's asking them to pray for him, while he agrees to pray for them—a far cry from the atheistic intentions so often attributed to him.[12]

His purpose in this 1802 letter was to assuage the fears of the Danbury, Connecticut, Baptists, and so he told them that this wall had been erected to *protect* them. Actually, he took the language from Roger Williams, the founder of the Baptist church in America who had settled Rhode Island, a colony known for its freedom of religion and conscience. Reverend Williams had talked about a wall being erected around the garden of the church to protect the right of conscience. Jefferson took that same phrase and said that this wall protected the church, not against hostile Indians or worldly things, but against the federal government.

In our time liberals have taken that and turned it around completely. It's an unfortunate metaphor, because it can be used two different ways. Unlike the First Amendment, which completely controls the government, saying that "Congress shall make no law respecting an establishment of religion, or prohibiting the free exercise thereof," a wall can inhibit people on both sides.

Yet the only time you hear this phrase used today, it's talking about what Christians can't do, what pastors can't do, what the church can't do—not what Congress can or cannot do.

Today's liberal interpretation minimizes the influence of Christianity in the public arena. That's not what Jefferson meant. It is not what his friend James Madison meant when he introduced the Bill of Rights into the Congress and stated very explicitly that the purpose of this was to interdict the federal government from interfering with the religion of the people. On June 12, 1788, Madison wrote, "There is not a shadow of right in the general [federal] government to intermeddle with religion . . . The subject is, for the honor of America, perfectly free and unshackled. The government has no jurisdiction over it."[13]

During Jefferson's entire public life, his view was that government could support religion. In fact, as you may know, the Constitution ends with the phrase "in the year of our Lord, 1787." Throughout the eight-year presidency of George Washington, all of his presidential papers ended "in the year of our Lord 17—— . . ." And when Adams came to the presidency, he followed suit for the next four years.

Jefferson changed that when he became president. I have a photocopy of the conclusion of one of many of the documents that he signed as president, and it says, "In the year of our Lord Christ 1804." He was the first president, and to my knowledge, the only president who did that. Jefferson, the anti-Christian, the irreligious infidel, said that it is Christ who is our Lord, and no one else.

Jefferson's letter to the Danbury Baptists has been greatly perverted and distorted. The ACLU has fought vigorously to keep out any reference to God in our public lives, including the prohibition of religious expression in any public building. Is this what Jefferson intended?

I don't believe so. Consider these facts. Jefferson wrote his letter to the Baptists on Friday, January 1, 1802. Two days later, Thomas Jefferson went to church. He said he was going to throw the influence of his position as chief magistrate, president of the United States, in favor of the public display and support of the Christian religion.

How did he do that? He went to church. But not just any church. He went to the largest church in America at the time.

Every week, Christian worship services were held in the chambers of the House of Representatives in Washington. The Capitol building took a long time to be completed; the cornerstone was laid in 1793, and the building was revised for the next half a century and beyond. Meanwhile, worship services were held on Sundays at the same place congressmen met on Mondays. (Decades later, worship services continued in the completed building in the Rotunda of the United States Capitol, the most visible public building in America, bar none.)

So each week for seven years, the rest of his presidency, Thomas Jefferson sat in the front row. He wasn't pleased with the music, so he ordered the marine band to come to church on Sunday. They were paid out of the federal treasury to support the singing of hymns and psalms in the church. How is that for "separation of church and state" Jefferson-style?

Some may say, "But that was in the Congress, and he didn't directly control the Congress." Well, that's about as feeble an argument as you could have, but let's take a look at it. He did control the War Department, which is part of the Executive Department. He also controlled the Treasury Department, and another church was holding services in the War Department and yet another in the Treasury Department. Who was in the Treasury Department? Well, you see, these Scotsmen who came over here and started the Presbyterian Church knew a good place to start a church—right in the Treasury.

Well, that may be the Congress and the Executive Office, but what about the Supreme Court? They would never allow anything like that. As a matter of fact, the chief justice of the Supreme

Court, one of the most famous of them all, John Marshall, ordered that the facilities of the Supreme Court be turned over every Sabbath Day to yet another church to hold Christian worship, which included not only prayers and hymns, but also the preaching of the Word of God.

As far as the concept goes that "there shall be no religious activities in public buildings," Jefferson never even dreamed of such a thing. This is a total distortion used by the ACLU and their ilk to suppress and demolish Christianity and remove it altogether from the public square.

In fact, one of the justices in recent times, taking the separation-of-church-and-state metaphor, said that the "wall must be kept high and impregnable. We could not approve the slightest breach."[14] Well, I guess you could say that Thomas Jefferson had a few slight breaches in his wall, breaches so big you could drive a truck through them. In fact, you could drive a whole company of tanks through those walls.

Madison, who introduced the Bill of Rights, said that the government was forbidden from establishing a national religion. The First Amendment was given, as all of the testimony indicates, to do two things: (1) to prevent the Congress from establishing a state church, like the Anglican Church in England, from which they had mostly fled, and (2) to prohibit interference with the free exercise of religion. Here are Madison's own words on what's intended by the establishment clause ("Congress shall make no law respecting an establishment of religion . . ."): "No national religion shall be established by law."[15] This has been grossly distorted in our day.

The whole separation statement of Thomas Jefferson has been turned into a total distortion and perversion, and it is a lie.

Well, now, thus saith the preacher, James Kennedy, you might be thinking. But what saith an authority on the matter? "The metaphor of a wall of separation is bad history and worse law. It has made a positive chaos out of court rulings. It should be explicitly abandoned."[16] Who said that?

Jerry Falwell?

Dan Quayle?

Jesse Helms?

No, it was William Rehnquist, chief justice of the United States Supreme Court.

I hope that Americans will wake up to the realization that they have been deceived, that the Jefferson who has been presented to them is a fabrication. He was a definite friend to the Christian faith, and he viewed it as the finest religion that God had given to man.

But Did He Believe the Gospel?

Now, someone may point out to you that several ministers wrote letters highly critical of Jefferson. Yes, there are five of them. But on the other hand, Jefferson had 110 personal friends who were clergymen. In fact he encouraged nine of them to run for public office. And while he was in the presidency, he financially supported ten different churches and numerous others for the rest of his life. He was not the anti-Christian agnostic that the ACLU makes him out to be.

Well, what did he lack? Was he really a Christian? That depends on what you mean. He did attend church regularly all of his life. But he did come to question and doubt one of its major tenets later in his life, long after his entire public career was over.

I don't think that we could say that Jefferson was a genuine Christian in the sense of one who had been transformed by the regenerating power of the Holy Spirit, one who trusts in the death of Jesus Christ for his salvation. Like millions of church members today, he had never gotten beyond seeing in Christianity anything other than a code of ethics, a system of laws—albeit the most elevated and wondrous system known to man.

But that is not real Christianity. Real Christianity involves a supernatural transformation of the heart. Jesus said that it is a "rebirth." He declared to Nicodemus, who was an extraordinarily religious man and one of the religious leaders of Israel, that "except a man be born again, he can in no wise enter into the kingdom of heaven" (John 3:3). That is what it means to be a real Christian. Hence, Jefferson was a nominal Christian—in name only—as are about half of the professing Christians in America today.

But even as a nominal Christian, what Thomas Jefferson did is totally antithetical to everything the ACLU and others have told the American people. For example, summing up, author Mark A. Beliles has assembled an impressive list of some of Jefferson's actions as president:

- Promoted legislative and military chaplains

- Established a national seal using a biblical symbol

- Included the word *God* in our national motto

- Established official days of fasting and prayer—at least on the state level

- Punished Sabbath breakers

- Punished marriages contrary to biblical law

- Punished irreverent soldiers

- Protected the property of churches

- Required that oaths be phrased by the words "So help me God" and be sworn on the Bible

- Granted land to Christian churches to reach the Indians

- Granted land to Christian schools

- Allowed government property and facilities to be used for worship

53

- Used the Bible and nondenominational religious instruction in the public schools. He was involved in three different school districts, and the plan in each *required* that the Bible be taught in our public schools.

- Allowed and encouraged clergymen to hold public office

- Funded religious books for public libraries

- Funded salaries for missionaries

- Funded the construction of church buildings for Indians

- Exempted churches from taxation

- Established professional schools of theology. He wanted to bring the entire faculty of Calvin's theological seminary over from Geneva, Switzerland, and establish them at the University of Virginia.

- Wrote treaties requiring other nations to guarantee religious freedom, including religious speeches and prayers in official ceremonies[17]

No, my friends, the *real* Thomas Jefferson is the ACLU's worst nightmare!

FIVE

LIBERTY OR LICENSE?

"For certain men have crept in unnoticed,
who long ago were marked out for this condemnation,
ungodly men, who turn the grace of our God into lewdness
and deny the only Lord God and our Lord Jesus Christ."
—JUDE 4

ONE DAY, JERRY NEWCOMBE, THE COAUTHOR OF THIS book, came across a memorable sight at the beach. At the time, in August 1994, hundreds of desperate Cubans risked their lives trying to flee from the Communist island on makeshift rafts. Jerry stumbled across one of these rafts off the shores of Deerfield Beach, just north of Ft. Lauderdale, about three hundred miles or so away from Castro's "Paradise." This raft, composed primarily of three wooden doors, reflected the desperation that its makers must have felt. The raft's bottom consisted of a wooden door, which was attached to two doors, one on each side. Pieces of wood, including window shutters, served as crossbeams to hold the two side doors together. Some sort of white flotsam or Styrofoam was attached to the bottom to keep the raft afloat. It was as if someone had torn apart his own home to put this precarious vessel together.

Then the refugees had to float or row over treacherous waters, in the grueling sun, with the potential threat of sharks along the way, to try and get to America so that maybe—just maybe—they might get a chance to enjoy what you and I have every day. Freedom. The chance for a better life.

People the world over seek freedom. Some seek it desperately and will literally risk their lives to attain it. Where the gospel of Jesus Christ has gone and taken root, political, social, and civil freedom has usually followed. Ironically, in America and other Western democracies, we suffer from an overindulgence of freedom. Billy Graham once declared, "We have confused liberty with license—and we are paying the awful price. We are a society poised on the brink of self-destruction."[1]

The founders of our nation put a great deal of stress on liberty. But they also warned that liberty is not the same as licentiousness or license to do whatever your bodily passions want. Yet today, there is a cry from virtually every quarter for this type of liberty.

WHAT IS LIBERTY?

What is freedom or liberty? Author Charles Hummel, former head of Barrington College, wrote an excellent booklet on the subject. In it he says that real liberty can only be conceived in terms of the purpose for which we were made. That is why the humanist and the evolutionist cannot really define liberty; instead they always end up with license because they have no purpose. Evolution has no purpose, no teleology, no end, because no Creator is involved in the process.

But freedom and liberty cannot properly be defined without considering purpose: that for which something was made. For example, says Hummel, consider a modern diesel locomotive flashing across the country at high speed on shiny rails. Is that train most free when it is speeding across the countryside on the rails, or when it leaps the tracks and thunders by, smashing barns and houses and scattering cars and people? Obviously, it is most free when it is where it was meant to be.[2]

Liberty as the founders understood it meant liberty under God—the freedom to do what is right.

Then what is license? you might ask.

WHAT IS LICENSE?

The dictionary defines license as "excess," and the thesaurus provides these substitutes for *license*: "immoderation," "abandon," "lack of control," and "lawlessness." First John 3:4 says sin is lawlessness. License is the freedom to do what is wrong.

License says I can do anything I want to do—anything my sinful little heart desires; and there will be no restraints whatsoever upon my conduct.

In some cases, professing Christians confuse license with liberty. They believe they can do whatever they want and God will forgive them. After all, they have made professions of faith and they believe the gospel, so they will go to heaven, regardless. As one cynic said, "I can do anything I want and God will forgive me because, you see, God is in the forgiving business." How tragic, how fatally tragic, an idea that is.

Just recently I visited with a man who told me that, yes, he knew he was going to heaven. Why? Because he believed that Jesus Christ died on the cross for his sins. Did he go to church? No. Had he been to church? No, not in years. And to him, that was not a problem. After all, he did believe the gospel and, therefore, of course he would go to heaven, would he not? No. That is not the gospel. That is license, and salvation is not a license to sin. It is a deliverance from sin.

In the second to last book of the New Testament, Jude tells us about "ungodly men, who turn the grace of our God into lewdness and deny the only Lord God and our Lord Jesus Christ" (Jude 4). Though we expect the world to throw off all restraints and law, including the law of God, which it detests, again, the tragedy is that this same tendency is found in certain segments of the church. In fact, I believe much of the license existing in our society today must inevitably be traced to the church and to the antinomian teaching that has been prevalent in some sections of it.

Antinomianism comes from the Greek word *nomos*, which means "law." Antinomianism is that attitude of mind that is against the law. It says, in effect, that Christ has redeemed us from the law; therefore, the law has nothing whatever to say to us. We are under no obligation to obey it or to keep it.

The early church considered antinomianism a heresy. The apostle Paul deals with this concept in Romans 3 when he asks "Do we then make void the law through faith?" (v. 31). The antinomian would rise up and say, "Yes, and amen. We get rid of the law of God." Incidentally, the devil has attempted to do this since the very beginning when he told Eve, "You will not surely die" (Gen. 3:4). He lied to get her to disobey the law of God—and both she and her husband disobeyed—and died.

"Do we then make void the law through faith?" Note Paul's answer in the same verse: "Certainly not! On the contrary, we establish the law." The Old Testament promised through the prophets that God would write His law upon our hearts. God gives us new hearts. He also gives us a new motivation of love to want to keep the law. Yes, we establish the law through faith; we do not destroy it.

At times there is a great deal of confusion concerning this truth. We do not gain eternal life by faith *plus* keeping the law. These two horses do not pull the chariot of salvation. The truth is that we are saved by grace alone through faith in Christ. This inevitably leads to a life of obedience performed out of love and gratitude for Christ. As Jesus said, "If you love Me, keep My commandments" (John 14:15). But if we love Him, then His commandments, His laws, are written on our hearts.

Unfortunately numerous teachers and writers in this country say the law ended with Christ. They are going to have to deal with the apostle Paul on this matter, because the law did not end at the cross.

Recently I learned of a young man, working at a Christian radio station in the suburbs of one of our large metropolitan cities, who believed that we are free in Christ—that is, free from the commandments. The Ten Commandments, he proclaimed, have been done away with. In fact, one day he attended a church where they read the Ten Commandments aloud, and he chose not to participate. The person who invited him to church asked him afterwards why, and his answer was, "The Ten Commandments are not for today. We live under grace."

The station fired him when they found out he slept around with several of his female radio fans. His wife divorced him because of this constant infidelity. The state jailed him because of intentional check kiting. He was a chain smoker and a glutton. His life was a mess in every way. *But he claimed to be free from the law* in Christ—free to practice any and every sin. His pagan lifestyle was simply an outworking of his bad theology.

No, the commandments have not been abolished. Do not believe those who say Christ has done away with the law and that we are under no obligation to keep it. Certainly, the founders of this country did not think so.

THE FOUNDERS' ASSUMPTION—THAT WE WOULD REMAIN A VIRTUOUS PEOPLE

Read the writings of the founding fathers, and you will find it abundantly clear that they expected us to be a virtuous people. Let's consider a sampling.

- John Adams—our second president, signer of the Declaration of Independence, chief architect of the Massachusetts constitution (the world's oldest constitution still in operation), and one of our chief founding fathers—once declared that our constitutional form of government assumes that Americans are virtuous: "We have no government armed with power capable of contending with human passions unbridled by morality and religion. Avarice, ambition, revenge, or gallantry, would break the strongest cords of our Constitution as a whale goes through a net. Our Constitution was made only for a moral and religious people. It is wholly inadequate to the government of any other."[3]

- James Madison, the father of the Constitution, would take issue with the idea of abandoning good and evil. He said, "To suppose that any form of government will secure liberty or happiness without any virtue in the people, is a chimerical idea."[4] That is, it is imaginary.

- In a well-known quote, George Washington, the father of our country, the first president, the man who presided over the Constitutional Convention, gave our nation some final warnings as he retired from public service. His Farewell Address, one of the most important messages ever given in the history of the republic, sums up his admonition to the budding new nation. In that address, he declared, "Of all the dispositions and habits which lead to political prosperity, religion and morality are indispensable supports. In vain would that man claim the tribute of patriotism, who should labor to subvert these great pillars of human happiness . . . And let us with caution indulge the supposition that morality can be maintained without religion."[5]

Over and over, in various ways, the founders declared that our republic was designed to work with a virtuous people.

Michael Kammen, an authority on the Constitution, says this about the men who gave us our founding document: "Even though they often spoke of liberty, they meant civil liberty rather than natural liberty. The latter implied unrestrained freedom—absolute liberty for the individual to do as he or she pleased. The former, by contrast, meant freedom of action so long as it was not detrimental to others and was beneficial to the common weal."[6]

Political science professor Donald S. Lutz, author of *The Origins of American Constitutionalism*, said, "And the most fundamental assumption [of the Constitution] is that *the American people are a virtuous people.*"[7] Furthermore, he adds something that would shock today's secularist, clamoring for the right to engage in all sorts of perversions: "Without the belief in a virtuous people, the federal republic would not have been tried."[8]

About seventy-five years after our nation began, U.S. Congressman Robert Charles Winthrop, descendent of the great Puritan leader John Winthrop, made a classic speech at the Annual Meeting of the Massachusetts Bible Society in Boston, reflecting the idea that we must be self-governed (through Judeo-Christian morality) or we will be governed by tyrants. He declared:

> All societies of men must be governed in some way or other. The less they have of stringent State Government, the more they must have of individual self-government. The less they rely on public law or physical force, the more they must rely on private moral restraint.
>
> Men, in a word, must necessarily be controlled either by a power within them, or a power without them; either by the word of God, or by the strong arm of man; either by the Bible or by the bayonet.[9]

There it is: men will be either governed by the Bible or the bayonet. We will have self-rule or we will be ruled by a tyrannical state. As Paul Harvey likes to often say, "Self-government won't work without self-discipline."

The lack of virtue on the part of millions is the reason for much of the chaos we see today. Furthermore, sins like abortion and pornography have become entrenched in our political and cultural landscape.

Today's Problems

Author Charles Hummel provides a telling anecdote about liberty and license. At his home, an aquarium sits at the foot of the stairs. He said that not long ago a cry went out from one of his daughters: "A fish has leaped out of the tank!" There it was, flopping on the floor. His daughter picked the fish up, put it back into the tank, and it began to swim again. On other occasions, when no one was around, other fish had leaped out of the tank and were found dead on the floor hours later. The fish leaped beyond their restraints. They were free—but they were also dead, because their freedom was contrary to the parameters for which they had been created.[10]

So it is with our sex lives. Who is most free sexually? The profligate? The promiscuous person? The pervert? The person who feeds his soul on pornography? Psychologists tell us that recent discoveries show pornography to be addictive—that a person involved with it wants more and more, and ever more explicit, lewd, and savage depictions and actions. That person is no more free than the heroin addict who is enslaved by his own passions. With about thirty sexually communicable diseases rampant in society today, I assure you that he will soon be dead—probably from his own excesses. When he leaves this world, he'll find himself in hell. Is that person freer than the person who confines his sexual life to the monogamous marriage God created him for? I don't think so.

Charles Hummel elaborates further:

Is Christianity a straitjacket? Many people think so. Over the years in fraternities, sororities and residence halls, I have heard students frankly express their opinion. Many think Christianity is an intellectual straitjacket restricting our reason or a social straitjacket squeezing the fun out of life. From the outside Christianity, like any condition of existence, may appear restrictive, but from the inside we find this is what we were made for. Yet even Christians sometimes consider complete commitment to Christ as a restriction. "If I'm obedient to God, he'll make me do things I don't want to do." As we consider our dating, career, hobbies, money or time, we are reluctant to commit all to God for fear that we will lose out. Jesus Christ frees us from this warped idea of Christianity.[11]

The Statue of Liberty, holding high her torch, is a great symbol of the liberty that made America great. Our fathers came to this country to establish a nation where people would be free to worship and serve Christ, to do what they believed to be right, according to the Word of God. They gave us liberty and law. But that liberty has always been endangered—and has been under increasing assault—by those who are not free in Christ.

The modern humanist is daily on his platform crying out for license. He does not want freedom *under* law—he wants freedom *from* law, unless he can remake the laws into decrees that legalize license. That is precisely the direction our country has been taking for a number of decades. Every form of immorality has not only been condoned and practiced, but if the humanists have their way, these excesses will be enacted into legislation and given official sanction by the government. As decisions about pornography show, as decisions about abortion show, as decisions about any relaxed moral issue show, the situation immediately becomes worse because of man's natural inclination downward.

As of this writing, Sweden, a most liberal country, is poised to inscribe acceptance of homosexuality in their constitution to the degree that any public opposition to it will result in fines and jail time. This includes opposition from the pulpit.[12] The Swedes have taken liberty, perverted it into license, and then made it so that objection to that which is wrong will now be illegal.

Aleksandr Solzhenitsyn describes one of the great problems of our time in the West in this way: "We hear a constant clamor for rights, rights, always rights, but so very little about responsibility, and we have forgotten God. The need now is for selflessness, for a spirit of sacrifice, for a willingness to put aside personal gains for the salvation of the whole Western world."[13]

How few people today are willing to sacrifice for the salvation of the Western world. We are letting our whole Western civilization slide over the precipice, while people are concerned with their own "rights," their own hedonistic pleasures, their own selfish rush of acquisitiveness in order to gain more and more.

Although our morality has plummeted of late in virtually every category, we have a great increase in ethicists—a whole new breed.

An Increase in Ethicists

Some eleven thousand courses are now being taught in American colleges about ethics, mostly by psychologists or academics, and virtually all of them are relativists. They are trying to do the impossible—teach morality without certainty and ethics without absolutes. It cannot be done, and the more classes they teach, the worse the situation becomes.

While the humanists have been transforming liberty into license, they have been screaming loudly to Christians: "Oh, you can't legislate morality."

"You Can't Legislate Morality"

To say that morality cannot be legislated is just a lie. The truth is you cannot legislate anything *but* morality. We have laws against rape, incest, bestiality, and adultery because they are immoral. We have laws against murder and stealing because they are immoral. The question is simply, Whose morality is going to be legislated? It is either going to be God's morality, as expressed in the Judeo-Christian tradition of the Ten Commandments, or it is going to be man's morality, as expressed in the *Humanist Manifesto*, which sanctions everything that used to be called immorality.[14]

Remember the tremendous outcry over Watergate? No one should have been so surprised. Watergate was situation ethics, and this theory has been taught in colleges and universities for decades. Why, they were only doing that which suited their own needs, and the situation dictates the morals, we are told.

The same principle applies to all the school shootings. For decades we've been telling our public-school children that morality is relative—there are no rights and wrongs—and that essentially life is meaningless because we evolved by happenstance. Lo and behold, some kids brought guns into school and picked off some of our best and brightest in random school shootings. They're simply acting on that which adults have been telling them for years.

We have forgotten the belief held by the settlers and founders of America that it is only by the Spirit of the Lord that there is real liberty. And so, over the past forty years in this country a purblind Supreme Court has taken the Bible, prayer, the Ten Commandments, and the Creator from our young people. We wonder—and we hear television commentators and newspapers columnists wondering too—what has caused the dramatic rise in crime and every sort of evil in our country.

FROM LIBERTY TO LICENSE TO ANARCHY

Only a people committed to God are capable of being free. Wherever that commitment diminishes or is destroyed, then liberty will inevitably turn into license, license into anarchy and chaos, and chaos into tyranny. When the French revolutionists threw off the monarchy of France, they set out to create liberty. This soon degenerated into license, bloodshed, and chaos. Within a decade Napoleon came on the scene to restore order; France then suffered under tyranny.

Aleksandr Solzhenitsyn once said in one of his writings that when he was just a young boy, the Communist revolution was going on—millions of people were being slaughtered, the streets were running with blood, and fear stalked the land. He overheard two peasants arguing as to why all this was happening. He said he will never forget what one of the peasants said: "It is because we have forgotten God! That is why all this is happening to us. We have forgotten God!" In spite of all the education and experience Solzhenitsyn had gained, including the years in the Gulag, he never forgot the wisdom of that simple peasant.

I am afraid that peasant demonstrated a wisdom that far exceeds that of many of the leaders of our nation, schools, and courts today. That incisive critic and columnist in England, the late Malcolm Muggeridge, very precisely put his finger on the problem when he said, "Since the beginning of the Second World War, Western Society has experienced a complete abandonment of its sense of good and evil."[15] He added, "The true crisis of our time has nothing to do with monetary troubles, unemployment, or nuclear weapons. The true crisis has to do with the fact that Western man has lost his way."[16]

Good and evil provide the theme of the drama of our moral existence. When we lose sight of that and when we call evil good and good evil, destruction is not far behind. Not only is this true for nations, but for individuals as well. "The wages of sin is death" (Rom. 6:23). That is as true as the fact that the nation that forgets God shall be turned into hell. Because of sin:

- Adam and Eve lost their lease on Paradise,

- Moses was denied admission into the promised land,

- Samson degenerated to total dependence upon his Philistine captors,

- Saul lost his kingdom,

- David forfeited peace in his own family,

- Solomon sacrificed the most glorious reputation of all,

- Elisha's greedy servant traded his good health for Naaman's leprosy, and

- Jonah served his sentence in the belly of a large fish.

In the New Testament, the same truth is taught over and over again.

We will only see change in our culture when godliness prevails. And a new birth of freedom will not take place until there are multiplied new births in the hearts of Americans.

We need to rise up and take our stand. We need to shake off the lethargy that exists in the church, as well as the nation. For too many, Sunday morning and Wednesday evening services have become our leading spectator sport. We need to be doers of the Word and not just hearers (James 1:22).

REPENTANCE

As we have seen, part of our problem rests within the church. We have been promoting easy believism, a type of Christianity that does not demand repentance. But such a "Christianity" is not true to the Bible.

Jesus told us to repent. "Unless you repent you will all likewise perish" (Luke 13:3). Repentance is the other side of the coin of faith. You can't have faith without repentance, just as a coin can't have a head without a tail. It is not possible; it just doesn't exist. Repentance is a turning from sin and turning to God—with repentance toward God and faith in Jesus Christ.

There are some bright spots in the picture—some illumination upon the horizon.

CHRISTIANS EFFECTING CHANGE

I was happy to see that the largest drugstore chain in America has thrown out pornography, *Playboy* and *Penthouse* and the like. A number of other chains are following their example.

Several years ago, I heard Hugh Hefner's announcement that in one quarter the Playboy conglomerate had lost $2 million. They are selling off many of their Playboy Clubs. Well, Hugh, old boy, things are tough all over; and as far as you're concerned, I hope they are going to get tougher. By the grace of God, our voices are beginning to be heard.

Similarly, *Penthouse* magazine has hit hard times. In the last few years, its circulation has shrunk from five million to less than one million. Unfortunately, this loss largely reflects the great increase in Internet pornography.

As things stand right now, we recognize that, tragically, some Christians, including pastors, are addicted to Internet pornography. Thankfully, ministries to help wean Christians and others off such pornography are rising up. Focus on the Family, the American Family Association, and other groups minister to men—and generally, they are men—caught in the snare of pornography.[17]

I believe things are beginning to change and are going to continue to change even more. I am encouraged by the hundreds of thousands of children being taught in Christian schools or godly home-school environments. I am encouraged by the number of outspoken evangelical candidates, congressmen, senators, and our current president, George W. Bush.

I am encouraged by the incredible success of well-done, family-friendly films at the box office over the well-publicized, trashy fare. Hollywood has slowly begun to get the message that Americans want more family-friendly fare and less garbage on the silver screen. I am encouraged that the number of abortions per year has decreased from about 1.5 million to less than 862,000 for

1999, the most recent year reported.[18] I am delighted in the alternative media that is mostly conservative, often Christian, which has broken the monopolistic stranglehold of the liberal media in this country. Above all, I am encouraged by the quiet growth of evangelism, one on one, doing its work week after week, leading people to personal faith in Jesus Christ.

I believe that we can get out of this cesspool of license and back onto the solid ground of liberty in Jesus Christ.

We need to continue to make our voices heard. We can make a difference. I would urge you to not let an opportunity go by. Make a call, write a letter, stand up, express your mind, and by the grace of God we can return this nation to what it was in the beginning. God grant that we may see that victory in Christ.

If America is to become a Christian nation again, we will need to clarify the point that the founders intended us to enjoy liberty under law. We close this chapter with the words of the apostle Paul to the Galatians. He shows us clearly that Christ sets us free, but not so that we may abuse that freedom:

> Stand fast therefore in the liberty by which Christ has made us free, and do not be entangled again with a yoke of bondage . . . . For you, brethren, have been called to liberty; only do not use liberty as an opportunity for the flesh, but through love serve one another. For all the law is fulfilled in one word, even in this: "You shall love your neighbor as yourself." But if you bite and devour one another, beware lest you be consumed by one another! I say then: Walk in the Spirit, and you shall not fulfill the lust of the flesh. For the flesh lusts against the Spirit, and the Spirit against the flesh; and these are contrary to one another, so that you do not do the things that you wish (Gal. 5:1, 13–17).

This brings us to the end of Part One of this book, where we have seen just a fraction of the vision of the original settlers and founders of this great nation. The majority of these settlers came to escape religious persecution and to worship Christ according to the dictates of their own consciences. There never would have been an America as we know it without this religious thrust.

Now we want to shift gears and take a look at some of the burning issues of today. From education to the media, from abortion to gambling, from the threat of the militant secularists in our culture to the threat of Islam, America is being torn apart in different ways, mostly from within. We need to get a handle on some of these key issues and apply the mind of Christ to them.

Although Christians have lost much ground in this nation that was largely founded by Christians, we owe it to our forefathers who sacrificed so much to establish this nation on godly principles to gain back this lost territory. We owe it to the generations yet unborn and we owe it to our Lord to do all we can and not give up simply because we have supposedly lost the cultural war. Then we leave the results up to the Lord. I agree so much with President John Quincy Adams, who reminded us that, "Duty is ours. Results are God's."[19]

PART TWO

★ ★ ★ ★ ★

Where We Are:
The Culture Clash—from
Leave It to Beaver *to*
Beavis and Butthead

SIX

WHOSE VERSION OF
TOLERANCE?

*"Woe to those who call evil good, and good evil;
Who put darkness for light, and light for darkness;
Who put bitter for sweet, and sweet for bitter!"*
—ISAIAH 5:20

EVERY ONCE IN A WHILE, MILITANT HOMOSEXUALS AND others come out and surround my church to protest something I said or did on one of my broadcasts. During such times, coauthor Jerry Newcombe quips, "Here come the 'shock troops of tolerance' again."

Have you ever noticed how some of the most intolerant men and women are those who clamor the loudest *for* tolerance? Their view of free speech is that you can have complete free-speech rights—*if* you agree with their views and toe their line. Woe to you if you dare say, for example, that homosexuality is wrong.

Christianity gave birth to the good type of tolerance, as summarized in Christ's Golden Rule: "Therefore, whatever you want men to do to you, do also to them, for this is the Law and the Prophets" (Matt. 7:12). This implies respect for others—even if they're different. But today's version of so-called "tolerance" in reality is anything but broad-minded. If America is to ever become a Christian nation again, it's time to get back to the traditional definition of tolerance and to promote it. It's also time for us to discern once again between good and evil. As the Scripture from Isaiah quoted at the beginning of this chapter points out, God does not take lightly those who label evil things good and vice versa.

DISCERNING BETWEEN GOOD AND EVIL

In this country we are very much involved in a "culture war," a war for the minds, souls, and lives of every American, which has been going on apace and growing in its intensity. You may hear this described in many other ways, but ultimately this is a battle of faith against unbelief, a battle for God or against Him.

Goethe, the great German writer, said that the only struggle in this world worth our attention and energy is the struggle between faith and unbelief. Well, we are living through just such a period in our country today. Mortimer Adler, editor of *The Great Books of the Western World*, said that more consequences for life and action stem from belief or disbelief in God than from any other factor.[1] So this is a pervasive, all-inclusive war.

The first phase of any war, as a general will tell you, is the semantic phase, and we have been in that for the last century. It's a war of words. It's a war that defines the war. The twentieth century, in almost its entirety, saw the unfolding and development of this semantic war. And I must tell you that Christians are very definitely losing it. We have been outgeneraled, outstrategized, and outmaneuvered on every side. So far. But the war is not over yet.

I'm somewhat reminded of George Orwell's famous classic, *1984*, which describes a tyrannical government where Big Brother was watching you, and there were various, never-before-heard-of departments, like the Department of Truth. This department consisted of people working twenty-four hours a day, transforming truth into lies.

We have just such a department in this country today. Now, I can't take you to a building in Washington, D.C., where such a department is housed, but I can show you a little bit of their handiwork so that you can judge for yourself. In fact, I would like to share a couple of the most strategic words in this semantic battle and the consequences of the changes and distortions in those words.

"THERE ARE NO ABSOLUTES"

A myth that's prevalent in our society is this: "There are no absolutes. All truth is relative." I'm sure you've heard it a thousand times. This is currently believed by 62 percent of adults. If young people between the ages of eighteen and twenty-five are included, the figure rises to 74 percent.[2] A hundred years ago, or even fifty years ago, that would have been unthinkable. A century ago, I'm sure 99 percent of Americans believed there were absolutes and truth was not relative.

Some think and say that Einstein proved we live in a relativistic universe and that everything is relative. That settles the matter. It must be so because Einstein said it.

No, he didn't. What Einstein said is that relativity applies to the realm of *physics*—not *ethics*. Paul Johnson, author of the blockbuster book *Modern Times,* points out, "Mistakenly but perhaps inevitably, relativity became confused with relativism. No one was more distressed than Einstein by this public misapprehension . . . Einstein was not a practicing Jew, but he acknowledged a God. He believed passionately in absolute standards of right and wrong."[3] So it is a travesty that Einstein's theory has been transported into every other discipline, and we have ended up with almost a total moral relativism.

Dr. Paul Vitz, professor at New York University, observes that the moral decline in America is directly related to the widespread acceptance of this myth: "One of the major characteristics of moral decline in the United States in recent decades has been the rapid growth of moral relativism. The idea is now widespread that each individual has some kind of sovereign right to create, develop, and express whatever values he or she happens to prefer."[4] Surely, this echoes what the Bible says about ancient Israel during the time of the judges: "Everyone did what was right in his own eyes" (Judg. 21:25). What the Bible said more than three thousand years ago is just as true today as it was then.

What "No Absolutes" Really Means

When a teacher or professor says there are no absolutes, you need to understand that he is also saying, "There is no God," because, you see, God is the ultimate absolute. He is absolutely supreme. He is absolutely infinite in His power and wisdom and knowledge—in all of His attributes. What He says is the ultimate and *absolute* truth. Keep in mind that when someone says there are no absolutes, this person is simply giving you a veiled and cloaked atheism.

Who Can Condemn the 9/11 Hijackers or the Nazis?
Somebody once made the point that relative morality died on 9/11. Millions of Americans woke up that day believing that there wasn't any objective right or wrong, but went to bed convinced that what the hijackers did *was* wrong. Wrong with a capital W. We rallied around the president when he declared that the unprovoked attack was evil.

And yet, not all Americans were willing to condemn the 9/11 attacks. For example, David Westin, then the head of ABC-News, raised quite a few eyebrows when he said we could not definitively condemn the hijackers' attack on the Pentagon. At a Columbia University Graduate School of Journalism event the month after 9/11, Westin was asked, "Do you believe the Pentagon was a legitimate military target, even if the missile was not?"

He answered, "Our job is to determine what is, not what ought to be . . . I can say the Pentagon got hit, I can say this is what their

75

position is, this is what our position is, but for me to take a position this was right or wrong, I mean, that's perhaps for me in my private life, perhaps it's for me dealing with my loved one, perhaps it's for my minister at church. But as a journalist I feel strongly that's something that I should not be taking a position on."[5]

Mr. Westin later apologized for this remark, but please note that he was only saying what he and millions of Americans have been taught for decades.

If there are no absolutes, if everything is relative, if everything is culturally initiated, if we cannot impose our culture upon another culture, then how dare we say that the Nazis were wrong for killing millions of people? Yet everyone knows that what they did was categorically monstrous.

THE NEW TOLERANCE

Next we look at the issue of *tolerance*. All of us know what tolerance means: that you put up with or bear with people who hold to views or beliefs or values or lifestyles that you don't agree with. And if you are a Christian, or for that matter even a gentleman or a lady, you will try to be tolerant and kind to them.

Not anymore. The definition of this word has gone through the "Department of Truth." It has been crushed and smashed until it means something entirely different, so much so that a father and son cannot discuss any moral subject today without arguing about tolerance. The father thinks of tolerance as it has been known for centuries, basically, the application of the Golden Rule. The son sees tolerance in the way Josh McDowell and Bob Hostettler describe it in their excellent book, *The New Tolerance*, which I recommend.

And what is the new tolerance? The new tolerance is that we are not only to put up with values, habits, lifestyles, and beliefs different from our own, but we are to *accept* those values, those lifestyles, those beliefs as absolutely equal to, and as valid as, our own. This new tolerance is being pounded into the minds and hearts of scores of millions of students every week.

So your religious beliefs are no better than anyone else's since, after all, everything is relative. And since your beliefs are not any better than theirs, and since your moral views are not superior to their moral views—no matter if they are little more than alley cats in their sexual lives—you cannot impose your views upon them. And if you don't accept their lifestyles, their beliefs, their habits, you are an intolerant bigot. Kids by the millions have been called that in front of their classmates in the classrooms of this country. Most of them, indeed, quake before such an assault.

Well, any person who gives up a belief in moral absolutes and the absolute truth of the faith will be incapable of distinguishing right from wrong and will, as McDowell and Hostettler say, be powerless to resist temptation and choose the right. This is what is happening in our schools today. We have moved from respect for a person to acceptance of wrong.

SERIOUS CONSEQUENCES

If you don't accept wrong as right, ah, my friend, serious consequences await you, because not only do sinners want your glad acceptance of all of their lifestyles, beliefs, values, and habits as equal to your own, but they also want you to participate in what they do. For example:

- In New York City's medical schools, effective June 2002, every student has to participate in on-the-job abortion training and must perform abortions, regardless of his or her opinion on the grisly trade of the abortionist. Failure to participate results in failure to graduate. Before this, it was an elective; now it is required. [6]

- In Ohio, several nurses were reprimanded and penalized because they protested participating in therapeutic abortion procedures on religious grounds.[7]

- At Stanford University, the gay and lesbian alliance promotes a shorts day each spring during which people are exhorted to wear shorts to show their support for homosexual lifestyles. It just so happens that most of the students wear shorts every day, so they are put in a position of either having to change their dress or appear to support what is being done.[8]

- In another college, students who indicated their disapproval of the homosexual lifestyle were forced to watch hours of XXX-rated pornographic homoerotic films while being observed by a professor. If the students showed any signs of disgust or revulsion, they were forced to watch more films. Sound like the Chinese communist's reeducation camps?[9]

A lot is going on in our country today that most people are not even aware of.

Similar to the term *tolerance* is the distortion of another word with which we are all familiar—*discrimination*.

NO CRITICISM OF HOMOSEXUALITY

I recently read of a totalitarian nation where they would not even allow the negative mention of homosexuality on television or radio. If anyone read Romans 1 or any of the many other passages in the Bible that condemn homosexuality, that person was going straight to jail; do not pass Go; do not collect $200.

What benighted nation would have such an immoral law? Canada!

When Coral Ridge Ministries and other ministries in the United States publish full-page ads in papers all over the country that simply say, "There is hope. Tens of thousands of homosexuals have found deliverance from this lifestyle. In Christ they have found a way to change their lives," some say it is hate and could be categorized as a hate crime. In fact, if we had taken out this ad in Canadian newspapers—in a nation that has taken the new tolerance to the extreme—we could have gone to prison. Homosexuals require that you validate not only their persons, but their beliefs and their lifestyles and their activities as well. It is not possible, they say, for anyone to do anything other than that.

Polls have repeatedly shown that high-school students in this country believe that you cannot criticize anything that anyone believes without finding fault with that person. Therefore, if you have a discussion of atheism with an atheist, you are finding fault with that man *and* criticizing his views. You can't separate the two. The same is true of a homosexual. You cannot have a rational discussion of the rightness or wrongness of homosexuality, because if you find any fault with it, you are finding fault with that person, who will tell you, "What I do is what I am," and you cannot divide the two.

Hogwash! Jesus did it. Does anyone question the fact that Jesus loved people? Does anyone question the fact that Jesus loved sinners? Yet He did not accept their sinful beliefs and lifestyles. Jesus told the woman caught in adultery, "Your sin is forgiven." But He also said, "Go and sin no more." We often hear the first part, but we rarely hear the second part—which implies the need for repentance.

Jesus also condemned *pornea* in Mark 7:21, from which our modern word *pornography* is derived. This word is translated as "sexual immorality" in some of our English translations, but it really stands for a laundry list of sexual sins, which a first-century Jew would understand: premarital sex, adultery, homosexuality, incest, and bestiality. People sometimes say that Jesus never condemned homosexuality. This only shows their ignorance. When He condemned *pornea*, He certainly condemned homosexuality.

But to say such things today makes you intolerant. It makes

you a hater, which I'm not. I love homosexuals more than their friends do because I don't want to see them cut down in the prime of their lives, and I don't want to see them burn in hell, which they will if they don't repent and turn to Christ. Thankfully, thousands of homosexuals have found freedom in Jesus Christ.[10]

Jesus confronted sinners, and we are to do it as well. But the day is coming when we might suffer persecution for doing so. For far too long Christians have been afraid to state their faith for fear of offending somebody. It's time for Christians to get out of the bleachers and onto the playing fields and get involved, or laws may be passed with consequences that will roost right in our homes and families. It's time for Christians to stand up and say, "When you take Christ out of Christmas, you offend me."

"BRING BACK THE LIONS!"

One time I was preaching about the new tolerance, and after the service someone who survived the Holocaust said to me, "You are exactly right. That is what happened to the Jews. They first ridiculed them. They laughed at them. They drew political cartoons with the Jews depicted as rats. And then they began to condemn them, then to silence them. They began to persecute them. And then they began to imprison them. Finally they began to kill them." The new tolerance truly leads to intolerance.

This reminds me of the protest in Madison, Wisconsin, a few years ago. Militant homosexuals surrounded a church that dared to speak out against the homosexual agenda. I have seen videotape of this protest, and there, plain as day, is one of the protesters yelling at the top of her lungs, "Bring back the lions! Bring back the lions!" The others around her clearly approved of her message: it's time for Christians to again be thrown to the lions.

In a similar vein, but with perhaps a little more subtlety, Denver columnist Reggie Rivers writes:

While I don't agree with the action, I can periodically understand the frustration and general fatigue that compelled the Romans to throw select Christians to the lions.

It's not just that the lions were hungry; it was that the Romans were tired of listening to the self-righteous babbling of the Christians who claimed to be experts on everything, and had egos the size of . . . well . . . God.[11]

Unfortunately those who clamor for tolerance are among the least tolerant when it comes to conservative Christians.

★ ★ ★ ★ ★

SEVEN

As the Family Goes ...

"For the LORD *God of Israel says
that He hates divorce."*
—MALACHI 2:16

CHARLES AND DORIS HAD BEEN MARRIED FOR ABOUT ten years, and for them it seemed like ten years too long. When Charles came home, he would slip in the back door, and his wife would be working in the kitchen. She was always surprised to see him and would say, "Oh, are you home already?" He said it always sounded like what she really meant was, "Don't tell me you're home already." And he always felt as though he'd done something wrong just by coming home.

Then he would go and greet his children, but it always seemed that he stepped between them and the TV set at the wrong moment. The only one who seemed happy to see him was his little dog, Susie. So he would pick up the dog and go outside and pet her. Charles felt like stomping his feet and saying, "Doesn't anybody care? Isn't anybody glad to see me?" But he was a gentleman, so he didn't stomp his feet. He just let these moments pass. But the resentment grew.

I have not kept up with Charles and Doris, but it would not surprise me if their miserable marriage ended in divorce, as so many millions have in America. Divorce is an all-too-easy out for millions of families. Even Christians have been very unfaithful in this arena.

If America is going to survive and thrive, it will require a renaissance of the American family. I truly believe the expression, "As the family goes, so goes society," because the family is the heart of our society. Whatever hurts the family hurts society. The family is the number-one department of health and human services in the nation. Therefore, government should do everything in its power to protect any familial authority. Government should get out of the way and let the family do its job—with rare exceptions, such as cases of genuine child or wife abuse. It's important for modern America to get back to the tried-and-true biblical principles of family relationships—including honoring our parents and recognizing the unique roles of mothers and fathers.

HONORING OUR PARENTS

Once there was a little old man whose moist eyes blinked more than they should have and whose hands trembled quite a bit. Since he had no place to live, he moved in with his son's family. Now, the son's wife was not overly thrilled with this new arrangement, but she tolerated it. Then one day the old man's hands were shaking so much that the clinking of his silverware on the bowls and glasses was more than the wife could bear. So the next day, she got an earthenware bowl, placed it in the corner, and put a chair there for him to eat. She said, "It's just not right that I have to put up with this sort of thing. Why, it's against the woman's right to happiness."

For some time he ate out of his earthenware bowl in the corner, looking wistfully at the family sitting at the table. Then one particular day his hands were shaking more than usual and the bowl fell out of his lap onto the floor and broke, spilling all of his meal onto her beautiful rug. "Well, now, that just does it!" she said. "If you're going to eat like a pig, we'll feed you like a pig," and she made a trough, put it down on the floor, and told him that he could kneel there and eat like a pig. And so he did.

And the days went by, and one day the very modern wife called her family to the dinner table, but their little boy didn't come. So the father called to his son. "Tommy, what are you doing? It's time for dinner."

Tommy came in with something he had made out of wood. "Look, Daddy," he said, "I am making a trough to feed you and Mama out of when I get big."

The husband and wife looked at each other, and their eyes filled with tears. Without a word they went over to the old man, lifted him to his feet, led him to the table, and let him sit down and eat. And it didn't seem to matter anymore how much clinking he made with his silverware or how much he spilled.

That story is from *Grimm's Fairy Tales*. You may have recognized it. And it tells a lesson that I think we need to hear again. Today we don't provide troughs for the older folks or our parents when they get old, but we usually get them out of sight and out of mind; we warehouse them in some semblance of decency.

THE ONLY COMMAND WITH PROMISE

Many of us have forgotten the scriptural admonition of the fifth commandment, which says, "Honor your father and your mother, that your days may be long upon the land which the LORD your God is giving you" (Ex. 20:12). This is called the first commandment with promise. There are actually two promises in it—one here, and then one in the repetition of it in the book of Deuteronomy, the second law. There it says "that your days may be long, and that it may be well with you" (5:16).

There was a time when this commandment was adhered to. I think of a young man who wanted nothing in life more than to join the navy and see the world. Why, someday he might even be the captain of a ship. That just made his mind spin.

His mother, however, was not too thrilled with the prospects of her son, then just sixteen, going off to sea. Still, she walked him down to the port (all of his goodies in a knapsack over his shoulder) and watched him put his clothes in the longboat that would take him out to the ship. As he said good-bye to his mother, she couldn't help saying, "Son, I just have no peace about your going off to sea. I just don't feel right about it. I have prayed a great deal about this, and, Son, I really wish you wouldn't go."

How do you think that scenario would play out today? I think we have a pretty good idea about how many young men would respond. Well, this particular young man went back to the longboat, got his sack of food and clothes, and said to one of the sailors, "I cannot sail off and break my mother's heart."

He never became the captain of a ship. He never even became an admiral. But he did come to command an entire navy, as well as an army and the marines. In fact, he came to command all of the forces of the United States.

That young man was George Washington, who had been taught the commandments of God as a child, including, "Honor your father and your mother, that your days may be long upon the land which the LORD your God is giving you." And God kept His promise, "that it may be well with you." Nineteenth-century senator and great orator Daniel Webster said of Washington, "America has furnished to the world the character of Washington. And if our American institutions had done nothing else, that alone would have entitled them to the respect of mankind."[1] What was the wellspring of Washington's character? He was a man who took the Word of God seriously, as taught to him by his parents.

Do you have that kind of respect for the law of God?

I have been amazed at how many homes I have been in where children seem bent on destroying everything in the house while company is there, including their parents' peace of mind, and the parents do nothing about it. Is it any wonder that those children don't grow up to honor their fathers and their mothers? They have not been taught to do so.

In our permissive age, some parents are saying that they don't want to force their children to attend church; instead the parents allow the children to decide for themselves when they're old enough. Let them decide when they are twenty-one whether they want to go to church or not. This cannot be left to the children any more than you can leave the decision to take a bath or to brush their teeth up to them.

The apostle Paul said, "Children, obey your parents in the Lord, for this is right" (Eph. 6:1). But the well-known pediatrician and author Dr. Benjamin Spock said that "children should do whatever they want to do. Parents, forget about it. The important thing is to let it all hang out. Creativity. Self-expression is the rule." And he helped produce the most rebellious, disobedient generation that ever walked upon this continent. (And in his old age he even admitted it and apologized.)

How many times has the world, in its supposed wisdom, told us to do *this*, which is exactly the opposite of the Bible, which told us to do *that*? A few years later we discover that *this* has been a recipe for catastrophe. When will we learn to take God's Word for what it is—the wisdom of the almighty, omniscient, and loving God?

A Nation of Individuals—All from Families

When a child does not respect his parents at home, he is not going to respect or obey his teachers in school. When he gets a little older, he is probably going to disrespect and disobey the law. He is going to discover that the law is not his "mama," and the law isn't going to let him do anything that his wicked little heart wants to do. Soon he is going to find himself standing in front of a judge. And the next thing you know he is going to hear the door clang shut on his cell. Then Mama and Daddy are going to say, "Where did we go wrong?"

Well, Mama and Daddy, you've got a monster because you raised him to be one. You didn't teach him to honor his father and mother, and his days have not gone well, and his life may not be long.

We need to heed the unique roles of mothers and fathers. Ignoring them has caused a breakdown in the family.

The Crown of a Godly Mother

"As American as apple pie or motherhood." So goes the saying. I am not sure what the status of apple pie in America is today, but I certainly know that motherhood has taken a terrible beating in the last few decades. We are going to have to change that saying to "as American as apple pie." Indeed, few people today even want to identify themselves as a mother or a housewife.

A young lady told me that once, at a social gathering, a gentleman approached and asked, "And what do you do?"

"I'm a housewife and a mother," she replied.

The man immediately turned his back on her and said to someone else, "Oh, and what do you do?" The young woman was sure this man thought to himself, *There must be somebody here who's got an interesting life.*

She was wounded deeply, and she asked me, "What should I say when asked that question?"

In a moment I'll tell you what I replied.

Motherhood in Disrespect Today

Motherhood has certainly had a difficult row to hoe in the last several decades. Betty Friedan, author of *The Feminine Mystique*—the book that launched the whole feminine movement—said that if you're just a housewife, you're "committing a kind of suicide."[2] She writes, "In a sense that is not as far-fetched as it sounds, the women who 'adjust' as housewives, who grow up wanting to be 'just a housewife,' are in as much danger as the millions who walked to their own death in the concentration camps."[3]

Women are told that they ought to get out into the men's world where the action is, where the real satisfaction is. There they will find life at its fullest. Today very few women go to college to study home economics. It's just not the "in" thing, we are told.

One time my wife and I were sitting in a restaurant, and my wife nodded in a certain direction and said, "Do you know who that is?" I looked over at what appeared to be the saddest, most miserable woman I had ever laid eyes on.

"No. I don't know who she is."

"That's Betty Friedan."

"That's the infamous Betty Friedan?" I took another look, and on closer inspection I could see that she was even more miserable than I had first thought. Perhaps the constant discontentment of her life had etched lines upon her visage. She looked very unhappy.

Years after Betty Friedan said housewives were living in "comfortable concentration camps,"[4] feminists have been making another definitive statement. Do you know what they have been saying? "I do." A goodly number of leaders in the feminist movement are rushing to get married, as their biological clocks seem to be ticking ever faster. Now they are the ones who feel they have missed out. A prominent example of this is Gloria Steinem, who once said that a woman needed a man like a fish needed a bicycle. Years later she had to eat her words as she walked to the altar. She, too, has said, "I do."

Interestingly, syndicated columnist Joan Beck put it very succinctly:

The most compelling reason why so many fast-track women drop out, or slow down is that their priorities change. They discover—usually to their surprise—that it's more satisfying, and important to do a personal job of mothering a small child than to make a two percent gain in the year-over-year sales of the packaging division of Widget Inc. Small children love you back. Computer printouts don't.[5]

Yes, satisfaction is not always what we are told it is.

SECOND THOUGHTS

Happily, things have changed somewhat. Indeed, it is interesting that even Betty Friedan admitted that the feminist movement was a failure.[6]

Ladies, I think you've been duped.

Where do you find real satisfaction? Well, if you would ask old Jochebed, she might have told you something different from the gurus of the feminist movement. You do remember Jochebed, don't you? You ought to remember her—she rules your life. She had a baby. Those on the fast track of the times wanted to kill that baby, so she finally put the infant in a little boat and set it out to sea—at least in a river.

The child was found by the daughter of Pharaoh and grew up in his household, with his mother Jochebed's identity hidden until he became an adult (Ex. 2). We know him, that son, as Moses, who brought to the world the commandments of God. Certainly there is a lot of truth in the saying that the hand that rocks the cradle rules the world.[7]

NANCY AND ABRAHAM

I think of another woman, Nancy, who was very godly and tried her best to rear her son as a godly boy. Unfortunately, she didn't have much time with him. She died when he was nine, but before her death, she would sit him on her lap each day and teach him the Word of God, especially the commandments: Thou shalt not steal. Thou shalt not commit adultery. Thou shalt not bear false witness.

Though this young man only knew his mother for a little while, he attributed his honesty to his following the commands of God as he heard them from his mother. In fact, he said, "All that I am, all that I hope to be, I owe to my angel mother—blessings on her memory."[8]

Later in life he was known as the most honest lawyer east of China. That covers a lot of territory. In fact, his reputation for integrity and honesty was such that he was elected president. His mother's name was Nancy Hanks Lincoln—his name was Abraham. Honest Abe. Yes, indeed, the hand that rocks the cradle rules the world.

"The Most Precious Asset of Any Nation"

Theodore Roosevelt was a wise president. He was also a godly man, and what he said on Mother's Day will give all mothers a reason to take heart. He said, "Mothers are the most precious asset of any nation. They are more important than statesmen, than business-men . . ."[9] How about that, gentlemen? Mothers, said Theodore Roosevelt, are more important than any of these powerful people. They have the most important occupation of any person in this nation.

This is a very different view from what was given to the young lady I mentioned earlier, who was totally ignored because she was "simply a mother and a housewife."

Women who have believed the lie that it isn't good enough to be "simply a mother and a housewife" have gone out to "have it all"—family and career. Often they have realized that their loyal-ties become divided. The husband and children are not their first priority anymore. A boss and a job have replaced their families. Because of overwork and extreme fatigue, no one cares for the family, so unhappiness, bitterness, and resentment grow. A lot of young people are very angry in our culture, and I believe it is ulti-mately because of the neglect of their parents.

This does not mean that a woman can't have a career, but she is the one who carries the burden of keeping the family together. She has to have her priorities straight if her family is to survive and thrive.

What Would I Have Said to the Impolite Man at the Party?

I promised earlier to reveal what I would have this young woman tell the very impolite gentleman who wasn't at all interested in her after he found out that she was a housewife and mother. When he asked her, "And what do you do?" I told her, "I think you should have said, 'Why sir, I rule the world'—then turned on your heel and walked away."

The Father in the Home

It doesn't take a lot of smarts to become a dad. Any man can do that. I recall seeing a movie about the life of the famous tenor Enrico Caruso. When his wife had just given birth to a baby, someone asked him, "What is it like to be a father and have a baby?" He said, "Oh, having a baby is very simple. There is nothing to it. We, of course, watched what we ate for the past few months and were careful about our diet. Then the other night there were some pangs, so I called the hospital and we went to the hospital. And then, shortly after that the baby came. I can assure you there was nothing to it."[10] That's childbirth from a father's perspective.

It is really very easy to become a father, as Caruso testified, but it is very difficult to be a godly father in the home. You must, first of all, be a godly man. Second, you must *be* in the home, because if there is one place where tens of millions of American fathers aren't today, it is in the home. Eighty percent of all families in the inner city are fatherless. Eighty percent. And 30 percent of the homes in the rest of the country are run by unwed mothers.

Divorce Is Not So Bad?

We have been told that there is nothing really so bad about divorce. "Children bounce back," and, after all, in the "me" generation when the great goal in life is self-fulfillment, we've got to

91

find the person who is going to help us do that. We are told, "If you made the wrong choice the first time, just keep choosing. Eventually you will find the right person"—at least so many famous people seem to tell us that. Who was it that said, "I never met a man I didn't like"? Elizabeth Taylor, I think.

So we have bought the lie of the world that divorce is really not so bad. And tragically, the flood of divorce has swept right under the doors of the church, and today church members are getting divorced as never before in history.

Whenever I talk about this in the midst of a country that has sunk into such immorality and degradation, there are always those who feel guilty. That is not my purpose. My purpose is to try to protect future mothers and fathers, husbands and wives, sons and daughters from the heartache that comes from divorce. But you can't stop a tidal wave—a flood—without creating some waves and backlash.

How often I have heard people who are getting a divorce say, "Well, after all, it is our own business, isn't it?" No, it is every-body's business, because everybody is paying for these millions of single-mother homes where men and women have ignored the teachings of God, who says, "I hate divorce" (Mal. 2:16). The Bible allows divorce for adultery and the desertion of a believer by an unbeliever. (And certainly, I would not counsel a woman being battered by her husband to remain in harm's way.) But most of today's divorces are for other causes.

So, let me tell you, dear friends, you have been lied to. Divorce is not the easy, no-fault kind of thing that the world has been telling you. Divorce creates all kinds of problems.

THE RESULTS OF A FATHERLESS AMERICA

Another modern phenomenon is expanding exponentially in our nation: the rise of gangs in our cities—over a hundred thousand teenage boys in gangs in the city of Los Angeles alone, and most of them armed.[11] All over the country this is true, both in the big cities and the smaller ones. Even upscale suburban communities are having tremendous problems with gangs. And there's no consequence to a fatherless home?

It is interesting that 70 percent of the teenage criminals in America come from broken homes, and 70 percent of the teenage murderers come from broken homes.[12] Yes, my friends, it is everybody's problem, and everyone pays a price.

THE GAYING OF AMERICA

You've probably heard about the "graying of America." But have you heard about the "gaying" of America? I believe this phenomenon is one of the consequences of the rise in illegitimacy and divorce. Developmental psychologists tell us that every child, male and female, that is born originally bonds with his or her mother, unless that woman dies in childbirth or is gone.

Then in years two and three, which these developmental psychologists call the "gender identity period," every male child begins to reach out to his father because of an inner drive to bond with the male of the species. But if the father is not there, or if the father ignores, rejects, or insults that advance in some way, the child is hurt and wounded. What does the boy do? He flees back to his mother. I believe that is the origin of much of homosexuality in our country today.

As one psychologist said, homosexual men are just little boys running around looking for the love of the fathers they never had. The problem, then, lies in the fact that so many men are not in the home where they belong. I admit that this is only one factor among others that cause homosexuality. The amoral experiential view of sexuality is another. Ex-gays have told us that about 75 percent of homosexuals and lesbians were sexually molested as children.[13]

Homosexuality, so rampant today, is just one symptom among many of the breakdown of the family. Pain is another.

The Pain

Years and years ago, my daughter dated a young man who was probably the best-looking young man I have ever seen. He had a physique like a Greek god and a face that would make a Hollywood star envious. Not only that, he had a brilliant mind. But in his teens, his father left his mother, which just tore that boy apart.

I remember him sitting at our breakfast bar one time, just staring off into the distance, which he did often. For about ten minutes he just sat there. Suddenly he slammed his fist on the bar and virtually shouted, "How could he have done that to us?" as if he was not even aware that anybody else was in the room. Do you think he was torn up inside? You had better believe it.

The Termites recently revealed another result of divorce. I am not talking about the little critters that crawl around and eat your houses; this was a group of fifteen hundred young people who were chosen for a longitudinal study approximately eighty-five years ago by a Dr. Terman. The doctor planned to study the entire lives of these California juveniles, who were at the time approximately eleven years old. These subjects chose for themselves the name "Termites." When Dr. Terman died, others continued his study to discover what affects longevity. They examined these people every way—forward, backward, and sideways—and discovered an interesting fact: Children from broken homes, male or female, live on average four years less than those who come from homes that are not broken.

Just a private matter between you and your wife? Think again, my friend. If you are going to be a godly father, you have to be in the home and you have to stay there.

Something to Tell Your Children

Every child is afraid of being left alone—being deserted by one or both of his or her parents. I think every parent should reassure his or her child as I did my daughter when she was about ten or twelve years old: "Jennifer, from time to time your mother and I will have an argument. After all, no woman is perfect. (I'm just kidding.) But there is one thing I want you to understand: We will never get divorced. Never!" I think you ought to tell your children that, and you had better mean it when you tell them. You will give them a security and a confidence that perhaps nothing else can give.

Second, let me say to you men that you need to love your wives. It has been said, the best thing a father can do for his children is to love their mother. That is very, very true. The vows say, "Forsaking all others, I will cling to thee alone. I take thee to be my lawfully wedded wife." Tragically, there are many men today with roving eyes. With the tidal wave of pornography titillating the senses all around, I think every man needs to guard his eyes, his ears, and his body from sexual temptation. We don't need to get out on the edge of the precipice and play around with temptation. We need to stay as far away from it as we possibly can. Flee temptation. Ben Franklin, with his incomparable wit, said in *Poor Richard's Almanack*, "Keep your eyes wide open before Marriage, half shut afterwards."[14]

A reporter once asked me if I had ever had an affair with another woman. I replied, "Have I ever had an affair with another woman? I've never even kissed another woman since I got married, and I don't plan to start." She really found that difficult to believe.

If you are going to be a godly dad, you need to forsake all others with heart, mind, and soul and love your wife. We are to love our wives as Christ loved the church and gave Himself for it (Eph. 5).

Men, do you know what the word *husband* means? It comes from two words: *house* and *band*—a band that goes around the house to protect it, to provide for it, to take care of it, to nurture it. This is what a husband is supposed to do. And a wife, therefore, can yield herself to such a protector, one who treats her lovingly.

But today, we have completely reversed God's order, and we have men who are saying, "I am the head of my household, I am the king of my castle, what I say goes, and you had better jump high when I say jump." They do not love their wives as Christ loved the church; they are loving their wives as a drill sergeant loves his platoon.

Unfortunately we have husbands who are tyrants and wives who are rebels (even though Scripture says that wives are to submit to their husbands), and they are locked together in an unending conflict for dominance. I say, "unending conflict," but really, the conflict does end—most of the time in the divorce court. Why? Because rebel wives and tyrant husbands are going right in the face of the commands of God.

And who really suffers as a result of our neglecting or disobeying God's Word? The children.

EIGHT

LIFE: AN INALIENABLE RIGHT

"These . . . things the LORD hates . . .
Hands that shed innocent blood . . ."
—PROVERBS 6:16–17

CAROL EVERETT OF AUSTIN, TEXAS, USED TO BE A SUC-
cessful abortionist. She got into the business because she had
had an abortion, and she felt the need to justify the procedure. She
said, "Nothing worked after my abortion."[1] So if in some twisted
way, she could talk other women into having abortions, then
maybe her own abortion wouldn't seem so wrong.

Once she got into the abortion business, she became hooked on
the money. She was well on her way to becoming a millionaire
through this means. Then something happened. She experienced a
new birth in Christ through a surprising occurrence.

Many problems had arisen between employees in the clinic, so
they called in a counselor who specialized in solving workplace
conflicts. What no one realized was that the man was also a Baptist
minister. During a private visit he shared the gospel of Jesus Christ
with Carol. She actually said the prayer to ask Jesus in her heart so
she could get back to her thriving business.

Little did she know what difference her commitment would
make. Her first day back on the job after accepting Christ, Carol
realized that each girl who came to the clinic was actually frightened that her parents would "just kill" her if they knew she was

pregnant. Abortion looked like a cheap, quick way out. Carol quickly talked three such girls *out* of aborting. One after another. It was then that she began to realize the fundamental incompatibility between abortion and her newfound Christian faith.

The Lord had truly changed Carol Everett's heart. There was no going back—no matter how much money she was making. After having materially profited from thirty-five thousand abortions, she soon left the business. She feels that Jesus Christ opened her eyes to the grisly trade she had been involved in.

This chapter will explore what I think is the single greatest evil of our time and what we can do to counteract it. If America is ever to become a Christian nation again, we can't ignore the millions of "silent screams." For millions yet to be born, abortion is literally a life-and-death issue.

And light needs to be shone upon this horrific procedure. The Bible says, "This is the verdict: Light has come into the world, but men loved darkness instead of light because their deeds were evil. Everyone who does evil hates the light, and will not come into the light for fear that his deeds will be exposed" (John 3:19–20 NIV).

When I was a young lad, I watched some boys at camp catch large grasshoppers. The boys pulled the legs off, one by one, and then crushed the insects. That appalled me. Then these same youngsters took more grasshoppers, put them in a bottle, threw the bottle into a campfire, and watched the insects jump and jump and jump until they were finally cooked. To this day, I can remember the absolute horror I felt. But this horror is nothing to compare to the abomination that we call abortion.

I'd like to expose abortion for what it is. The following descriptions are not easy to read, but more of us need to see what is happening inside the abortion clinics in our nation. Unfortunately the media does not picture this reoccurring procedure.

HOW IS AN ABORTION PERFORMED?

One of the most common types of abortion uses a high-powered vacuum cleaner to suck out the unborn baby, piece by piece, chunk by chunk. In another type of abortion, the "doctors" reach in with forceps and rip off a leg, then another leg, then an arm—all while the baby may still be alive and fighting to avoid the forceps. Then the abortionist rips off the other arm and reaches in to crush the baby's head so the doctor can pull it out.

The most horrific procedure is the partial-birth abortion, a late-term procedure in which the abortionist moves the baby into a breach birth position. The tiny body's backside faces his executioner, who pulls the feet out, and then the rest of the body. Everything but the head. Understandably, the baby is writhing in pain at all this. Now the doctor punctures the back of the base of the skull with scissors. He puts a tube into the baby's skull and sucks out the baby's brains with a vacuum. When the skull is largely empty, the abortionist pulls what's left of the head out of the womb, and the partial-birth abortion is "successful."

The media know that if any of these things were shown on television, this horror would come to an end. The Bible says that the Lord hates those who shed innocent blood (Prov. 6:16–17). And I say woe unto those people who have complicity in it.

Just think about the complicity of the media. It is virtually impossible to get any television station in America to show a picture of an aborted child, but how many tens of thousands of victims of the Nazi holocaust have been shown on television? How many pictures of slaves in productions like *Roots* have been shown? How many times did we see the burnt bodies of people from the Vietnam War brought right into our living rooms? Yet never a picture of an aborted child, because abortion proponents know that if the light were shone in that darkness, people would see the atrocities and would recoil in horror. "How could people allow such a thing to happen?" they would cry. "This must end!"

Shari Richard, an ultrasonographer, who takes sonograms of babies in the womb, said something I think is very, very perceptive: "If wombs had windows, abortion would end." Unfortunately abortion happens in secrecy behind the well-protected doors of abortion clinics and behind the walls of the mother's womb, unseen and unheard.

Carol Everett has firsthand knowledge of the deception at the heart of the abortion industry. She says, "In the front counseling room, the young woman is asking, 'Is it a baby?' And she's being told, 'No.' But in the back, every single baby, as early as it can be done, has to be put back together—arms, legs, hands, feet, the head, and the spine—to be sure it's all there. It is a baby."[2]

So we have semantic deception: "Not a person . . . It's something else. . . It's a glob of tissue. " Or "It's P.O.C., products of conception." Some clinics have even told women the fetus appears to have gill slits in various stages of development. They say, "You see, it's just a fish. We kill fish, don't we?" Yet these indentations are not gill slits and have nothing to do with fish; they never connect to the lungs. These marks eventually produce the ears and glands in the neck, but clinics have deceived people into believing the fetus is a fishlike evolutionary ancestor. And so the deception goes on.

Just as people today have asked, "What were the German Christians doing when the Nazis were slaughtering Jews?" our grandchildren may ask, "What were *you* doing during the American holocaust? Why did you not stop it?" Someday the mask of silence and secrecy and darkness will be taken away, and everyone will see all the ghastly details. Then they will say, "How could you have lived during all of that and never lifted a hand or your voice to stop it?"

The baby in the womb has as much a right to life as any of us.

Life, Liberty, and the Pursuit of Happiness

Our Declaration of Independence declares, "All men are created equal, that they are endowed by their Creator with certain inalienable rights, that among these are life, liberty, and the pursuit of happiness."[3]

In one of Dr. Francis Schaeffer's last messages he said that the right to life is more fundamental and basic than the right to liberty or the pursuit of happiness, or any other right, for that matter. Indeed, if you are lying in your coffin, you do not care how many shackles and chains have been wrapped around you to restrict your freedom. Nor do you care how much money you have in your bank account. Without life, nothing else really matters.

Ever since the Supreme Court legalized abortion in *Roe v. Wade* on January 22, 1973, almost 50 million unborn babies have been killed in the U.S.—some by having their brains sucked out in partial-birth abortions. This American holocaust is eight times larger than the loss of Jewish lives in Nazi Germany.

You might wonder how our nation could be involved in such a holocaust.

Semantic Manipulation

This atrocity begins, as always, with semantic manipulation. In 1857, in the now infamous Dred Scott Decision, the Supreme Court of the United States declared that slaves were not persons in the sense of constitutional law, and therefore were not protected by our Constitution or our laws.

We now look back at that decision and ask, "How could people have been so morally blind? How could there have been such moral turpitude as to suppose that these slaves were 'things,' which people owned and could do with as they willed, even to the point of killing them?" As in every decade of such atrocities, this was done in large measure in private, in secret, on large plantations and hidden from the eyes of many people.

However, men such as William Wilberforce of England did address the issue. He repeatedly appealed to the parliament. This devout evangelical also had a committee gather information on the treatment of slaves, and more light was shed, though men resisted it. Finally, the light invaded the darkness, and in 1807 parliament voted to abolish the slave trade. In the United States, it took a bloody civil war to end this bondage, after decade upon decade of largely Christian-led antislavery movements, including the Underground Railroad, which was run by the Quakers.

In 1936 another high tribunal, the Supreme Tribunal of Nazi Germany, declared that Jews were not persons and, therefore, not protected by the laws of Nazi Germany. This decision opened the gates to the Holocaust, and millions died. Again we say, "How could those people have been so morally blind? How could such moral turpitude have existed without the people doing something about it?" And again, in large measure this was done in private, hidden behind the electrified walls or fences of concentration camps. When the war finally ended, the gates were thrown open and the atrocities were revealed. Then people were aghast at what had taken place, but it took the light to invade the darkness.

Now let's take a look at the context in which the *Roe v. Wade* decision was made. Our nation had just come through the decade of the 1960s. The moral values, traditions, and laws of life that had governed Western civilization for two thousand years had been, it seems, suddenly jettisoned in one decade. Acting in that moral vacuum, the Supreme Court moved to provide what they felt was a solution to the problems created by the blatant and epidemic immorality in America. The solution: the sin engendered in the sexual revolution was to be covered up by the abortion revolution. So began the parade of the dead.

In 1970, a few years prior to the Supreme Court decision legalizing abortion, Dr. Malcolm Watts wrote the most revealing editorial for the California Medical Association, entitled "A New Ethic for Medicine and Society." This is brutally and painfully honest:

> The traditional Western ethic has always placed great emphasis on the intrinsic worth and equal value of every human life regardless of its stage or condition. This ethic has had the blessing of the Judeo-Christian heritage and has been the basis for most of our laws and much of our social policy . . . This traditional ethic is still clearly dominant, but there is much to suggest that it is being eroded at its core and may eventually even be abandoned . . .
>
> Since the old ethic has not yet been fully displaced it has been necessary to separate the idea of abortion from the idea of killing, which continues to be socially abhorrent. The result has been a curious avoidance of the scientific fact, which everyone really knows, that human life begins at conception and it's continuous whether intra- or extra-uterine until death. The very considerable semantic gymnastics which are required to rationalize abortion as anything but taking a human life would be ludicrous if they were not often put forth under socially impeccable auspices. It is suggested that this schizophrenic sort of subterfuge is necessary because while a new ethic is being accepted the old one has not yet been rejected.[4]

Well, there it is—in painfully honest detail. And this editorial predates *Roe v. Wade* by three years.

In 1973 the judges of the U.S. Supreme Court again demonstrated their "consummate" wisdom by passing *Roe v. Wade*. In that decision, they said that unborn children are not persons and are not deserving of the protection of our Constitution and laws. Thus, the American holocaust was unleashed.

Today those aborted babies would be out in the workforce, rearing children and changing our world. Many of them would be graduating from high school and choosing colleges. If you watched a graduation ceremony this past year, you should know that every fourth place would have been occupied by a cap and gown that was empty, for that child was not there—not there to be valedictorian, not there to become a doctor, lawyer, minister . . . perhaps even president of the United States. Some fifty million Americans are missing in this bloody action that has been such a dark blotch on the escutcheon of our country.

And this horrendous decision was based on lies, from its very inception, as legal affidavits show.

BASED ON LIES

It used to be *Roe* vs. *Wade*. Now it's Roe *agrees with* Wade. Sound confusing? Let me explain.

Roe v. Wade rested on a series of lies. To begin with, all Norma McCorvey ("Jane Roe") wanted was an abortion. She says the attorneys assured her they would get her one; they didn't. Lie number one. One of the feminist attorneys had had an abortion in Mexico, yet she never gave Norma this information. Why? She needed a pregnant plaintiff to sign the affidavit challenging the laws against abortion. When Norma asked if the decision would come in time for her to legally get an abortion, the attorney was evasive. She knew that the decision would never be handed down before Norma gave birth, yet she never told Norma that truth. Lie number two. In fact, Norma's baby was four months old when the court declared abortion legal on January 22, 1973. In *Roe v. Wade,* the attorneys argued that Jane Roe should be allowed to abort because she was gang-raped. This, too, was untrue. In fact, she was neither *gang*-raped, nor raped at all.

These attorneys simply used Norma for the monumental case. Lie number three.

Furthermore, *Doe v. Bolton*, the companion Supreme Court case that came out the same day as *Roe,* which allowed for second- and third-trimester abortions and made it legal for this procedure to be accomplished outside of a hospital (giving rise to the numerous abortion clinics throughout the United States), was also based on a lie.

Sandra Cano (who signed an affidavit as Mary Doe) was a poor pregnant woman seeking a divorce and the return of her two children who were in foster care.

But Sandra Cano never wanted an abortion and never had one, though her attorney arranged for her to get one at an out-of-state hospital if she had wanted one. So *Roe*'s companion decision, *Doe,* was completely deceptive. Lie number four. The affidavit in *Doe v. Bolton* also said that Cano's mental and physical health would be jeopardized if she didn't have an abortion. Not so. Lie number five. Sandra later gave birth to a baby girl.

Neither Jane Roe nor Mary Doe ever had abortions; they are now pro-life. Their two children are alive today. That's why I say Roe agrees with Wade. (Henry Wade, who opposed abortion, was the attorney general of Texas, the state from which *Roe v. Wade* came.)

Another major lie that the whole argument hinges on puffs up the number of women killed from illegal, back-alley abortions. Abortion rights advocates used to say ten thousand women a year died in such a way. Dr. Bernard Nathanson, cofounder of the National Abortion Rights Action League (NARAL), who is today pro-life, admits that they just fabricated the number: "I confess that I knew the figures were totally false. But in the 'morality' of our revolution, it was a *useful* figure, widely accepted, so why go out of our way to correct it with honest statistics."[5] The data impressed the media enough to report it, but they never took a close look at the details. Lie number six.

THE BIBLE REFERS TO THE "UNBORN CHILD"

What do the Scriptures say on this issue? The Bible is very clear. It constantly refers to the unborn child precisely as that: an unborn child. The same words are used to describe the child *in* the womb and *outside* the womb. In Greek, the word *brephos* is used for both the unborn child and the young child lying in a manger. The term *huios,* son (for one who is born), is also used for one in the womb. In the Old Testament the Hebrew word *yeled* is used for both a born and an unborn son. And the word *geber* means either the child in the womb or outside of the womb. Personal pronouns are used in the Scripture to describe a baby in the womb. It is "I" or "me" or "you," always referring to a person, not the pronoun *it,* which refers to a thing.

Furthermore, we are told in Scripture that both Jeremiah and John the Baptist were sanctified or consecrated from their "mothers'" wombs. Of Jeremiah, it is said, "Before I [the Lord] formed you in the womb I knew you; before you were born I sanctified you; I ordained you a prophet to the nations" (Jer. 1:5). You don't consecrate or sanctify a "thing," a "glob of tissue." You sanctify a person. When Mary, with Jesus in her womb, visited her pregnant cousin, the baby in Elizabeth's womb leaped for joy. "Things" don't have joy. No, the Bible is clear: a person, not a thing, is in the womb.

It is only by deceit and lies that "pro-choicers" and abortionists keep this ghastly horror going. A lawyer told me that according to Florida law, a corporation is a person, but a child in the womb is not. What hypocrisy!

"PRO-CHOICE" RHETORIC

Then there is the so-called "pro-choice" rhetoric—again a large measure of semantic deceit. *Webster's Ninth New Collegiate*

Dictionary defines the noun *choice* as "the power of choosing." And we all know that the prefix *pro* means "for." "Pro-choice" advocates are for the power of choice.

Yet surveys have shown that more than half of the women who have had abortions have not done so by their own choice. According to their testimony, they have done so under duress, under pressure from the fathers of their children, from their own parents, from friends, from schoolteachers, and from clinic administrators.[6]

What choice do the abortionists give these women? One man who is head of a pro-life organization was picketing an abortion clinic. When the clinic manager told him to stop picketing, he said, "Give me a small desk in an obscure corner, and just a few minutes to talk to each of the women to simply present the adoption option and explain to them what it is they are carrying in their womb, and I will call off the pickets."

The man replied, "Over my dead body."

"Pro-choice" indeed.

Abortion is the only surgical procedure for which a physician is not required to tell his patients of the dangerous complications involved in the surgery, or even the truth about what it is he is doing—removing a baby, not a lump of tissues.

The head of one of the largest pro-life organizations in this country told about speaking to a number of doctors and asking them this question: "Do you realize that you are killing a baby in abortion?" He said every one of them got mad. Why? Because they didn't believe that it was a baby? Absolutely not. They knew precisely what they were doing. They were upset because this man assumed they were so ignorant that they didn't know what they were doing. Abortionists *know* what they're doing; they just don't want the *women* to know what they are doing.

Abortion is based upon ignorance. It's no coincidence that the word *fetus* is constantly used. What is a fetus? The word *fetus* is a perfectly good Latin word that simply means an unborn child, but the average American doesn't know that. I think it is fascinating that Martin Luther felt that, for Christianity to flourish in Germany, it was absolutely essential to translate the Scriptures from Latin (the only scriptural language available in his day) into the vernacular of German so people might know what was going on. The abortionists purposely reverse this process. They insist on translating the word *baby* from the vernacular into Latin, *fetus*, so people *won't* know what's going on. Deception is essential for the abortion industry.

The only "choice" the abortionists ever give anybody is "Tuesday or Friday? When do you want to have the abortion?" Any of you who may be pro-choice, I just want to say this to you: "You ought to get down on your knees and thank God that your mother wasn't pro-choice."

Some people say, "Well, I'm personally opposed to abortion, but I can't impose my values on other people." Wait a minute, suppose Abraham Lincoln had had that view as president. "My fellow Americans, I am personally opposed to slavery and would never own a slave," he would have said. "However, I cannot impose my values on others. If others choose to own slaves, that, of course, is their prerogative."

I can assure you of one thing: if that had been the case, we would rarely hear of Abraham Lincoln. Instead he is considered the greatest and most famous of all American presidents, precisely because he took a firm, moral stand for that which was right.

I think it is also interesting that the "pro-choice" crowd is, for the most part, the same crowd that rose up in "holy" indignation when the Supreme Court ruled in favor of school vouchers, whereby families could turn in vouchers at any school of their choice so their children could be educated there. "Horrors," said the so-called "pro-choice" group. "This can never be allowed." You see, we must allow mothers the choice to kill their children, but we cannot allow them to choose where their children will go to school. Hypocrisy? That's what I would call it.

How about sex education? The most effective sex-education programs in this country have one thing in common: they promote abstinence. They teach children to respect their bodies. They teach abstinence until marriage and then fidelity in marriage. The American Civil Liberties Union (ACLU), Planned Parenthood, and others are rising up in "holy" horror that such things could be taught to our children. Wait a minute, these children are being given a choice, rather than just being told, "There's only one solution, and you're going to do it anyway, so this is the way to go about it."

What about the choice of evolution or creationism? Despite the scientific evidence for creationism, the same "pro-choice" group, led by the ACLU, says, "Oh no, students must not choose between the two theories. They must be force-fed evolution and nothing else." How pro-choice is that?

Or consider the school-prayer issue, giving children the choice to pray or not to pray silently or audibly in school. "No, we must never give them that choice" is the rhetoric of the pro-choice movement. The only choice these pro-choice advocates are in favor of seems to be the choice of sin and death.

Finally, think of the irony of the term *pro-choice* as it applies to abortion. Those who use it promote only one choice—the choice of abortion. By eliminating other choices, such as adoption or keeping the baby, they show that they really aren't pro-*choice* after all. Allowing only *one* choice automatically disqualifies you from being truly pro-*choice*.

"Pro-Choice" Arguments

Several issues cloud the discussion of abortion, beginning with the often-heard phrase *the woman's right to control her own body.*

THE "CONTROL-HER-OWN-BODY" ARGUMENT

Surely a woman has a right to control her own body. We certainly would grant that. However, we should note that this is not without limits. A woman doesn't have the right to kill her body. That is a crime. The most important thing to remember is the baby is *not* a part of a woman's body. Every single cell in the mother's body has the same set of forty-six chromosomes, exactly the same genes—except the baby, who has an entirely different set of chromosomes and genes. The baby makes his or her own placenta, umbilical cord, and nest. The baby also has his or her own blood supply, and in 50 percent of the cases, the baby is a different sex.

The baby is not a part of a woman's body. However, the baby is dependent upon her. Pro-abortionists say, "Well, as long as the baby is dependent upon the mother, she should have the right to kill it." May I remind you that a baby who is six hours or six months old is also totally dependent upon his or her mother. Leave the baby alone for a couple of weeks, and he will be dead. Shall we kill babies because they are dependent upon their mothers? How about old people who are dependent upon nurses and their children? Have they also lost the right to live?

I recall seeing a cartoon that showed two beautiful babies with halos around their heads sitting on a cloud in heaven. One of the babies says to the other, "She had no right to abort me. After all, it's my body." So, you see, the woman's right to control her own body is a fallacious argument.

Another matter that confuses the abortion discussion is the matter of rape, incest, and the life of the mother.

WHAT ABOUT RAPE? INCEST?

One thing you ought to get very clear: all three of these situations—rape, incest, and the life of the mother—together make up less than 2 percent of all abortions. Yet they give rise to 98 percent of the rhetoric *about* abortion.

Fine, I say, let's get rid of the 98 percent of abortions, and then we'll talk about this 2 percent. In the Bible, when somebody was raped, the rapist was put to death. Today, as we have seen repeatedly, the guilty rapists frequently get their wrists slapped or get off scot-free while the only incontestably innocent person, the unborn baby, is killed. Even if the woman had a part in it—which she didn't in most cases—surely the baby did nothing wrong. Yet the innocent party is killed and the rapist often goes free.

Less than 1 percent of all abortions are due to the threat of danger to the mother's life. This situation is very different from an abortion, and therefore should not be part of the discussion. In abortion, the abortionists are trying to kill the baby. Here, an attempt is made to save the life of the mother and the baby if possible. This is a totally different matter.

A final argument is the "every-child-a-wanted-child" theory.

"EVERY CHILD A WANTED CHILD"

For decades we aborted on average about 1.5 million babies a year in this country. At the same time, two million couples were looking for babies to adopt. (Thankfully, the number of abortions is down to less than nine hundred thousand. But that's still quite a number of innocent human lives snuffed out.) Meanwhile, these babies are not available to those seeking to adopt them. In fact, many adoption agencies have had to close down because of a lack of babies. They are all in the incinerator. Some childless couples have had to wait five to ten years to get a baby.

I recently heard about a child who was born with AIDS. The parents didn't want him; I think the mother was dying and the father was gone. Six or eight families lined up to take this child who had a sentence of death on him.

The "every-child-a-wanted-child" proponents say that children will be abused if they are not wanted, and they won't be abused if they are adopted by people who *do* want them. Yet studies have shown that the vast majority of children who are abused were wanted and planned.[7] Another one of the lies.

Finally, let's follow this argument to its natural conclusion. Since we have destroyed about fifty million unwanted children, child abuse should have virtually disappeared from America. Yet it is epidemic in our time.

I'd like to propose the real reason for such child abuse: our culture has devalued human beings, and children, in particular. We have destroyed children by the millions in the womb, and we are now moving toward destroying them after they are born. We have, in fact, become much more violent as a culture since the legalization of abortion in the early 1970s. The rate of violent crime has increased, and a recent headline proclaimed, "FBI Report Shows Rise in Crime Rate."[8] How many violent crimes were there last year? There were 1.4 million, about as many as the normal rate of abortions reported in America.[9] Surely, human life has become much cheaper in America than it was in 1973.

Mother Teresa asked a penetrating question that the "prochoicer" cannot answer: "And if we accept that a mother can kill even her own child, how can we tell others not to kill one another?"[10]

People who advocate abortion also propose that we jettison our sanctity-of-life ethic and replace it with a "quality"-of-life ethic.

QUALITY OF LIFE: A NONTHEISTIC ETHIC

First, let me point out that the word *sanctity* comes from the Latin word *sanctus*, which means sacred, holy, or sanctified, words that relate to God. It is only in the eyes of God that anything can be made sacred or holy or sanctified; therefore this word deals with a spiritual essence.

The word *quality*, however, deals with material things. We can examine the *quality* of a cloth or the *quality* of an automobile. Sanctity of life deals with a theistic concept; quality of life deals with a nontheistic concept, so we are being asked to abandon our theistic ethics and accept an atheistic, materialistic ethic. That, my friends, is a long step down a very slippery slope.

Thirty years ago, many of us throughout the country were saying that legalized abortion was the first step down a slippery slope that could lead to infanticide, suicide, euthanasia, and, of course, the final stop at the end of that path—genocide. Well, that was said to be ridiculous and absurd. Yet today infanticide is practiced in every major city in America. "Nothing by mouth" is a sign over the crib of many a baby. However, this is abbreviated so people won't recognize its meaning: "N.B.O." "Nothing by mouth. Let it die." But it's a baby. It's not even a fetus. It's out of the womb. It's alive, but it doesn't come up to the proper "quality" of life.

We should never forget that before Adolf Hitler ever killed a single Jew, he murdered 275,000 handicapped people. First, abortion was prevalent in Germany for over twenty years. Then there was infanticide, the killing of babies. And then there was the destruction of handicapped adults. Some pro-abortionists argue that Hitler was opposed to abortion. That's only partially true. He opposed abortion for Aryans, but he supported and in some cases forced abortions for non-Aryans: Jews, Gypsies, and Slavs.

In contrast with the pagan worldview of Nazi Germany and the beliefs of some quarters of modern America, in the sight of God every soul is equally sacred and can't be measured on some scale. Unfortunately we have slid down that slippery slope so that now suicide is becoming almost epidemic in our society, and doctor-assisted suicide is on some state ballots. Euthanasia, the killing of the elderly, is the big push in our time, and is already legal in one state, Oregon.

I think it is interesting to note that with almost fifty million aborted babies gone from our population, there just aren't going to be enough people on the workforce to provide Social Security for today's adults when they reach retirement age. And there's no security fund built up to fill the gap; the funding is taken out of current taxes. So there won't be enough to pay for their medical expenses. Then they will be told that they don't have the quality of life they ought to have, so therefore, kill 'em. Poetic justice. The generation that killed their unborn children will, in turn, be killed by the children they failed to kill.

I recently saw a cartoon that showed an old bedridden woman. A middle-aged couple was at her side. The man had a court order in one hand and a hypodermic needle in the other. They were getting ready to give her an injection to put her to sleep permanently. The man was her son. With great bitterness in her voice, the mother says, "I knew I should have aborted you, Wilbur, like all the rest."

Poetic justice at last!

PRACTICAL SOLUTIONS

So what can we do to stop the American holocaust? If we are to experience a new birth of freedom in this nation, we cannot proceed with business as usual. I believe several steps will make a significant difference here.

STEP ONE: CHRISTIAN CONVERSION

Who would have ever thought Jane Roe of *Roe v. Wade* would be pro-life? But she is today because Rev. Flip Benham and a seven-year-old girl, Emily Mackey, took the time to share the love of Christ and the gospel with her.

Imagine Norma McCorvey's surprise when the pro-life group Operation Rescue, run by Flip Benham, moved next to A Choice for Women, the abortion clinic where Norma was marketing director.

A few years earlier Flip Benham had confronted Norma at a signing for her book about abortion, *I Am Roe.* "You are responsible for the deaths of thirty-five million babies!" he shouted. "How dare you desecrate their blood by selling a book?"[11]

Yet the first Saturday after Operation Rescue moved beside A Choice for Women, Flip Benham told Norma, "I have wanted to apologize to you for what happened at the book signing a few months back," he said. "I saw my words drop into your heart, and I know they hurt you deeply. I'm sorry. Will you forgive me?"[12]

Norma was amazed by his apology. "Flip's apology was the most potent assault I had ever known. I was defenseless against it," she said.[13]

Soon Flip and Norma began talking on a daily basis, he about God, she about the goddess. Flip let her know that he was a great big sinner saved by a great big God.

Norma says that the Christians "never shoved anything down my throat. They simply passed along a cup of refreshing spiritual water, confident that I was thirsty and that I would take a drink whenever I was in a mood where I could receive it—which I occasionally did."[14]

The war that went on in front of A Choice for Women clinic became a war, Norma says, of love, not hatred.

And the love of a young seven-year-old, Emily Mackey, finally convinced Norma to go to church. The child's mother, Ronda, worked for Operation Rescue, and Emily often played outside the office. The engaging little girl befriended Miss Norma, and they soon spent time together. "In truth, though at the time I didn't know it, I was being won by love. I could handle the hatred. When people yelled at me and called me a murderer and a wicked witch and things that shouldn't be printed—that didn't affect me. I could handle that. But the love in Ronda's face, and the love pouring out of Emily's voice—well, that love just about ripped me apart."[15]

As Emily Mackey hugged Norma and said, "I love you, Miss Norma," over and over again, Norma McCorvey finally heard the truth of Christ's love for her and became a Christian.

And she's not the only "pro-choice" advocate who has been won over by Christ's love.

Today Dr. Bernard Nathanson is a Christian and a pro-lifer, but at one time, he cofounded NARAL. As we saw earlier, Carol Everett was responsible for thirty-five thousand abortions, but today she is "playing for the other team."

Aiming for conversions of people in the abortion field is certainly a significant step toward curbing abortion. But also significant is the conversion of regular American citizens, many of whom are mildly "pro-choice" by their own descriptions. Pollster George Gallup Jr. makes an interesting observation. He says that 20 percent of Americans are *strongly pro-choice*, and 20 percent of Americans are *strongly pro-life*. But he says that 60 percent are in the "mushy middle."[16] No wonder one poll comes out listing a majority of Americans as "pro-choice," and another poll says that a majority of Americans are pro-life. The 60 percent in the "mushy middle" helps explain the apparent contradiction. Winning over more Americans to the pro-life perspective is often a by-product of winning them over to Jesus Christ.

STEP TWO: GREATER EDUCATION ABOUT THE PRO-LIFE PERSPECTIVE

Not everyone who claims to be born-again opposes abortion. Some Christians agree that abortion is wrong, but they think it should remain legal because some women are going to have it anyway. Therefore, converting more people to Christ is not the only answer. We need to help these Christians understand that God is pro-life, as witnessed in the Bible.

We live in an information age, yet when it comes to some key social issues, such as abortion, there is a great deal of *mis*information. More Americans would become pro-life if they just knew a few basic facts.

STEP THREE: CONTRIBUTE TO THE PRO-LIFE CAUSE

We need to continue to fund the crisis pregnancy centers. Christians by and large operate these centers, which provide free care to the mother at all levels of the continuum. This network of mostly Christian pro-life centers saves thousands of babies' lives per year and spares their mothers from lifetimes of guilt and anguish. Any pregnant woman can get help simply by calling the toll-free number of 1-800-BETHANY. That service has been around at least since the early 1980s.

STEP FOUR: SUPPORT PRO-LIFE CANDIDATES AND PRO-LIFE LEGISLATION

Many times a lonely Christian congressperson sticks his or her neck out on behalf of pro-life legislation, only to receive a major attack from the secular media and the pro-abortion forces. The Christian community is too often silent in such conflicts, and we leave such a statesman twisting in the wind.

Supporting pro-life candidates presupposes keeping up with the candidates in the first place. This may seem so obvious, but often we find ourselves in the voting booth with little or no information other than the candidates' names and party affiliations. Personally, I like the voter guides that include a candidate's position on abortion and other issues. To me, abortion is a clear dividing line between right and wrong, between a civilized and a barbarian society.

STEP FIVE: DO NOT ADOPT THE ABORTION OPTION

I wish I didn't have to discuss this last option, but I'm afraid professing Christians are among those getting abortions. This is the height of hypocrisy. We will never stop or significantly slow down the number of abortions if we ourselves are supporting abortion.

In all these issues, we are never going to be a part of the solution if we are a part of the problem.

Suppose you found out your daughter was pregnant—out of wedlock. How would you react? Obviously, as parents we try to do everything we can to teach our children the right way to live. But they don't always follow it. Meanwhile, as Carol Everett learned, many young daughters think their folks are going to "kill them" if they find out they are pregnant. Obviously, we must not drive our loved ones or the young people in the church into the arms of the abortionist. That only compounds the problem.

HELP FOR THOSE WHO HAVE HAD ABORTIONS

Some of you reading this book have had abortions; others have encouraged them. Some others have actually taken a young lady by the elbow and led her to an abortion clinic to cover up her (or your) sin. Your conscience is smiting you now.

Well, there is mercy with the Lord. There are grace and forgiveness for those who will confess their sin and flee to the cross, asking Jesus to forgive them, to wash them and make them whiter than snow, to wash away the blood from their hands.

Carol Everett had the blood of thirty-five thousand and one babies on her hands—and that one was her own. She gave this aborted baby a name, Heidi. About eighteen years later, she wrote a letter to that baby. I think her letter speaks to each of us:

Heidi, I wish I could see you right now and hold you. But for now I can only share with you what's on my heart.

I hope you like the name I've given you. Precious, you were hidden from me for seventeen years. I'm sorry it took me so long to acknowledge you.

Although you have never physically lived on this earth, you have lived for more than eighteen years in my heart. It is true your father and I had no place for you in our home, but you have always had a home in my heart. You will live there as long as I live. I wear my gold "precious feet" pin everywhere I go to remind me of you.

Heidi, nothing can replace the loss of you, but I want you to know that your death has not been without purpose. The love God has shown to me in forgiving me compels me to work hard telling every mother and father I can about my mistake. I try to help them hear the cry of their unborn child saying, "I want to live. I want to have the opportunity to grow to my full potential, too. Don't shut me out before I have a chance to share my life with you. Don't shut your heart to me."

I am also trying to help all of the families who have been damaged by abortion. I want them to discover the power of love I know today and continue to see working in our family . . .

Heidi, you would be graduating from high school this year and preparing to go off to college. I would be helping you select a college just like I did your brother and sister. They would be right in the middle, helping us with your selection. You would really love Joe Bob and Kelly like I do.

I have a special request to make of you that I think you can honor. Please sing a joyful song of thanksgiving to the Lord for me because of all His love shown to our family.

Heidi, I love you and miss you with all my heart. I can hardly wait to hug you and to join you in our heavenly home.[17]

NINE

THE DUMBING DOWN
OF AMERICA

"And these words which I command
you today shall be in your heart.
You shall teach them diligently to your
children, and shall talk of them
when you sit in your house,
when you walk by the way,
when you lie down, and when you rise up."
—DEUTERONOMY 6:6–7

Several years ago, I had the pleasure of having lunch with the Honorable William J. Bennett, former Secretary of Education for the United States. He told me some of his concerns about what is happening in education in our country today. Truly, my friends, the situation has gone from deplorable to catastrophic.

An example of this might be reflected in some statements taken from papers turned in by high-school students across the country. These are the facts they remember:

- "A triangle which has an angle of 135 degrees is called an obscene triangle."

- "A virtuoso is a musician with real high morals."

- "The Gorgons had long snakes in their hair. They looked like women, only more horrible."

- "Zanzibar is noted for its monkeys. The British governor lives there."

- "To collect sulphur," says one of our budding scientists, "hold a deacon over a flame in a test tube."

But their real forte is in ancient history:

- "Socrates was a famous Greek teacher who went around giving people advice. They killed him. Socrates died from an overdose of wedlock. After his death, his career suffered a dramatic decline."

- "It [The Middle Ages] was an age of great inventions and discoveries. Gutenberg invented the Bible."

- "Christopher Columbus was a great navigator who discovered America while cursing about the Atlantic. His ships were called *The Nina*, *The Pinta*, and *The Santa Fe*."

- "Abraham Lincoln became America's greatest precedent. Lincoln's mother died in infancy, and he was born in a log cabin which he built with his own hands."

- "Gravity was invented by Isaac Walton. It is chiefly noticeable in the autumn when the apples are falling off the trees."

- "The sun never sets on the British Empire because the British Empire is on the east and the sun sets on the west," as every educated person knows.

Well, I don't want to talk about the educational accomplishments or the lack thereof; I want to talk about rearing godly children in an ungodly world. Certainly that is the kind of world we live in today. A few years ago I read in the Ft. Lauderdale newspaper that in a recent year 1,425 crimes were committed in Broward

County's public high schools alone. What happened to spit balls, paper airplanes, and talking in class?

Today in our secularist education in America we have a world-and-life view that was not prevalent in this country fifty or a hundred years ago, a world-and-life view without God. When God is simply removed, He does not have to be denied. He simply has to be ignored, and students imbibe almost by osmosis a world-and-life view that is godless. And so they learn about a world in which God has silently and effectively been banished from the cosmos.

In 2001 a television documentary aired that included an interview of serial killer and cannibal Jeffrey Dahmer. He said that evolution in school undermined his faith that human life had any value, and that when he accepted that view, it totally devalued his opinion of his fellow man, and, since it taught him there was no God to whom he would be accountable, it gave him permission to do as he pleased. His father confirmed this change in Jeffrey's outlook from what he learned at school.[1]

We have forgotten that children will simply live out what they learn. Garbage in, garbage out.

A TUG-OF-WAR IN THE CLASSROOM

In 1983 *The Humanist* published John Dunphy's prize-winning essay that proclaimed, "The battle for humankind's future must be waged and won in the public school classroom . . . between the rotting corpse of Christianity . . . and the new faith of humanism."[2] Unfortunately, even though there are far more Christians than humanists in America, the educational elite in this country have systematically excluded God from our public schools.

And the results are the fodder for today's newspaper . . .

"READING, CHEATING, AND 'RITHMETIC"
Fast-forward to the year 2000. At Piper High School in Piper, Kansas, teacher Christine Pelton, who had assigned her students a

semester-long biology project, discovered that 28 out of 118 had plagiarized their work. Entire sections were copied from the same Internet Web sites. She gave each student a zero on the project and a failing grade in the class. However, the parents did not stand behind her; in fact, they were outraged and went to the school board, who demanded she give the students partial credit. The next day Pelton told the *Kansas City Star*, "I went to my class and tried to teach, but the kids were whooping and hollering and saying, 'We don't have to listen to you anymore.'" Since she had no authority, Pelton quit.[3]

Studies made by Rutgers University professor Donald McCabe found that more than 75 percent of college students cheat and that the professors don't seem to care. In another study he made in 1999 of one thousand professors in twenty-one colleges, one-third of them said they were aware of what was going on.[4]

Another outworking of the completely secular environment in so many of our public schools is the rampant discrimination against Christians.

PREJUDICE AGAINST CHRISTIANS

Earlier I told how the one great sin of our culture is the sin of intolerance. Yet the very people who clamor for tolerance are completely intolerant toward Christians. Consider these recent examples from David Gibbs Jr., of the Christian Law Association of Seminole, Florida:

- A public-school bus driver in New York was fired for witnessing to a student when he answered the student's questions about religion and gave him a Bible.

- A student in Utah was told to cover his Bible when he brings it to school.

- Christian students in Missouri have been told they may not pray over their meals or pass out gospel tracts in school.

- The state of Washington forbids public university students from student teaching in private religious classrooms.[5]

None of these anti-Christian acts were constitutional. And what has been the academic fallout of the secularization of the schools? Poor reading and writing skills.

ACADEMIC RESULTS

A recent study found that four out of ten elementary-grade students in Illinois cannot write an organized essay using basic grammar and spelling. It has continued to increase since the new Illinois Standards Achievement Test was introduced in 1999. Educators and experts say the students don't get enough instruction in writing, and that many teachers are not adequately trained to teach it.[6]

But it isn't just grade-school and high-school students who have been impacted by what William Bennett has called "the dumbing down of America." Even many college students today are faring poorly. In its November 2002 edition, the *Education Reporter* pointed out, "More than 600,000 college freshmen need remedial courses this fall. Courses in reading, writing and math cost U.S. taxpayers approximately $1 billion and contain material that should have been mastered in high school. By next year nine states will have drastically cut back or eliminated remedial classes in four-year public colleges."[7]

Another fallout of the secularization of the schools has been the rewriting of history.

NO MORE AMERICAN HEROES

If the educational elites get their way, not only will schoolchildren not know about the Christianity of the founders of this country, they won't even learn about our founders. Period. Consider this example from California: "California's state list of recommended books for students excludes American heroes and founders. While many great literary works appear on the twenty-seven-hundred-title list, books about Washington, Jefferson, Paine, and John Paul Jones are missing, as is the Bible, stories about America's war heroes, inventors, and the taming of the American West. Christopher Columbus is represented in only one book as an exploiter of native Americans."[8]

Another symptom of the secularization of our schools has been antipatriotism.

ANTIPATRIOTISM

To commemorate the first anniversary of the September 11, 2001, terrorist attack, the NEA Web site presented more than a hundred antipatriotic lesson plans that teachers could use in elementary, middle, and high schools. In these plans the NEA took a decidedly blame-America approach, urging educators to "discuss historical instances of American intolerance" so that the American public could avoid "repeating terrible mistakes." The lesson plans were developed by Brian Lippincott, affiliated with the Graduate School of Professional Psychology at the John F. Kennedy University in California.

William S. Lind, director of the Center for Cultural Conservatism for the Free Congress Foundation, a conservative policy think tank, said, "A lot of what's stated in these lesson plans are lies. There is no such thing as peaceful Islam. It says the followers should make war on those who believe that Christ is the Messiah." Phyllis Schlafly, president of Eagle Forum, said, "There is nothing that schools can add to what happened on September 11 that the children haven't already seen in the media. They should stay off it and teach what's true. They should leave it alone."[9]

These lesson plans are not the only way curriculum is changing.

GOD IS OUT, YOGA IS IN

Aspen Elementary School students in Aspen, Colorado, in grades one through four, have a new subject added to their curriculum this year: "Yoga Ed." On September 9, 2002, the school board approved yoga lessons, supposedly to help students "relax" and adjust to the new school year. A controversy arose when some parents objected to the lessons on the grounds that yoga is based on Hinduism and other Eastern religions, and therefore violates the so-called separation between church and state. The objecting parents, including First Baptist Church of Aspen Pastor Steve Woodrow, insist that yoga is more than a stretching exercise, and that it cannot be separated from its religious roots. At a public meeting before the lessons won final approval, Woodrow pointed to a number of religious terms in the curriculum, including *mantra*, *mandela* (a Buddhist spiritual term), and *meditation*. The parents also objected to the use of nonteacher instructors who may view the lessons as "spiritual."[10]

Another symptom of the secularization of our schools is the disparaging of traditional Judeo-Christian morality.

NEA AGAINST ABSTINENCE

How the subject of sex is brought up in the schools is hotly contested between those with a secular and those with a Christian worldview. We know which side the leadership of the teachers' union is on. For example, the New Jersey Education Association (NEA), which held its annual conference in Trenton on November 9, 2002, canceled three of its workshops because it discovered that the sessions would be conducted by an educator and two medical doctors who favor abstinence-only sex education for youth. Those scrubbed were Bernadette Vissani, director of the New Jersey Coalition for Abstinence Education; Joanna Mohn, an internist and member of the New Jersey Physicians Resource Council; and retired physician James Thompson, a member of the New Jersey Advisory Council on Adolescent Pregnancy. Replacement workshops were given by members of the Network for Family Life Education at Rutgers University, who train teachers in "comprehensive" sex education,[11] which includes such goals as: Give the kids condoms and show them how to use them.

If the public schools have not been bad enough in the last few decades, it's entirely possible that they could get worse.

FED ED: A BLOODLESS COUP

Perhaps the most alarming development in American education is the complete restructuring of our schools by the federal government. Allen Quist, professor of World Politics at Bethany Lutheran College in Minnesota, has blown the whistle on the new program in his concise, uncompromising exposé, *Fed Ed: The New Federal Curriculum and How It's Being Enforced*, calling it a "bloodless coup" because it happened without public debate.[12]

The takeover, swift and silent, began in 1994 with Congress passing three laws that year:

- Goals 2000 (G2000), which created a partnership between government and education by mandating dumbed-down national educational standards, a national curriculum, and national teacher licensure;

- The School to Work Opportunity Act (STW), which changed the purpose of education from acquiring knowledge to supplying workers for business, so that schools have become job-training centers, offering narrowly defined career choices; and

- The Workforce Investment Act (WIA), which mandated that the program be managed by one nongovernmental organization (NGO), the Center for Civic Education (CCE).

The CCE has total authority over what will be taught in our schools.

Who Is Writing the Fed Ed Textbooks?

When the CCE was appointed in 1994, it already had its plan worked out: its standards and a textbook.[13] The CCE wrote the textbook, *We the People: The Citizen and the Constitution*, to teach the relationship between citizens and government because civics and government form the core curriculum for the entire new Federal Curriculum. Each school must integrate *We the People* into its existing curriculum, which means the school will have to rewrite its curriculum.

You may be wondering why I'm so against the Fed Ed curriculum. Let's take a quick look at its contents.

What's Wrong with the Fed Ed Curriculum?

First of all, attitudes will be more important than subject matter. For example, traditional mathematics is often being replaced with what critics call "fuzzy math." The short version of the math war is that parents and the public generally want a back-to-the basics approach to math, where students first learn to calculate, memorize, and drill. The reformers consider that a waste of time, calling the traditional approach "drill and kill." The reformers want students to work in groups and use calculators to solve "real-world" problems—without first learning basic math facts.

Joy Hirokawa, a concerned parent from Quakertown, Pennsylvania, whose children are in ninth, sixth, and seventh grades, voiced her dissatisfaction at a recent school board meeting, "We're very concerned because we have children who are honor students who come into the ninth grade and now absolutely hate math. These kids are your best and brightest, but they don't have a clue of what they're doing in their math classes." Peggy Cohen, whose children are in ninth, sixth, and second, agreed: "[The teachers] are stopping science class to teach math because [the students] don't have the math skills needed to do the science."[14]

Second, the teacher will no longer be an expert in a subject area, but merely a facilitator. That's because under the new plan, academics takes a backseat. Quist points out that under this new plan for restructuring our schools, "the new curriculum is not organized around academic subjects. Those subjects are still there in a superficial way, but they don't make up the real curriculum."[15]

Third, subject matter will be restructured to embrace these themes:

- undermining national sovereignty,

- redefining national rights,

- minimizing national law,

- promoting environmentalism,

- requiring multiculturalism,

- restructuring government, and

- redefining education as job skills.[16]

Quist devotes one chapter to each of these. Let's examine a few of them briefly. Perhaps you are thinking that promoting environmentalism is not such a bad idea, but here is how it is presented. Rather than advocating that the students be good caretakers and stewards of the earth, the students are to become "one with the environment."[17] This is religious environmentalism, and it is now standard fare in national textbooks. Here is an example from a fourth-grade language-arts book, published in 1999 by Harcourt, Brace and Company: "Before she left the forest, Anrita kissed her special tree. Then she whispered, 'Tree, if you are ever in trouble, I will protect you.' The tree whispered back with a rustle of its leaves . . . As Anrita grew, so did her love for the trees. Soon she had her own children, and she took them to the forest with her. 'These [trees] are your brothers and sisters,' she told them."[18]

How are national rights redefined in the Fed Ed Curriculum?

We the People states, "The primary purpose of this text is not to fill your head with a lot of facts about American history and geography. Knowledge of the facts is important, but only insofar as it deepens your understanding of the American Constitutional system and its development."[19] That may sound good to the gullible. But on closer examination, the new curriculum will provide a history that emphasizes politically correct people and situations. Everything that is "traditional" will be downplayed, altered, or left out. The role of the founding fathers will be grossly downplayed. Any good that America has done will be left out of history or modified. What brought on various problems, such as the 9/11 terrorist acts, will be adjusted to be politically correct.

Now look at redefining education as job skills. In order to turn the educational system into a job skills–training program, students will be set on a career path by the time they are in the eighth grade. This is supposed to cut down on wasted resources, meaning time and money spent on people who do not necessarily use their education in a way that directly benefits the employer.

HOW WILL THE GOVERNMENT ENFORCE FED ED?

Private schools and home schools will be brought under the umbrella of the new curriculum by altering the ACT, SAT, and the Iowa Basics Tests to reflect the federal curriculum. For example, in the past the SAT tested for *aptitude,* looking at the future, that is, successfully graduating from college. In June 2002 the Trustees of the College Board for the SAT voted to change it to an *achievement* test, which will align it with the federal curriculum. All state-level tests and the Graduate Record Exam are also realigning to the federal curriculum. "The implications of this realignment of the SAT are profound. The new federal K–12 curriculum requires little more than minimum competencies in knowledge-based learning. Attitudes and beliefs are the core curriculum of the new federal standards. The federal curriculum is based on creating a new global citizen, not educating children with broad-based knowledge."[20]

The future does not look promising if we don't turn things around quickly. But there are a few bright spots out there, like the "Golden Rule School."

"GOLDEN RULE SCHOOL"

An example of a Christian providing a positive alternative to the public-school mess is what has been called the "Golden Rule School." Mrs. Orlean Koehle, a parent and president of Eagle Forum of California, was inspired to create the program as she sat with other parents at a "Hate-Free Schools" meeting at Santa Rosa's Maria Carrillo High School. You've probably never heard of "Hate-Free Schools." I hadn't either. The administrators at Maria Carrillo High School claimed the program was necessary because of two incidents of "hate" at the school. They explained that if 60 percent of the students and 60 percent of the faculty would undergo a "diversity" training program, the school would receive a banner pronouncing it "Hate-Free."

Mrs. Koehle said, "As I listened to the Hate-Free Schools presentation, it occurred to me that we could save a lot of time and money if we would just return to the Golden Rule, the concept that influenced our schools and our society for over two hundred years: 'Do unto others as you would have them do unto you.'" She drafted a handbook, composed of sixteen principles and procedures, to teach children to respect one another, their teachers and principals, and their school rules. The first step in implementing the Golden Rule program was to post the Golden Rule in every classroom and have every teacher explain that it was the main rule of the class. Then teachers taught one positive character trait each week, incorporating it into their English, literature, history, science, and music classes. They did this by choosing famous quotations, holding class discussions, making writing assignments, or having the students create posters. Other aspects of the Golden Rule program included setting up a student government and adopting a school dress code.

Student reaction was very positive. One student wrote that with the use of famous quotations in class "we are being taught great moral truths that we would not hear otherwise."[21]

WHY A CHRISTIAN EDUCATION?

Because of all the terrible things I have described, millions of parents have yanked their children out of the public-school system and placed them into private Christian schools. Furthermore, hundreds of thousands have gone the route of home schooling. Consistently, the children educated in the Christian and home schools test one year higher on average than their counterparts in the public schools.[22]

Many Christian schools offer four specific objectives: a spiritual factor, academic strength, discipline, and patriotism.

A Christian school says that a child must first become reconciled to God. Once he is reconciled to God, he will then be reconciled to himself and others, entering into wholesome relationships with other people and really adjusting himself to his environment and the world in which he lives. This is the meaning of a Christian world-and-life view. Many of the children in Christian schools come to know Jesus Christ personally as their Savior, and often when someone comes to know the Lord, he or she becomes motivated to learn for the first time. I'm reminded of what the Bible says: "The fear of the LORD is the beginning of knowledge" (Prov. 1:7).

Not only is there a spiritual factor to Christian education, there is also academic importance. We believe that anything that bears the name of Christ should be excellent. Unfortunately Christian schools have not always been excellent. But many certainly are. Years ago, our church founded Westminster Academy in Ft.

Lauderdale, and more than 60 percent of the teachers now have master's degrees or beyond. Recently, a majority of our first-grade students ended the year reading on a third- or fourth-grade level.

It is interesting to note that in our first year most of our students came either from other Christian schools or other private schools. Now roughly half of them come from the public-school system. And an interesting dichotomy appeared. We had students who made A's and B's and students who made D's and F's, and we had practically no students who were making C's. There was a very strong correlation between the fact that the students who came from Christian and private schools made A's and B's and those who came from the public-school system made the D's and F's.

So we see that the academic excellence of the public-school system continues to decline as the disintegrating forces of a godless world-and-life view continue to produce more and more discipline problems and false concepts of education, depriving the student of the kind of education he should have.

The third objective in many Christian schools is proper discipline. We live in an age that may be characterized by lawlessness. We see lawlessness everywhere in the world, but I think much of it grows out of the permissive parental attitude of the last several decades. The Bible calls us to discipline—we are called to be disciples of Jesus Christ, which involves discipline and means that there will be boundaries, places beyond which we do not go. Children may rebel against these barriers, but they actually make them feel secure.

Finally, there is a balanced emphasis on patriotism. Our nation is far from perfect. It has many flaws, many things that are wrong, but there is no doubt that it is the most blessed nation that has ever existed on the face of the earth. It has more freedom and abundance than any land has ever enjoyed in the entire history of this planet. The poor man in America would be rich in most of the lands of this world. Why does America enjoy this tremendous abundance?

If you look at any other nation around the world, you will find that what the Bible says is true—they are what they are because of what they believe. "As [a man] thinks in his heart, so is he" (Prov. 23:7). Look at India—a nation that has stagnated in its poverty for several millennia. Why? Because its Hindu religion teaches through pantheism that there is no reality—the external, visible world is unreal, and therefore you do not try to correct an unreal world; you try to escape it. Consequently progress dies.

For centuries North Africa has been sunk in poverty, superstition, and ignorance. Why? The fatalism of Islam has kept the people from any significant progress since Allah has fated all that is; therefore nothing can be changed and North Africans are left in perpetual stagnation.

In many nations of the East, their religion is Buddhism, which teaches that life is irreparably evil and cannot be changed. Man's only hope is to rid himself of all desire for any improvement. The goal is not a more abundant life but extinction altogether, and so the very roots of social amelioration are severed.

Conversely, much of what America has enjoyed can be traced to its adherence to faith in Jesus Christ and the Bible. Until the middle of the nineteenth century, most of the education in this country was explicitly Christian, and the Bible was the chief textbook, in one way or another. Universal public education did not come into being until the middle of the nineteenth century. I believe that departure from the Christian faith led to the ungodly, secular, materialistic educational system that now threatens to overwhelm the spiritual foundations that made this land great.

Does that mean that all Christian schools are good and all public schools are bad? No. Some Christian schools have failed to do what they ought to do. And some public schools are still doing a good job. Many godly teachers are teaching in them, and I thank God for those godly men and women in our public-school system. But their hands are tied.

Does that mean that everyone who goes to a public school is going to end up overwhelmed by the evil forces that underlie its teaching? No. Some will get through and will survive because of the strength of what they receive from their churches and the teaching in their homes. But may I say to you that the overwhelming odds are in favor of training up the child in the way he should go?

Parents come to me in tears. "I cannot understand it—little Johnny—I sent him off to college. All those years of Sunday school, and he comes back an atheist. What did we do wrong?"

I'll tell you. These parents sent Johnny to an atheistic school where a bunch of professors with impressive degrees and tremendous influence and persuasiveness tore him apart. But Johnny had to go to that school, because he would get a much better job after he graduated from this prestigious college!

Unfortunately some students who are turned out of the Sunday schools and into the secular high schools and colleges are overcome by the unbelief, the immorality, and the ungodliness that prevails. As the twig is bent so goes the tree, and we as Christian parents are responsible for determining how that twig is bent.

TEN

IS GAMBLING A SIN?

"You shall not covet."
—EXODUS 20:17

A SECURITY GUARD AT AN ATLANTIC CITY CASINO THOUGHT he had seen it all. Then one day a man who kept feeding a slot machine keeled over from a heart attack. His wife literally stepped over his body to continue playing the machine. Her reasoning was that her husband had "invested" so much money in the slot machine that it would be a shame to have it all go to some other player.

She didn't attend to her husband's needs. She didn't talk to him as he was dying, or even call out for help. She just kept feeding the machine. Her husband's heart attack proved fatal; he died right there, as she continued to feed the slot machine.[1] This may seem like an extreme example of how obsessed some people can be with gambling, but gambling often appeals to obsessed people.

Gambling has become a national epidemic. Dr. James Dobson, founder of Focus on the Family, points out that Americans spend more money on gambling than we do on groceries.[2] Today more than a hundred million Americans admit to being gamblers of one sort or another. In fact, 51 percent of the American people now say they see nothing wrong with gambling. This is not too surprising, since numerous states have been spending tens of millions of dollars in propaganda that teaches people that nothing is wrong with gambling. (Think of all the lottery ads.) They have even changed the name to the more innocent-sounding word *gaming*.

Pastor and author John Piper reports on how disturbing and widespread gambling has become:

In 2001 Americans wagered $57 billion on lotteries, $18 billion on horses and dogs, $592 billion in casinos, and $150 billion on other gambling. (Total: $817 billion.) This is a blot on American life. Break it down to individuals. Massachusetts sells more than $500 worth of lottery tickets each year for every man, woman, and child. Think how many do not gamble, and you will begin to imagine what thousands are throwing away to have a 1-to-135,145,920 chance for the jackpot.[3]

Gambling has become so prevalent throughout our culture that even many professing Christians think nothing of gambling a dollar here and there or enjoying a "junket in Vegas." But the question is, Is gambling a sin?

Once when I preached a sermon entitled "Is Gambling a Sin?" a man challenged me after the service. "You just show me one place in the Bible where it says, 'Thou shalt not bet on the lottery.'"

I can't. I cannot show you a single Scripture that says, "Thou shalt not bet on the lottery." But neither can I show you a single Scripture that says, "Thou shalt not attend a pornographic film." Yet the Bible does talk about the sin of lust. And the sin of covetousness. Those who can't see the connection between lust and pornography are certainly purblind, and they probably won't be able to see the connection between covetousness and gambling either.

COVETOUSNESS

The truth is that gambling is nothing other than institutionalized covetousness. That is precisely the reason people gamble. It is the old desire for something for nothing—the "get-rich-quick" scam—which has been a plague upon the human race since man first fell into sin. The oldest dice, made from the anklebones of sheep, are more than two thousand years old. The Roman Caesars were notorious gamblers. One of them even had his chariot rigged so he could gamble while riding.

Let me make this very clear: people don't give money away gladly when they gamble. This is not voluntary giving. In fact, Caesar Caligula would sometimes have people murdered and their property confiscated if they beat him in gambling.

Gambling is a sin. It is a violation of the tenth commandment: You shall not covet. Jesus Christ also warns us to beware of covetousness (Luke 12:15). Paul writes that covetousness is idolatry and brings on God's wrath (Col. 3:5–6). Gambling is a sin, and like all sin, it is addictive. Highly addictive. In 1970 there were a million gambling addicts in this country. Today it is estimated that there are between 12 and 15 million, and that figure is escalating rapidly, with some 60 million family members, employers, employees, and friends who are seriously and adversely affected by the sin—60 million people. A large section of the American population.

One magazine put it this way: "Coveting is desiring, anxiously yearning to possess something that belongs to another without due compensation." That is exactly what gambling is. Covetousness is desiring what belongs to our neighbor. The covetous man has put "things" in the place of God; he is mired down in the mud flats of materialism and has forgotten the kingdom.

The greatest example of this in history is the picture of the Roman soldiers—the gamblers at Golgotha—surrounding the cross of Christ. They are down on their knees with their faces to the mud, casting dice for the garments of Christ, while above them the Savior of the world is dying. Gambling has a pernicious effect upon people in every conceivable way.

One expert, who spent thirty years as a compulsive gambler

and has written a book on the subject, gives this composite description of a compulsive gambler:

> He is a male in his thirties who is without any financial resources. He is deeply in debt to banks, loan companies, credit card companies, friends, business associates, and his family. He is behind in mortgage payments, car payments, utility payments. He has no life insurance, disability insurance, or hospitalization insurance. The family's basic needs are provided by parents, welfare, or income from the wife's employment. His employment is lost due to absences, inefficiency, irresponsibility, or theft. His business is lost due to legal action by unpaid creditors. He possibly has a history of bankruptcy.[4]

As if that isn't bad enough, his wife threatens divorce; she complains about the shortage of funds, the constant calls from creditors, and the total lack of communication with her husband. The children are upset and become discipline problems. The gambler of the family sleeps poorly, eats poorly, is no longer interested in sex, drinks more alcohol, has no friends or social life, and takes no pleasure in life. The stress causes him to be tense, irritable, critical, and slovenly. He considers suicide or the committing of a crime to obtain money to support his gambling, which he thinks about constantly, even though he loses regularly.

Gambling has become his god, his life, his all. He is an idolater, and he is on his way to hell. Up to 15 million people in our country are just like the man I just described.[5]

Many years ago, Mario Cuomo, former governor of New York, was quoted in *Time* magazine as saying, "There's something going on in this state. It's called greed."[6] He had been standing in line in the rain for twenty minutes to buy a five-dollar lottery ticket. Yes, it is greed. It is covetousness. It is gambling.

Ironically, though gambling is so popular, the odds against

winning are astronomically high. I once asked a group of older men who obviously had been gambling most of their lives this question: "On the whole, have you won or lost?" They all laughed at me, as if to say, "You poor, young, ignorant slob." Then they all said, "Of course, we've lost."

What Really Is Gambling?

What is gambling? According to people on the inside who run it, gambling is a business, the business of separating the sucker from his money, and they are experts at doing it. Someone once said that many of those people who sing in Nevada and Atlantic City do so simply to pay off their gambling debts; they are virtually indentured servants to the casino and will be singing as long as they can yodel a tune.

One of the all-time champs was probably not Pete Rose, who lost an average five thousand dollars a day for years, or even the late Walter Matthau, who gambled $1 million per year. Or Omar Sharif and a number of other famous stars reported to be gambling addicts. The all-time champ is probably a woman named Gitti Millinaire.

Gitti is around fifty years old. Many years ago, when she was much younger, she inherited $20 million. Then she started gambling. She was betting $200,000 to $300,000 on the turn of a card. She went through $20 million in cash in five years. She even borrowed $2 million from an ex-boyfriend and then promptly lost all of that. She sold her apartment in Paris for $200,000 and lost that too. She lost everything she had. Finally, she said, "I gambled too much."

Pete Rose's comment, after losing his money, his job, and his place in the Baseball Hall of Fame, was, "I don't think I have a gambling problem at all." So it is with most addicts; they deny there really is a problem.

The Real Cause of the Chicago Fire

We all know how the Great Chicago fire of 1871 began—or do we? Tradition tells us that the Chicago fire started when "Mrs. O'Leary's cow kicked over the lantern." At least that is what was thought, in spite of the fact that Mrs. O'Leary swore in court under oath that she never went into the barn that night to milk her cow. She was, in fact, asleep in bed.

So this mystery was not solved until a few decades ago when a man by the name of Louis M. Cohn died and left a large sum of money to one of the local universities. Included with that money was a letter. Cohn said he was leaving this money in partial payment for the damage he had caused when he knocked over that lantern. He said, "I and some of my friends had gathered in the barn that night." No, it wasn't a prayer meeting like the famous haystack prayer meeting. Rather, he and his friends had gathered to shoot craps. When asked "Why did you knock over the lantern?" he explained, "I was winning. I got so excited, I knocked over the lantern."

He may have won a few dollars that night, but thousands upon thousands of people in Chicago lost everything—some even their lives. I think that is a miniature picture of what gambling is like: a few people win, but a large number of people lose.

A Social Problem

Gambling is not only a sin, not only a personal problem, not only a financial problem, not only a spiritual problem, it is also a social problem of tremendous dimensions. Wherever legalized gambling goes, law enforcement reports a great increase in crime. For example, the FBI said that six years after casino gambling started in Atlantic City, the crime rate had quadrupled.[7] This is typical.

A SOCIAL BLESSING . . . OR A CURSE?

Is gambling a social blessing that increases the tax base, or a curse? Let's take a closer look at Atlantic City. Ovid Demaris has written a book entitled *The Boardwalk Jungle*, a story of Atlantic City with the advent of casinos. He first visited that city back in about 1984. The state had passed the Casino Control Act in 1977. He tells of hailing a taxi in broad daylight. He noticed the driver looked him over very carefully, as if the cabbie were used to watching out for someone who might mug him. Seeming satisfied, the driver motioned for him to get into the cab. After a few minutes Demaris thought he would open the conversation. With a rather jovial comment, he said, "Well, what has casino gambling done for you?"

The driver whirled around in his seat, glared at Demaris, and said, "I'll tell you what it's done for me. It's turned my daughter into a hooker and my son into a hustler." I'm afraid he was not alone in that.

What has gambling done to Atlantic City? If you have never been there, I recommend a quick trip. The scene a block from the casinos is reminiscent of a trip I made to East Berlin some time after the war. Many, many buildings are burned out, torn down, boarded up. It is now called the "Slum by the Sea," with casinos, of course.

Pacific Avenue is one block from the Boardwalk, and as Demaris says:

> It is crawling with hookers, pimps, pickets, pickpockets, drug pushers, car strippers, thieves, toughs, and a growing number of former patients from nearby Ancora State Psychiatric Hospital. Loan sharks are having a field day, and muggers attack people in broad daylight. Everybody is chasing fast bucks, which eventually wend their way into the casinos' coffers.
>
> Real-estate values and property-tax assessments have sky-rocketed . . . By 1985, nearly 90 percent of the city's businesses had vanished.[8]

Slum landlords, unable to evict tenants, burned down their buildings to collect the insurance. The population shrank from forty-five thousand to thirty-seven thousand. And in this once-prosperous city, there is now only one supermarket, no department stores, and one theater, which showed nothing but X-rated films, until it burned down.

Demaris concludes by saying, "Gambling is a parasitic enterprise that thrives on the weaknesses of people. It leaves in its wake corruption, debasement, despair and the subversion of moral authority."[9]

Does organized crime get into the picture? In 1977 Gov. Brendan Byrne of New Jersey said as they passed the Casino Control Act, "I've said it before and I will repeat it again to organized crime; keep your filthy hands off Atlantic City." Now, of course, hearing that serious warning, all of the organized crime lords crawled under their beds and trembled for a week—not quite. They have been thriving. In fact, former FBI Director William Webster said he knew of no place with legalized gambling that did not eventually have organized crime. Not one.[10]

Not only has organized crime stepped in, but gambling turns gamblers into criminals. Two doctors who wrote an authoritative book on the subject visited hundreds of Gamblers Anonymous meetings across the country and listened to thousands of testimonies by gamblers. They said they never heard one single person in all of those thousands who did not only acknowledge that gambling had wrecked his life, but also admitted to stealing to support the habit. We have created 15 million thieves, as well as gamblers.

As far as tax revenue generated from gambling, states and municipalities end up losing far more money in the long run because of the many costs associated with gambling. Dr. John Kindt, professor of economics at the University of Illinois, Champaign-Urbana, points out:

Legalized gambling activities are not like any other type of business coming into a community. Legalized gambling activities, particularly casino style gambling, brings in costs which other businesses do not bring in. That includes increased costs to the criminal justice system, increased regulatory costs, which other businesses do not have, and very large social welfare costs and just the social welfare costs alone will cost you three dollars for every one dollar in new tax revenues coming in.[11]

Gambling is, indeed, no blessing, but a curse to the state. Or put another way, gambling is not a good bet.

As far as jobs are concerned, gambling produces jobs in the casinos, which are notorious for low pay. But at the same time, it has destroyed most of the businesses around the casinos. They become walled fortresses—universes unto themselves. Gambling sucks up and takes out.

Yet, I am surprised to sometimes hear of church members who gamble or buy lottery tickets. Beware of covetousness. Be content with such as you have, says the New Testament (Luke 12:15; Heb. 13:5). Don't seek the fast buck. That devil's delusion has been around ever since man fell into sin. Yes, my friends, gambling is a sin. It is also unbelief. Christians believe that the Lord will provide all our needs. Gamblers do not think that what they have been provided is enough.

Besides the money, there is a secondary motive, gamblers say, for gambling. Excitement. When gamblers are not gambling, they only feel half alive. That's true because large sums of money are on the line.

But if you want real excitement, then cast your life down for the kingdom of God and follow Jesus Christ. The apostles who followed Christ were often scared out of their wits. Their lives were often in danger, but they were never, ever bored. Christ calls us to the greatest adventure in the history of mankind: to become co-laborers with Him in the redemption of the world, to be His witnesses, to seek first the kingdom of God and His righteousness. A Christian who is following Christ will never be bored.

"Isn't Gambling Just Like Wall Street?"

In ignorance, some people compare investing on Wall Street to gambling. "What's the difference?" they ask, since both involve risk—although the degrees of risk are much higher for the gambler. The differences are huge. When you invest in a company, although it may indeed be a "gamble," your money is normally used to provide goods and services for our nation. Most who invest can win, including those customers who benefit from the product or service they are able to purchase. The investment into the economy is not only less of a gamble than plunking down chips at a roulette wheel, but it is theoretically doing good for society at large (except when the investment is in pornography or something destructive).

Practical Steps

Gambling may be likened to a leviathan looking to devour whomever it will. What can the body of Christ do to combat it?

Step One: Mobilize the Church Vote

A few years ago, the state of Alabama was poised to adopt a state lottery. As a state it was one of the last holdouts. It seemed a foregone conclusion that this state was going to adopt the lottery because the voters rejected a governor opposed to the lottery and voted in his opponent who was in favor of it. But the people had one last chance in 1999 to directly vote for or against the lottery.

This gave the Christians of Alabama a new chance to oppose this expansion of legalized gambling. The odds, so to speak, were completely against them. But, as *Citizen* magazine points out, the church made all the difference on this issue: "Hundreds, if not thousands, of Alabama pastors preached against gambling from the pulpit in the weeks leading up to the vote. Churches conducted prayer vigils, registered voters, and even contributed significant amounts of money to help counter the pro-gambling propaganda. Five days before the election, 460 ministers from various denominations gathered on the statehouse steps to denounce the lottery plan."[12]

On October 12, 1999, the people voted 54-46 percent against the lottery referendum. The Associated Press reported, "The proposal—a constitutional amendment to allow gambling—had once enjoyed a 20-point lead in the polls but came under increasing fire from church groups who said it would exploit the poor."[13] Because of this vote and a defeat against video poker machines in South Carolina (where Christians also played a key role), gambling expert William Thompson, a professor at the University of Nevada-Las Vegas, called it "the biggest anti-gambling week in American history."[14]

This reminds me of the Methodist minister, Tom Grey, who retired from his pulpit in picturesque Galena, Illinois, to fight the expansion of legalized gambling. It all began for him when a riverboat casino became a fixture in his town through a back-room deal. We featured Tom on our program, *The Coral Ridge Hour*, and he credits our initial exposure as a platform that launched his message nationwide.

Tom Grey chafes at comparing gambling to harmless entertainment, like going out to a movie or taking in a show. The "gaming" establishment makes this argument all the time. Here is Tom Grey's response to that: "You could see *The Sound of Music* a hundred times and you wouldn't walk out in the parking lot and blow your brains out."[15]

Tom Grey has been most successful mobilizing communities, churches, and individuals across the country against the expansion of legalized gambling. Because he is a Vietnam vet, the gambling forces derisively call him "Riverboat Rambo." Would to God there were more godly men and women like him.

STEP TWO: DON'T BE FOOLED BY THE GAMBLING FORCES

The gambling forces in this country have expanded immensely in the 1990s, so much that you often see billboards for casinos in all sorts of places throughout the country, even in the Bible Belt. The "gaming forces" have fed these municipalities the lie that gambling is good for the local economy. In the short run, gambling may bring money into a community, but as I've shown, it brings so many other undesirable results that even in the short run, gambling is a disaster for a community.

We should stop the spread of gambling. Go to the commission meetings. Sign the petitions against gambling. Vote no on the casino referendums. Oppose politicians, whatever their party affiliation, who are beholden to the gambling interests. Gambling is a cancer to our society, and we owe it to our neighbors, our children, and our children's children to not give away the farm for a handful of empty promises.

STEP THREE: DON'T PARTICIPATE YOURSELF

If every professing Christian stopped supporting gambling in its various outlets, we could make a large dent in this problem. Instead, millions of Christians help contribute to the problem by buying lottery tickets and playing the slot machines. Sometimes churches even sponsor "casino night" or hold weekly Bingo games. Whatever funds they may raise, they sacrifice integrity in the process. I don't see how you can justify this from the Bible.

Americans need to rediscover the economic principles that made us great. They are found in the pages of the Bible, and they conform to human nature and all of history:

1. Don't steal—private property rights should be protected.

2. Don't covet.

3. If you want to eat, you must work.

4. Be generous with your goods to help your family, your neighbor, and the poor. But such charity should always be voluntary, never forced.

5. Above all, remember that God owns it all, and we are but stewards of what He has given us. One day, each of us shall give an account of how we have managed His property.

ELEVEN

CHRISTIANITY AND THE MEDIA

"You once walked according to the course of this world,
according to the prince of the power of the air, the spirit
who now works in the sons of disobedience."
—EPHESIANS 2:2

CRASHES, CHASES, EXPLOSIONS, EXPLICIT SEX, BLAS-phemy, pornography, adultery, homosexuality, and all manner of such themes barrage us nightly from our television sets. In fact, it became so bad for one man that he put a bullet right in the center of his screen.

Now, some would say that man was obviously some sort of right-wing reactionary, refusing to go along with the current of the times. Undoubtedly a puritanical prude. No, he happened to have been Elvis Presley. Television even got to be too much for him.

And many today are beginning to come to the same conclusion. Groups as diverse as the National Council of Churches, the American Family Association, and *Ladies' Home Journal* are combining to say that television is becoming a menace to the public health of America.

Syndicated columnist and author Michael Novak says that television has become much more secularized than its American audience. "In the face of the public media," he says, "countless devout Americans feel as if they are strangers in their own land." I wonder how many of us have had that feeling of loneliness and isolation. Novak concludes by saying that "our own public moral culture formed pre-eminently by television, cinema, and music is a disgrace to the human race."[1] Now, that's about as strong language as anyone could utter, and yet Michael Novak, winner of the prestigious Templeton Prize, is one of the most thoughtful analysts of the current scene today.

These are "Tasteless Times," stated the *Ladies' Home Journal,* and television is a key component. "The American people appear to be unshockable now, desensitized to genuine brutality—not to mention the lack of simple civility—and possessed of an insatiable appetite for whatever might once have been thought unsavory, crude, crass, and even decadent. At a moment in history when we are supposedly becoming more conservative, more mindful of enduring values, our popular culture is becoming flashier, trashier, more vulgar, and exploitive."[2]

THE TRUE CENSORS

The media is always decrying censorship, especially when Christians take exception to titillating or profane programs. Ironically, one of the most phenomenal pieces of censorship in the history of the world is going on today, and many Christians are not even aware of it. For some reason the modern media moguls seem to have decided that Christianity is to be censored from today's television and movies, in spite of the fact that more people go to church in America than ever before.[3]

Several years ago reporter Barbara Reynolds wrote an excellent column in *USA Today* calling religion the "greatest story ever missed." She asked, "What does the press have against Jesus? Is there a bias against Christianity?" Then she closed her column with this point: "By concluding that God isn't important, the press is trying to play God itself."[4]

A telling example of Christianity being ignored by the media can be seen by comparing how the media covers homosexuality versus Christianity. The statistics tell an incredible story.

"GAYS" VS. CHRISTIANS

Christians of one stripe or another make up a sizable group in our nation: 78 percent of Americans claim to be Christians, according to a study reported in *Time* magazine.[5] The Gallup poll, a more reliable source of statistics, reports 85 percent are at least nominal Christians. Yet this fact is clearly ignored on network television. In the vast programming of network TV, including seven evenings of prime time a week, one would think there could be more Christians on television. Instead, one is hard-pressed to find many positive Christian characters on network TV in a nation where a huge percentage of the population are evangelicals. Clearly Hollywood is not reflecting life as it is. According to Gallup, 46 percent of Americans report having had a born-again experience involving Jesus Christ. You wouldn't know it from prime-time programming.

In contrast, in recent years there have been about two dozen positive homosexual or lesbian characters on prime-time network shows. That number went down to six in the 2002 prime-time season. Why? Because the American people just weren't watching these shows.[6] The most scientific, exhaustive study on sex in America today, conducted under the auspices of the University of Chicago in the early 1990s, found that a much smaller percentage of men and women are homosexual than we've been led to believe. The researchers report, "About 1.4 percent of the women said they thought of themselves as homosexual or bisexual and about 2.8 percent of the men identified themselves in this way."[7] But if you watched prime-time television, you might think that about 30 percent of America was "gay" and less than 3 percent were Christians.

And if Christians are portrayed at all, they are portrayed as fanatics, as hypocrites, as extremists, as ignoramuses, as back-woodsy fundamentalists, as the uneducated and the bigoted.

The extent of prayer on television nowadays occurs during a tragic moment when the wounded party cries out, "Oh, God!"—if that is supposed to be a prayer, or maybe it's just an exclamation or a bit of profanity.

BIAS IN THE MEDIA?

Bernard Goldberg, a twenty-eight-year CBS veteran, committed professional suicide in 1996 by committing the unforgivable sin. Did he kill someone? Rape someone? Embrace the pro-life cause? No, he wrote an op-ed piece (a guest editorial) on media bias for the *Wall Street Journal*.

Goldberg, who describes himself as a political and social liberal, believes nonetheless that the mainstream press should be more fair and balanced. In his *Wall Street Journal* piece, he wrote:

> There are lots of reasons fewer people are watching network news, and one of them, I'm more convinced than ever, is that our viewers simply don't trust us. And for good reason.
>
> The old argument that the networks and other "media elites" have a liberal bias is so blatantly true that it's hardly worth discussing anymore. No, we don't sit around in dark corners and plan strategies on how we're going to slant the news. We don't have to. It comes naturally to most reporters.[8]

Bernard Goldberg called Dan Rather to tell him about the upcoming editorial before Rather heard about it elsewhere. Goldberg recounts Rather's response: "I hadn't given him any particulars yet, so before I could go on, he assured me that it couldn't be that bad. 'Bernie,' he told me, 'we were friends yesterday, we're friends today, and we'll be friends tomorrow.'"[9]

But when "Bernie" told him the "particulars," Rather said, "I'm getting viscerally angry about this."[10] That was the last time they spoke.

For this op-ed piece, Dan Rather and Goldberg's other professional cronies never forgave him. Overnight he became persona non grata at CBS. So, a few years later, Goldberg quit and eventually wrote a best-selling exposé on the media in general, entitled *Bias: A CBS Insider Exposes How the Media Distort the News*. The book went on to top the *New York Times*' best-seller list.

Note that Goldberg was not disowned because he said anything different or more shocking about the media than many Americans were saying. He was disowned because he was an insider, and insiders are supposed to be loyal, to cover up, to take an oath of silence. Because Goldberg broke the *omerta*—that oath of silence—the media labeled him a traitor.

ONE-PARTY MEDIA

We live in a country with a two-party political system, but as one writer pointed out, we have a one-party media. Here is a profile drawn up by three researchers who surveyed 104 of the "most influential television writers, producers, and executives." The researchers were Robert Lichter, a research professor in political science at Georgetown University, his wife, Linda, the codirector (with her husband) of the Center for Media and Public Affairs in Washington, D.C., and Stanley Rothman, a professor of government at Smith College. This Lichter-Rothman report on the "media elite" found that

- 93 percent "seldom or never attend religious services."

- 75 percent "describe themselves as 'left of center politically,' compared to only 14 percent who place themselves to the right of center."

- 97 percent "believe that 'a woman has the right to decide for herself' whether to have an abortion."

- 80 percent "do not regard homosexual relations as wrong."

- 86 percent "support the rights of homosexuals to teach in public schools."

- 51 percent "do not regard adultery as wrong."

- only 17 percent "strongly agree that extramarital affairs are wrong."[11]

In a very real way, the most telling of these statistics is the first. While slightly more than 40 percent of the population attend church every week, according to pollster George Gallup,[12] only about 7 percent of the media elite ever darken the door of a church.

I'm reminded of a candid remark from the former editor of the *New York Times*, Max Frankel. He said, "I have grown certain that humanity invented God."[13] Hearing him be honest about his atheistic worldview does not surprise me, in light of the godless vacuum often found in that paper of record.

Another study made in 1996 by the Freedom Forum and the Roper Center, which surveyed 139 bureau chiefs and congressional correspondents based in Washington, D.C., found that the journalists were far more liberal and far more Democratic than nonjournalist American voters. Here is how they voted in the 1992 presidential election:

- for Bill Clinton: journalists, 89 percent; nonjournalist American voters, 43 percent

- for George Bush: journalists, 7 percent; nonjournalist American voters, 37 percent

- for Ross Perot: journalists, 2 percent; nonjournalist American voters, 19 percent.[14]

Peter Jennings, described in a *Reader's Digest* interview as "an exacting editor and polished anchor of ABC's *World News Tonight*," adds to this profile by giving his opinion about truth.[15]

Reader's Digest: Americans tend to see the world in black and white. Yet you pride yourself on delivering gray.

Jennings: After living in the Middle East, I have become convinced there is no one truth, nor two; there are often several truths. One reason we are struggling over what is fundamentalist Islam and what is Muslim, who is the enemy and who is not, is that the answers are not black and white. As a journalist and as a person, I want people to pay attention to the gray.[16]

When Peter Jennings was asked on *Larry King Live* on May 15, 2001, about the media's general bias, Jennings stated, "I think bias is very largely in the eye of the beholder."[17] Jennings once again affirmed that for the journalist there is no such thing as absolute truth.

A manifestation of the bias in the media is reflected not only in their sins of commission—denigrating the Christian faith, promoting sexual perversion, profanity, blasphemy, and obscenity—but also in their sins of omission.

SINS OF OMISSION

The media ignores some important stories. For example, how many reports did we hear about Matthew Shepherd, the unfortunate young homosexual who was shamelessly beaten and left to die by two thugs in Wyoming in September 1998? Without doubt, quite a number. In contrast, however, how many reporters covered the story of two homosexuals who brutally murdered Jesse Dirkheising, a thirteen-year-old boy in Arkansas in September of 1999?

Let me give you both the details of this story and a warning: these details are not for the faint of heart. Two homosexual adults stuffed a pair of underwear in Jesse Dirkheising's mouth and taped his mouth shut. Then they tied him to the bed, facedown, spread-eagle. As one molested him, the other watched, enjoying the spectacle. Leaving Jesse in this position, the two men went to get a sandwich from a convenience store in the neighborhood.

When they returned, they found Jesse had suffocated. The chief of police of Rogers, Arkansas, where this took place, said this case was so shocking that he had all the police officers receive mandatory classes and counseling to work through the stress within a few weeks of the investigation.[18] If you ask people, "Have you ever heard of Jesse Dirkheising?" the answer is no. But the whole world knows Matthew Shepherd.

If you do not have an alternate source of gathering news, here are some other stories you would not know about. They are swallowed up because they reflect Christian values or a Christian worldview:

- *Women who have abortions have a higher risk of dying in years following the procedure than mothers who give birth.* The reasons range from suicide, which places women at a risk 154 percent higher than nonabortive moms, to death by accidents, which accounts for an 82 percent increased risk of death.[19]

- *Michigan posted "In God We Trust" in their schools.* After September 11, 2001, Michigan passed a law allowing school officials to post our national motto "In God We Trust" in their schools. Other states, including Florida, Utah, Arizona, Virginia, Louisiana, and New Jersey, are considering doing the same.[20]

- *Religious people are more generous with their time and money.* People who attend services regularly gave twice as much as others on average last year—$2,141 compared to $965. The more religious also volunteered at a much higher rate—54 percent versus 32 percent from nonreligious families. Overall, 89 percent of American adults gave to some form of charity last year, while 44 percent volunteered.[21]

- *The Salvation Army reversed its decision and decided against giving its employees domestic partner benefits.* "We will not sign any government contract or any other funding contracts that contain domestic partner benefits," the group said. The Salvation Army had been swamped with criticism from within and without after one chapter decided to provide such benefits.[22]

- *The Horatio Alger Foundation's "State of Our Nation's Youth" release in August 2001 indicates that family relationships are of the utmost importance to teens.* Eighty-four percent of over one thousand students surveyed agreed that their future success would be determined by whether or not they have close family relationships. More students would pick a family member as a role model than a sports star or entertainer.[23]

BIAS SEEN IN LABELING (AND NONLABELING)

The media is often eager to point out who belongs to the right-wing camp. With tongue in cheek, Bernard Goldberg says, "Everybody to the right of Lenin is a 'right-winger,' as far as the media elites are concerned."[24] In a more serious vein, he writes, "During the Clinton impeachment trial in 1999, as the senators signed their names in the oath book swearing they would be fair and impartial, Peter Jennings, who was anchoring ABC News' live coverage, made sure his audience knew which senators were conservative—but uttered not a word about which ones were liberal."[25]

Christians are "fatheads," according to one gracious columnist. In the wake of Columbine, Mary McGrory wrote, "But when it comes to preventing violence in our schoolyards, some fathead is bound to say that prayer is the solution."[26]

However, labeling does not always work in a political multi-cultural environment. An openly homosexual sociology professor, Pim Fortuyn, was shot to death in the Netherlands. The *Baltimore Sun* called him a "right wing leader"; the *New York Times*, a "rightist"; and the *Austin-American Statesman*, "far right." How so, when most homosexual candidates are often on the left? Fortuyn criticized Muslim immigrants, which would make him "far-right," but he criticized them because they were opposed to homosexuality and feminism, which would put him on the left.

Commenting on this case for *World* magazine, Marvin Olasky writes, "Journalists in the United States have long had a labeling problem . . . But the problem will grow more severe, as the assumption by American leftists that Third World voices are on their side no longer holds up."[27]

Maligning Christians has been going on quite a bit these days. A couple of years ago, Salon.com reporter Jake Tapper was covering a pro-Christian "Presidential Rally for Family, Faith, and Freedom." Later he described his gut reaction to the whole event: "And when they were all done, a bunch of reporters went into town, got drunk and ended up at a local strip joint called Big Earl's Gold Mine. There's only so much sanctimony a guy can take."[28]

Media bias against Christians is one thing, but when that bias turns against our Lord and Savior, the gauntlet has been thrown down. I want to take a moment to deal with such an attack on the person of Jesus Christ under the guise of news and information programming.

PETER JENNINGS'S SPECIAL ON JESUS CHRIST

A few years ago, Peter Jennings hosted a special presentation on Jesus Christ on ABC-TV. Technically, the program was well produced, but there was a heavy reliance on overly skeptical Bible critics. About 70 percent of the time was given to experts of a radical, antibiblical bent.

If the radical views of those guests were known, they might not have appeared as credible as they seemed on the program. For example, John Dominic Crossan was featured on the program as much as any guest. He looked good and sounded as though he knew what he was talking about. But Peter Jennings never bothered to identify him as a nonbeliever in the virgin birth and resurrection of Christ (which, according to 1 Corinthians 15:1–4, would make Crossan a nonbeliever in Jesus). Crossan believes it's likely that the body of the Lord was eaten by dogs—though historically, there's not a shred of evidence for that. Crossan is so liberal that in 1995, Bill Buckley, when introducing a debate on the resurrection, quipped, "If during the course of this debate you see Dominic Crossan disappear in a puff of smoke, you will know that Jesus has just cleared His throat."

Unfortunately, Peter Jennings relied too heavily on scholars like Crossan.

And too often there was an overly skeptical spin on the issue. After a while, if Jennings intoned in a voice-over that "the Gospels say . . . ," it was a tip-off that "it ain't necessarily so."

The documentary cast doubt on several particular points:

- Was Jesus really born in Bethlehem? Not necessarily, according to this show.

- The program implied the Gospels weren't written by eyewitnesses. Excuse me? Matthew and John were eyewitnesses. It's widely held that Mark's gospel was written with the direct input of eyewitness Peter. And Luke tells us that he painstakingly went back and interviewed the key players to provide us with a historically accurate account of the events that changed the world.

- The special gave the impression that Christ's temptation in the desert in which the devil appeared to Him was mere delusion caused by His forty-day fast.

- His healings were basically psychosomatic. Tell that to Lazarus, whose corpse rotted in his tomb for four days before Christ raised him up.

- Jesus perhaps intended to be more of a political savior than the Savior from our sins. His death thus caused His mission to fail. This is utter bilge. Christ Himself said, "My kingdom is not of this world" (John 18:36).

At least four of the guests (including Crossan) were members of the radical Jesus Seminar. The Jesus Seminar, you will recall, was a very controversial group of some seventy-four "scholars," which several years ago sat in judgment on the authenticity of the words of Christ. They voted anonymously on these words in the Gospels and concluded that Jesus only said for sure 18 percent of what is attributed to Him. For instance, they claim that of the Lord's Prayer, the only thing authentic from the lips of Jesus was the opening, "Our Father." But the fact of the matter is that the New Testament documents are very reliable; the material in the Gospels where manuscripts differ in spelling or in words applies to maybe 1 or 2 percent of the text. Instead, the Jesus Seminar rid the Gospels of 82 percent of the text. Textually, they stand on quicksand.

Peter Jennings's program didn't deal with the "findings" of the Jesus Seminar, nor did he indicate how radical these scholars were. However, to his credit, there were many sound bites from N. T. Wright, who is a conservative Bible scholar. At least he believes Jesus rose from the dead bodily, which is the most critical, watershed doctrine. Those who don't believe Christ walked out of the tomb are not Christians (again according to Paul in 1 Corinthians 15:1–4)—despite the number of theological degrees they may have after their names.

Mike Licona, who wrote *Cross-Examined*[29] (a book that proves the resurrection of Christ without touching the New Testament), counted the number of times on the show that skeptics vs. believers appeared. The four men from the Jesus Seminar were on camera 38 times (Marcus Borg, 10; John Dominic Crossan, 17; Robert Funk, 4; Marvin Meyer, 7), while the only evangelical scholar, N. T. Wright, was cited 11 times. When you add up all the comments from the liberal scholars (including those beyond these four), the total equals 54 times on camera. When you compare that number with those comments from the one evangelical, you end up with a ratio of 54:11—about a 6:1 ratio of liberal to evangelical scholars.

After watching this unbalanced presentation, the audience was left with this impression: scholars, experts who are in the know, don't believe in orthodox Christianity anymore. While I admit there are many liberal Bible scholars who deny some or many tenets of the faith, at the same time, there are also many scholars—thousands of them—who hold a much more conservative position. Tragically, through this television program, the faith of perhaps millions of people was made mincemeat—and all because of an unspoken bias.

I lost sleep after seeing this travesty, and I decided we had to respond. So by the grace of God, we produced an award-winning program[30] that aired on the major CBS-affiliates throughout the country at Christmastime 2000, "Who Is This Jesus?" We featured a wide variety of scholarly viewpoints, including the skeptical and Jewish, and, of course, believing scholars. We set out to show the ample historical evidence that the Gospels are reliable, that the New Testament is the best-attested book in antiquity in quantity and quality of manuscripts, that Jesus is who He said He is, and that He rose from the dead.

We received great feedback on this program, and we retooled it for Easter 2001, calling it "Who Is This Jesus: Is He Risen?" I am very grateful that the combined audience for these two programs was more than 20 million people. The original Jennings special had about 14 million viewers. Richard Ostling, religion writer for the AP, wrote of our program:

> Surprisingly, Kennedy achieved more journalistic success than Jennings at one point. Four of the five Americans on Jennings' program belonged to the "Jesus Seminar" of Santa Rosa, Calif., which promotes skepticism and took pro-and-con ballots that rejected the truth of many details in the Gospels.
>
> Jennings' viewers were told almost nothing about that context, or the reasons why the Seminar is spurned by many moderates and liberals at blueblood campuses. Kennedy gave viewers that information, and rather fairly. (Of the Seminar's two leaders, John Dominic Crossan agreed to be interviewed but Robert Funk declined.)[31]

So it isn't enough to curse the darkness. We must constantly light candles or turn on floodlights. We must provide alternatives. Thankfully, more and more Christians are rising up to do that.

WHAT CAN BE DONE?

I've talked to newspaper and magazine writers who have told me, "I know that my editors [or publishers] want something much more negative, and I hope that I might be able to get this in." They feel constrained to write negative things about Christians or about ministers, knowing that if they don't, the editors won't even publish their stories. We need to realize that because we retreated from the media and from politics and government and science and higher education, we have left these fields to the unbelievers. Now we need to begin to get more young people into the media to affect it. We need to have more Christian studio heads, anchormen, news writers, producers, and directors to affect the culture, since these people influence the thinking of so many others. This is not going to happen overnight, but over a period of several decades.

Secondly, we need to pray for these people—for their conversions. I wonder how many of you pray for actors, directors, producers, and writers? I must confess that I have prayed very little for them. We should also pray that those who are Christians will be strengthened as they attempt to lead godly lives and to have some influence.

We also need to evangelize—not just people in the media, when we have an opportunity, but we need to evangelize, period. Because the church has failed to fulfill the Great Commission in evangelizing the culture and to fulfill the cultural mandate to affect the spheres of society, our culture has produced a vast audience for these people that allows them to go on.

Do you realize that Hollywood is one of America's largest exporters? But what are we exporting to the world? Denigration of Christian beliefs and morals. Promotion of the homosexual lifestyle, which generally cuts a person's life span in half.[32] Promotion of all sorts of sex outside of marriage. Promotion of stealing, lying, and cheating when you can get away with it. Promotion of every profanity and blasphemy you can imagine. Promotion of gratuitous and disturbing violence. All these themes and many more are marketed to the world.

If millions of dedicated Christians turned off their sets at the onset of objectionable programs, stopped purchasing movie tickets for unacceptable movies, and stopped buying objectionable CDs, things would change rapidly. Too often we're part of the problem instead of the solution. Please do a little research before purchasing a movie ticket. You can find out about a movie before you decide to see it at www.movieguide.org or www.screenit.com. Generally, you don't get burned if you do your homework.

MISSIONARIES TO HOLLYWOOD

Think about this question. Who wields more influence? The leaders in Washington or those in Hollywood? Robert Knight, author of *The Age of Consent: The Rise of Relativism and the Corruption of Popular Culture,* believes the answer is the latter: "If I had my choice to controlling Washington or Hollywood, I'd pick Hollywood in a heartbeat. Hollywood . . . has enormous influence on our culture. Political institutions don't operate in a vacuum, they arise out of culture. I'd rather control the high ground of culture than the political superstructure that grows out of that culture."[33] Therefore, one way we can effect positive, long-term change is to support the missionaries to Hollywood (and New York).

One of my heroes is Larry Poland, who left a comfortable job as the president of a Christian college to start a missionary project. He founded Master Media in the 1980s to minister to Hollywood executives, writers, producers, and so on. And he also reached out to New York City media executives. At the same time he mobilized millions of Christians in the rest of the country to pray for all these people, including the "stars."

The work has been slow, but his organization has built bridges of friendship with many people over time. For instance, one Jewish man was miraculously converted. This man called Larry Poland and told him he was on the brink of signing a deal that would yield multimillions of dollars in profits. There was only one catch: pornography was at the heart of this venture. The Jewish convert told Larry, "Somehow I don't think Jesus would be pleased if I go through with the deal." Larry gently counseled the man, so that he could see for himself that, no, the Lord would not be pleased. Because of his new Christian convictions, the man turned down the deal.

Another man who is a type of missionary to Hollywood is Ted Baehr, founder and publisher of *Movieguide.* Year after year Ted Baehr documents information that shows that anti-Christian movies generally bomb at the box office, while well-done pro-family movies, including those with Christian content, generally do well.[34]

I commend the work of these two missionaries. Since Hollywood exports to the rest of the world, these and similar efforts are extremely important. Please keep these men in your prayers and consider supporting their efforts. In the long run, this could easily have worldwide impact.

EFFECTIVE PROTESTING

Do you know the name of the most active protest group to the media? It is the Gay Media Task Force. Directors and writers say that if they put anything on television that even in the slightest way is uncomplimentary to homosexuals, an unending string of phone calls comes into the station. And they will have a visit by several prominent homosexuals in the next forty-eight hours. That has an impact.

When was the last time you called a station and protested the way they portray Christians? We need to call the stations and write the networks.

There is also a need for solidarity. Unfortunately, too often Christians think, *That wasn't my particular group, my particular denomination. They attacked somebody else.*

That reminds me of what resistant Pastor Martin Niemoller said about the Nazis:

> In Germany they came first for the Communists, and I didn't speak up because I wasn't a Communist. Then they came for the Jews, and I didn't speak up because I wasn't a Jew. Then they came for the trade unionists, and I didn't speak up because I wasn't a trade unionist. Then they came for the Catholics, and I didn't speak up because I was a Protestant. Then they came for me, and by that time no one was left to speak up.[35]

We need to stand together as Christians, just as the Jewish people now do. If anything is said derogatorily about Jews, there's a tremendous outcry. It doesn't matter if the insult is against Reformed, Orthodox, or Conservative Jews; it is an attack upon

Judaism. Yet we'll see the name of Jesus Christ dragged through the mud and Christians portrayed as idiots, hypocrites, fanatics, and worse, and we say nothing at all.

We also need to discuss what's going on with our youngsters. We can't protect our children from this media bias. They're going to get it some way, but they need to be taught to test what they are hearing.

Finally, we ought to watch less television. You know, television is addictive, according to psychologists. And some of you are addicted to television. In fact, I wonder if they took the television away altogether, would you know how to live your life? Someone said that merely trying to improve programming is like taking an alcoholic and telling him not to drink cheap whiskey, but Chavis Regal.

CONCLUSION

Thankfully, over the last few decades, millions and millions of Americans have been tuning out the dominant networks and turning to alternative sources of news. Fox News, which strives to allow for conservative voices, is beating the competition per capita everywhere it goes. Conservative radio host Rush Limbaugh has far more listeners than any liberal commentator.

To counteract media bias, Christians are fighting back by finding alternative sources for news. This has inspired the founding of Christian radio and television stations that present another kind of news, and the rise of Internet sites.

Conservative columnist Michelle Malkin says:

> NPR liberals are horrified. Across the country, thousands of radio listeners are tuning out conservative-basher Nina Totenberg, and tuning in conservative heroine Phyllis Schlafly . . . For years, National Public Radio has gotten away with the smearing of religious groups and individuals, as it did earlier this year when NPR

reporter David Kestenbaum falsely suggested that the Traditional Values Coalition, a Christian political action group, was responsible for the anthrax letters sent to Sen. Tom Daschle, D-S.D., and Patrick Leahy, D-VT. Now religious groups are fighting back by taking over NPR's turf. American Family Radio, based in Tupelo, MS, now operates more than 200 stations nationwide and has applications pending with the Federal Communications Commission for hundreds more noncommercial radio outlets."[36]

Stay tuned, the best may be yet to come.

TWELVE

"THE FASTEST-GROWING RELIGION IN AMERICA"?

"Yes, the time is coming that whoever
kills you will think that he offers God service.
And these things they will do to you because
they have not known the Father nor Me."
—JESUS CHRIST, JOHN 16:2, 3

THE MUSLIM LEADER OF SANTA MONICA, CALIFORNIA, once distributed a booklet explaining Islam to Americans. The guide explained that non-Muslims (including Christians and Jews) who come to learn about the true faith (Islam), but then choose not to convert, should be put to death.[1] This booklet was disseminated on American soil. After 9/11, the mosque quietly took the booklet out of circulation.

Did that booklet accurately reflect the teaching of the Koran or was it aberrational? We'll see shortly.

I believe that if America is to ever achieve a new birth of freedom, we will need to rediscover our *Christian* roots. American renewal will require clarification of our genuine history, our institutions, and our traditions. We will also need to keep in check the negative and evil side of Islam, which wants to take over the whole world, including the United States. Meanwhile, Muslims are welcome to this country, thanks to our Christian heritage.

This chapter contains much that is politically incorrect, but it must be said. Please note that I have no desire to needlessly offend anyone, but I have a great desire for everyone who doesn't know Jesus Christ to come to know Him.

"A RELIGION OF PEACE"?

A year after 9/11, Jerry Falwell was tricked by a CBS-TV producer into making a remark against Mohammed. (The hour-long interview focused on Israel and Christians; the producer asked the question as an aside, and Falwell answered it as an aside, little realizing it would be broadcast.) Jerry Falwell made the unfortunate remark that the prophet of Islam was a man of violence. Halfway around the world, this remark caused Muslims and Hindus to riot in India, leaving five dead. For making such a remark, a *fatwah* (an Islamic "holy" death warrant) was declared against Falwell, who quickly apologized. But note the irony here. Major portions of the Muslim community threatened to treat him with violence for daring to say their religion was violent. They're saying in effect, "We're *not* violent . . . Take that back or we'll kill you." He took it back, and they still want to kill him.

Pat Robertson and Franklin Graham are other evangelicals who have offended Muslim sensibilities by speaking the truth about Mohammed and the Koran. They, too, have fatwahs against them.

Soon after 9/11, we were told repeatedly that Osama bin Laden and Al-Qaeda had hijacked the religion of Islam, just as the terrorists hijacked the planes they flew into buildings. But I'm afraid that's not accurate.

Islam has been violent for the bulk of its fourteen-century-long existence. From the very beginning, Islam gained much of its territory by wielding the sword. When you read history, you learn that by about A.D. 1000, half of what *had been* Christendom had been conquered by Islam. Half. All of the churches to which Christ sent letters in the book of Revelation are in territories now dominated by the Muslims. Much of the New Testament was written in, and to, places now in Muslim hands. This includes Galatians, Ephesians, and Colossians. The Christians were first called Christians in a place (Antioch) now under complete Muslim control.

Christians have been forever condemned for the Crusades. How often do we still hear that charge brought up, even though they officially ended some seven hundred years ago? Of course, aspects of the Crusades are totally inexcusable from a Christian perspective. But when someone brings up the Crusades, my first question to them is, *Which* Crusades? Do you mean the Crusade when the Muslims conquered the Holy Land the first time in the 600s or do you mean when the Christians finally decided to go there and take it back close to the year 1100, nearly five hundred years later?

"THE FASTEST-GROWING RELIGION IN AMERICA"?

Some people claim that Islam is the fastest-growing religion in America. That is debatable, except for maybe in our prisons, where Saudi money has helped gain tremendous inroads among disenfranchised members of minorities—many of whom have enormous pressure put on them to convert. Studies on the growth of Islam in America reveal that the greatest growth in the number of Muslims is through birth or immigration—not conversion.

Also debatable is the oft-heard phrase that describes Islam as "a religion of peace." I believe that an honest examination shows that the teaching of jihad is *embedded* within Islam itself. Here we have a clash of civilizations. And I am not a "hater" for saying so, although some in the media might call me that.

ALL ARE WELCOME HERE BECAUSE OF CHRISTIANITY

America's doors are open for people of all faiths—or of no faith—to live here and practice their religion unmolested. But that's not *despite* our Christian heritage—it is an *outgrowth* of it.

Someone once said persecution is an outgrowth of religious insecurity. I agree. If you know that what you believe is the truth, then you do not need to fear or persecute or kill the opposition.

I believe we should let the truth win out in the marketplace of ideas. Historically, not all Christians have believed or practiced that. To wit, the Inquisition. But using the sword to settle doctrinal disputes has brought nothing but dishonor to our Lord Jesus Christ. Reformation leader Martin Luther once said this about those who light fagots (the bundles of sticks used to burn heretics at the stake): "If fire is the right cure for heresy, then the fagot-burners are the most learned doctors on earth; no need we study any more; he that has brute force on his side may burn his adversary at the stake."[2]

No Reformation Within Islam

Thankfully, a great deal of progress has occurred in this area within Christendom in the last few centuries. Not so with Islam. Dr. Walid Phares, a professor of Middle East Studies at Florida Atlantic University in Boca Raton, says that part of the problem with Islam—as it is now—is that it has never experienced a Reformation.

Here's a telling contrast. Throughout America, some fifteen hundred mosques dot the landscape. But in Saudi Arabia, the main home of Islam, there is not one legal Christian church. Not one.

There's a true story about the underground church in Afghanistan that's rather humorous. That fiercely Islamic country refused to allow any church on its property. In the early 1970s, the authorities relented because of the strong suggestion of former U.S. President Dwight D. Eisenhower. A few years later, they changed their minds and destroyed the church. Then they used the bulldozers and earth-moving equipment to dig deeper and deeper into the ground of the ruined sanctuary because they had heard there was "an underground church" in Afghanistan. They dug at least twelve feet into the ground before they realized there was nothing deeper.

VOTING WITH THEIR FEET

There's no comparing religious freedom in America with what happens in other non-Western countries. I'm reminded of something the Orthodox rabbi, Daniel Lapin, said in our nationally televised special, "What If Jesus Had Never Been Born?" (Although Rabbi Lapin is Jewish and does not believe Jesus was the Christ, he nonetheless has a healthy respect for Jesus and for the positive contributions of Christianity in history.)

> The easiest way to answer whether life on planet earth is better because Jesus walked Jerusalem or not is very simple. And that is: Just watch the way people vote with their feet. Watch where the net flow of immigration is in the world today. Is it from Christian countries to non-Christian countries or the other way around? It is so obvious.[3]

Millions upon millions of people around the world would love to live in America. But frankly, I don't see people standing in line at the embassies of Pakistan or Afghanistan or Saudi Arabia.

Muslims and other non-Christians are guests in this country, and now they are citizens. But no one has the right, like the booklet distributed by the imam from Santa Monica cited at the opening of the chapter, to declare that I must convert to his religion or be killed. And yet our media seems to see little difference between the approach of Islam and of evangelical Christianity.

THE SONS OF ISHMAEL

To understand the Muslims, we need to go back to Genesis. (That's true for a lot of things—to understand them, we have go back to the first book of the Bible.) You will recall that God promised Abraham a son, a son of promise. Even though he and his wife, Sarah, were old, the Lord said that they would have a son. From the time of this promise to the time of its fulfillment, roughly twenty-five years elapsed. (God is not in a hurry.)

Meanwhile, Sarah got impatient because she wasn't getting pregnant. So she offered Hagar, her handmaiden, to Abraham in order to help God out with the fulfillment of His promise.

This proved to be a disaster, the implications of which still plague us today. Hagar bore a son, Ishmael, and this is what the Bible says about that son: "And the Angel of the LORD said to her, 'Behold, you are with child, and you shall bear a son. You shall call his name Ishmael, because the LORD has heard your affliction. He shall be a wild man; his hand shall be against every man, and every man's hand against him; and he shall dwell in the presence of all his brethren'" (Gen. 16:11–12). According to the Bible, Ishmael was not the son of promise; that honor was bestowed on Isaac, the son who later was born to Sarah herself.

Today, the sons of Abraham are battling with the sons of Ishmael on the streets of Jerusalem. The sons of Ishmael cannot get along with the sons of Isaac, and vice versa, and there seems to be no sign of letup in the conflict anytime soon.

THE DAY THAT CHANGED THE WORLD

The prophet Isaiah wrote of "the day of the great slaughter, when the towers fall" (Isa. 30:25). Obviously, he wasn't foreseeing 9/11/01 in modern America per se. But when the tragic attack took place, I found that Scripture quite striking.

Before 9/11, who could have imagined such an event? Except for the hijackers themselves, none of us had the faintest inkling of the catastrophic events that would transpire. Indeed, how true the Scripture is when it reminds us that we know not "what a day may bring forth" (Prov. 27:1).

In the wake of 9/11, we join with millions of others across the nation, in spite of our differences—Americans all—to share the grief and mourn the loss experienced by more than three thousand families who have had ones they perhaps loved more than life itself ripped from their bosoms. Some of those killed were Muslims.

But how could such things happen to America? We were not at war—at least most of us didn't believe we were at war. I'm afraid that most have forgotten that several years ago, in August 1996, Osama bin Laden declared war on the United States. And so, unbeknownst to most of us, we have been at war for some time and are now experiencing some of the horrors that war always brings—surely beyond our description.

It has often been said by those who have experienced it that "war is hell." Now many Americans right here at home have discovered the truthfulness of that statement.

One of the truly shocking things came to light a month or two later, when our troops captured a videotape in Afghanistan showing Osama bin Laden laughing and rejoicing at the destruction he had ordered. How demonic. Yet some portions of our news media equate religious fundamentalists of any type with Islamic fundamentalists. So suddenly, Jerry Falwell is no better than Osama bin Laden. They are two sides of the same coin, religious fundamentalism. Tragically, this type of nonsense is widely believed by many in our culture today.

The war Osama bin Laden declared against America saw different attacks through the last half decade of the twentieth century. In 1998 two of our embassies in East Africa were bombed, and again the evidence pointed to Osama bin Laden—the man who inherited a fortune and has been using it to carry out his own twisted ideas of justice and righteousness. This is, indeed, tragic.

What kind of man would mastermind such a gruesome, unprovoked attack as 9/11? Of course, he is descended from Ishmael, who, we are told in Scripture, would "be a wild man; his hand . . . against every man, and every man's hand against him" (Gen. 16:12).

It is interesting that bin Laden may have wanted to give the idea that the whole Islamic or Arabic world is against America, but there were people in the World Trade Center from fifty other nations. There were people there from Australia, and they are very angry with him. This one person succeeded in turning almost the entire civilized world against him.

NOT THE VIEWS OF ALL MUSLIMS

Now, let me make it clear that though this man is a radical follower of Islam, his views are not held by all Muslims. I am sure there are many Muslims in this country who are very grieved about what has happened and would not think of doing such a thing. There have also been Christians in past times who have killed people, but the interesting and important thing to remember is that when Christians have done this, they have done it in violation and opposition to the teachings of Jesus—not in obedience to them.

That is not the case in Islam. You are familiar, no doubt, with the "jihad," which is the declaration of a "holy war." Some Muslims point out that the main meaning of jihad is struggle with one's self. This would be similar to the Christian idea of dying to one's self or denying the flesh. That definition of jihad may well apply to hundreds of millions of Muslims—maybe even the majority. Meanwhile, there are legions of fanatical Muslims who define jihad as "holy war," and frankly, that would seem to be the plain teaching of the Koran.

THE TWO MOST IMPORTANT COMMANDS PER
ISLAM AND PER CHRISTIANITY

Some people say that all religions are alike. Don't you believe it. Just do a little research on religions, and you can see how incorrect this is. For example, consider this great contrast.

In the Hadith, which is a record of Mohammed's life and sayings, second in authority to the Koran, Mohammed was once asked, "What is the best deed?"

He replied, "To believe in Allah and his apostle" (Mohammed was supposedly his apostle).

The questioner then asked, "What is the next [in goodness]?"

He replied, "To participate in jihad [religious fighting] in Allah's cause" (Sahih Bukhari vol. 1, bk. 2, no. 25). That was their second most important commandment.

Christ was asked what is the greatest commandment. He answered, "'You shall love the LORD your God with all your heart, with all your soul, and with all your mind.' This is the first and great commandment. And the second is like it: 'You shall love your neighbor as yourself'" (Matt. 22:37–39).

If one cannot see a radical difference between those two statements, he is utterly blind. Yet our politically correct media has chosen to generally give favorable press to Islam, whatever they do, and to condemn Christianity for virtually everything that comes down the pike.

Just recently, CNN reported "religious rioting between Christians and Muslims" that rocked Nigeria. (This was in the wake of the ill-fated choice to hold the Miss World contest in that African country.) By listing the Christians first, the implication was that they started it, which they did not.

"FIGHT THE INFIDELS"

Mohammed commanded Muslims to fight against all infidels, if they do not embrace Islam, as well as against the people of the book (the Scriptures), that is, Jews and Christians. Furthermore, the Hadith[4] speaks of conversion to Islam by compulsion.

Mohammed said, "I have been ordered to fight against the people until they testify that none has the right to be worshiped but Allah, that Mohammed is Allah's prophet, that they offer prayers and give obligatory charity. If they perform all of that, they save their lives and their property" (Sahih Bukhari, vol. 1, bk. 2, no. 24).

Mohammed warned the king of the Byzantines: "If you

become a Muslim, you will be safe" (Sahih Bukhari, vol. 1, bk. 1, no. 6). But if the king did not convert, he and his kingdom would be destroyed and enslaved. The Muslims finally accomplished that in 1453. They besieged Constantinople, invaded it, and slaughtered untold numbers of Byzantine Christians.

Mohammed further said, "Whosoever has killed an enemy and has proof of that will possess his spoils" (Sahih Bukhari, vol. 4, bk. 53, no. 370).

Concerning Jews and Christians, Mohammed said, "Any Jew or Christian who heard about me and did not believe in me and what was revealed to me of the Holy Koran and my traditions, his ultimate destination is the [hell] fire."[5]

He says further that, "Allah has cursed the Jews and the Christians because they took the graves of their prophets as places for worship" (Sahih Bukhari, vol. 2, bk. 23, no. 414).

Dear friends, there is an infinite gulf between these teachings and the teaching of Jesus Christ that "you shall love your neighbor as yourself." Jesus even said, "Love your enemies" (Matt. 5:44)—not that Christians have always fulfilled this, by any means. But that's the ideal given us by our Master. The teachings of Christ contrast greatly with those of Mohammed, the prophet of Islam.

I don't know about you, but I have never personally done anything against Muslims. I have prayed for them. I have sought to share the Good News of the gospel with them, but I have never tried to hurt them in any way. But they believe that we Americans are the great Satan, that we are evil, and that we need to be destroyed. They have the teachings of their prophet Mohammed to encourage them to do just that.

September 11, 2001, was the largest foreign attack on American soil that has ever been seen in our nation's history. It was a cowardly attack by people who saw no reason for living, but were willing to give their lives for the vain hope that they might gain admission to paradise and the attentions of some seventy-two houris, or virgins. And all for naught.

The hijackers thought they would wake up in paradise by dying for Allah (and taking others with them). Instead, they woke up in an eternal inferno just as bad as the ones they caused in New York and Washington, D.C.

EVIDENCE FOR FAITH

Islam is a religion that has no real evidence to support it, whereas Christianity has the evidence of Jesus Christ, the evidence of His miracles, the evidence of His perfect life, and most importantly, the evidence of His resurrection from the dead. We have incredible evidence, more so than we have of any event in ancient history, historians have told us. For example, Dr. Thomas Arnold, nine-teenth-century professor of history at Oxford and the author of *History of Rome*, once said, "I have been used for many years to study the histories of other times, and to examine and weigh the evidence of those who have written about them, and I know of no one fact in the history of mankind which is proved by better and fuller evidence of every sort, to the understanding of a fair inquirer than the great sign which God hath given us that Christ died and rose again from the dead."[6]

Did you ever know what evidence Mohammed gave to prove that he was a prophet sent by Allah? Well, it was this: a large mole in the center of his back. That was considered to be the sign of a prophet in that superstitious time in the deserts of Arabia—a mole on his back.

- Our Savior walked on water and evidenced His divinity . . .

- He stilled the raging waves of a storm . . .

- He opened the eyes of the blind so that they saw . . .

• He fed five thousand from three little loaves . . .

• He walked out of a tomb after three days being dead . . .

but Mohammed had a mole on his back.

And therefore, people are willing to blow themselves up and kill innocent people in some deluded hope of a paradise promised by a man with a mole on his back. Incredible. Astonishing, to say the least.

That is why it has always been said that Islam was the religion of the sword. Ripley always said, "Believe it or not." Mohammed said, "Believe it or else"; either you would believe what he said or you would die. In one hundred years, with the sword, his followers conquered all of North Africa into Spain, across the Pyrenees into France, and all the way to the middle of France and the city of Tours before they were stopped by Charles Martel. A couple of centuries later the Islamic hordes went through Turkey into the Eastern part of Europe and came all the way through Constantinople and up into the eastern borders of Germany, taking at one time all but a narrow slice down the middle of Europe.

It was the goal, and continues to be the goal, to conquer the whole world, to Talibanize the world. Taliban, by the way, means "learner." A *talib* is a learner. The Taliban is a country full of learners. What are they learning? They are learning a radical form of Islam called Wahhabism, which is being taught to them by the Saudis.

You may recall that about five-sixths of all of the hijackers were Saudi Arabians—not Afghans. And the Saudis are funding some of this terrorism. They raised many an eyebrow in 2002 when Saudi television held telethons to raise money for the families of Palestinian suicide bombers. Although the Saudi government officially disputes it, research has shown that many gifts from wealthy Saudis have helped finance some of Al-Qaeda's operations.[7]

No, this is not a peaceful religion. As Samuel Huntington of Harvard University said, "Islam has bloody borders." Whenever a country is taken over, immediately hostilities begin along its borders as the next country is taken over, until finally, ten, twenty, thirty, forty countries have been completely dominated by them. And in any one of those forty countries, there will be no liberty, no freedom, no rights for women, and always present is the goal to Talibanize the rest of the world.

And the great impediments to that ages-long scheme are Christianity, America, and Judaism, which they see as their great enemies.

PERSECUTION OF CHRISTIANS

What New Yorkers experienced on 9/11 was just a taste of what the Christians have endured in many Muslim nations for a decade or more. In two types of nations, there is a horrendous persecution of Christians in our time: the radical Muslim nations and the remnant Communist countries, such as China. Consider the African country of Sudan, where the Muslim north has been waging war on the Christians and animists in the south. Eric Reeves of Smith College points out, "On gruesome statistical average, southern Sudan endures roughly the equivalent of a World Trade Center bombing every week and has for almost nineteen years."[8]

Sudan has now become the worst place in the world in terms of persecution against Christians. The Arab north has declared jihad ("holy war"—which is an oxymoron) on the south. The National Islamic Front, the power in the Arab north, has enslaved tens of thousands of Christians; they have kidnapped the Christian children and forced them into Koranic concentration camps. They have crucified some Christian leaders on trees. They have bombed hospitals, churches, and schools. Since 1983, the Islamic regime there has killed approximately two million people, mostly Christian.[9] Those who call Islam "a religion of peace" seem to ignore Sudan, not to mention Indonesia, Pakistan, and so on.

In a church in Sudan, the government troops of the National

Islamic Front swept down upon a small congregation and took them into prison. Their Muslim captors tortured them, but let the pastor go free. Wasn't that gracious? Just let him go. They said, "There's the door. Go on out." But first they pulled his eyes out. Then, with blood streaming down his face from his eyeless sockets, he staggered blindly down the road as an object lesson to other Christians as to what would happen to them.

A jihad has been declared against Christians in Indonesia as well. Laskar jihad warriors have entered Christian villages and slaughtered Christians, unless they "converted." They have burned countless church buildings.[10] Much of this slaughter received scant attention in the mainstream press. Why? Because the victims were Christians.

The extremists in Islam—and there are millions of them—not only persecute Christians and other non-Muslims in those countries, they often kill moderate Muslims. Dr. Walid Phares estimates that fanatical Muslims kill even more Muslims (moderate or non-practicing) than they do Christians or Jews. For example, in Algiers, extremists have killed Catholic nuns and priests and other Christians and have also slaughtered fellow Muslims who don't agree with their particular brand of Islam. I remember seeing a photo spread on this in *Time* magazine in 1997. The fanatics not only massacred several members of a village, they polluted the well by tossing corpses down there. One of the victims was a baby whose throat they slit. Anwar Sadat, former leader of Egypt, is an example of a famous Muslim killed by radical Muslims.

The only places in the world today where you have black chattel slavery are Islamic countries, according to a report recently released by the United Nations. Muslims are still enslaving blacks. Nothing novel. Mohammed traded and owned black slaves. You may recall that the Arabs renewed slavery after the Christians had ended it during the time of the early church. Mohammed also married a girl of six and consummated the relationship when she was nine. We have a word for that over here, and it isn't *religion*, and it isn't *noble*.

Alcohol or Worship Services?

It is outrageous the way our government and our State Department have often refused to even listen to the stories of Christians who have been persecuted in other countries; instead, they give them back to their persecutors to be killed. The U.S. government's influence brought an end to the persecution of Jews in the Soviet Union. It could also bring an end to the persecution of Christians in most nations of the world. Nina Shea of Freedom House in Washington, D.C., says that the number-one human-rights violation in the world today since the end of the cold war is the persecution of Christians.[11]

If our government had to choose between alcohol or Christian worship services to be available for American citizens living in Saudi Arabia, which would it choose? This is not a theoretical question. In 1995 the Saudis gave the American embassy such a choice. Our vacillating, spineless, faithless State Department, at least many of its members, was outraged when the Saudi Arabians wanted to close the nightclub and end the worship services we had there for Americans. They put up such a strong fight for the nightclub that it is still open, but they allowed the church service to cease.[12]

A Great Challenge

Dear friends, we face a great challenge—a challenge that almost conquered all of the world in the 700s.

Now, again, especially in the last fifty years, with the tremendous increase in oil wealth, Islam is on the move. I talked to a teacher of Islamic studies who told me that most Islamic studies teachers in America are funded by the "objective," "neutral" Saudis, who are giving Americans their understanding of what Islam is—a peaceful religion that wouldn't hurt anyone.

In the twentieth century, we faced both Nazism and the Japanese threat. America, though unprepared for those, showed itself able to stand up and meet the test. We are now being tested again with yet another great adversary. Thus far, our armed forces have done incredible things. The question is, Do the American people have the stomach for a long, drawn-out engagement?

Again, let me make it very clear that not every Muslim holds to extremist views. However, these views are in their Koran, and millions are daily being indoctrinated in these teachings when they are just boys from nine to twenty-five. And this fanatical strain of Wahhabi Muslims has practically no end to the recruits they are raising up in these schools. That means that we must have the backbone and the courage for a *long* engagement.

This is similar to what Israel has been facing. Young Palestinians count it a privilege to die for Allah, killing as many Israelis as they can in suicide bombings. For example, on Friday, April 12, 2002, the Palestinian Authority imam preached a message to a packed mosque including this line: "Whoever has not merited Martyrdom in these times should rise in the night and ask, 'My Lord, why have you denied me Martyrdom?'"[13]

One Palestinian mother of a twelve-year-old son said of giving her children to martyrdom, "This is a holy duty for all Palestinian people." Her son remarked, "I hope when I get to 14 or 15 to explode myself."[14]

Bill O'Reilly, syndicated columnist and host of the popular Fox News show *The O'Reilly Factor,* points out, "America will sooner or later have to defeat the Muslims who hate us, or be subjected to continuous terror and violence. If you think I am overstating things, consider this: Our so-called friends, the Saudis, are paying the families of suicide bombers thousands of dollars for their 'sacrifice.'"[15]

Are Americans cowards? Are we frightened? Well, one thing we know: If we are Christians, we know that we have eternal life. We know that the Son of God came and gave Himself for us. Jesus said, "Put up your swords." Mohammed said, "Draw them out." We are to win them with the Good News of eternal life, with the truth that God loves them, even our enemies—and we are to love our enemies. We must present to them that the Son of God died, even for mass murderers, and that He is willing to forgive them and cleanse them, and indeed, take them to paradise. This reward is not earned by shedding other men's blood, but by the Son of God shedding His own blood for us.

A PUBLIC-RELATIONS COUP?

Amazingly, because of our politically correct milieu, 9/11 turned out to be a PR coup for Muslims in some ways. Conversions to Islam are on the rise. Criticism against Christianity is fully allowed, while any dark word about Islam—even if it's totally true—is frowned upon. It is the equivalent of a "hate crime." Now, I'm not in any way advocating the violence that briefly came about against foreigners in the immediate wake of 9/11. But I am saying that the truth about Islam should be spoken.

Dr. George Grant, speaking on the subject of "Moslems in Your Neighborhood," stated that after September 11, 2001, the Reuters News Agency told its staff not to use the words *Islam* and *terrorist* in the same sentence unless it was a direct quote, and that preferably they should not use the word *terrorist* at all.[16]

Too often there's a sugarcoating of Islam in America. Let me be blunt. If all you know about Islam was learned from Oprah, you don't know much.

Columnist Kathleen Parker wrote a column on this post-9/11 public relations coup on the part of Muslims: "So it goes in post-9-11 America, where Muslims have become the new approved victim class. Here's how the knee-jerk drill goes: A journalist writes or otherwise depicts Muslims or their Prophet Muhammad in some way other than soft-focus, peach-toned Hallmark words or images, and thousands of American Muslims become like a battalion of whitewashers unleashed on urban graffiti."[17]

A year after 9/11, the University of North Carolina, Chapel Hill, required incoming freshmen to learn about the Koran. Only it was not a true representation. It was an idealistic presentation without a hint of the jihad in the Koran or Hadith that flew those planes into the World Trade Center and the Pentagon. At Christmastime 2002, American PBS viewers were treated to a pro-Islamic documentary that even *Time* magazine said painted a "too rosy picture of a humanitarian faith and its founder."[18]

I just recently heard that one of our public schools in California is teaching seventh-grade students to pray, to read and memorize the scripture, and to act and dress like religious adherents. But the religion is not Christianity; it's Islam. It's not the Bible; it's the Koran. Shockingly, this took place *after* 9/11. Daniel Pipes writes, "Students study the Koran, recite from it, design a title page for it, and write verses of it on a banner. They act out Islam's Five Pillars of Faith . . ."[19]

The difference between Christianity and Islam is enormous. Mohammed said that people were to give their sons for Allah. The Bible says that God gave His Son for you and me. You can't get more different than that.

So far in this book, we have seen how America began as a Christian nation, and how far we have drifted from that Christian base in the last few decades. In Part Three we will explore the steps that must be taken if America is to ever experience that new birth of freedom.

PART THREE

★ ★ ★ ★ ★

Where Our Nation Could
Be Headed: A New Birth
of Freedom

THIRTEEN

RELIGION WITHOUT REGENERATION?

"These things I have written to you who
believe in the name of the Son of God,
that you may know that you have eternal life."
—1 JOHN 5:13

THE YEAR WAS 1943, DURING THE MIDDLE OF WORLD
War II. The place was half a planet away. A young pilot was
flying his Corsair above the scattered islands of the Pacific, along
with several other American planes. They came out of the clouds
and didn't see the Zeroes. One of them was on this young man's
tail before he knew it. He rolled his plane over and dove for the
deck, back up again, turning, twisting, diving, doing everything—but he had an expert fighter pilot on his tail. At last a
burst of machine-gun fire pierced not only his plane, but his
body.

Mortally wounded, the young pilot managed somehow to
bring his disabled plane into something vaguely resembling a land-
ing on one of the jungle islands of the South Pacific. He barely
crawled out from the plane to get away, in case it exploded. Five
days later his body was found. When they pried open his fingers,
there was a scrap of paper on which he had written his last words:
"When peace like a river . . ." That was all.

When peace like a river attendeth my way,
When sorrows like sea billows roll;
Whatever my lot, Thou hast taught me to say,
It is well, it is well with my soul.[1]

Here was a young man who somewhere—whether in his home, his church, perhaps in the air force—learned the real meaning of a new beginning; a new beginning with God; a new birth in his heart. *The* new birth that is only available in Christ. When we know who holds the future, then whatever comes—even the worst—is transformed into a blessing.

THE FAILED MISSIONARY

A few centuries before, another young man was sailing, not the blue expanse of sky, but the blue waters of the North Atlantic. He was a missionary going home after a failure in the colony of Georgia (pre-American Revolution). He was a man who did not know who held his future.

The ship on which he was traveling encountered a great storm at sea. The wind howled as angry waves broke on the deck. The sails were torn to shreds. The young missionary was filled with horror and dread as he looked into what was certain death. There was no "peace like a river" for him; instead there was nothing but fear and terror.

Then he heard singing. On the other side of the deck three men were holding on to the railing and singing a hymn. The sight astonished him. He staggered over, against the howling wind and the crashing of the waves, and said to them, "How can you sing? You're going to die this very hour."

The three men turned, smiled, and said, "If the ship goes down, then we go up to be with the Lord."

The young missionary staggered away saying, "How can they know that? What more have they done than I have done?"

Later, this young man discovered that it was not what these three men had done, but whom they knew that brought peace to their hearts. The name of this young man was John Wesley. He finally discovered a new birth of freedom in his heart when he was born again.

It's amazing to consider that John Wesley (1703–91), the great founder of the Methodist Church, and one of the great preachers in the history of the Christian church, actually began his ministry *before* he was converted. Wesley, who was from England, crossed the Atlantic Ocean to serve as a missionary to the colony of Georgia, only to discover later that he didn't really know the Lord. He knew *about* God, but he didn't know Him as Savior and Lord.

Watching the Moravians (a Christian group active in missions at that time) so bravely face death made a huge impression on Wesley. He returned to England, and in London at Aldersgate Street, he heard a message delivered by a layman who was reading a sermon written by Martin Luther. That message told him it was possible to know for sure that one could have eternal life, and this could be done only when one trusted in the Christ who suffered and died to pay for our sins.

Wesley turned from trusting in his own good deeds, his own religiosity, his own morality, his own accomplishments, to placing his trust in the Savior who suffered to purchase a place for us in heaven. John Wesley, a failed missionary who had been filled with dread as he contemplated leaping out into the blackness of forever, went home and wrote these words in his journal:

> About a quarter before nine, while he [the lay preacher] was describing the change which God works in the heart through faith in Christ, I felt my heart strangely warmed. I felt I did trust in Christ, Christ alone, for salvation; and an assurance was given me that He had taken away my sins, even mine, and saved me from the law of sin and death.[2]

Wesley declared, "I knew He had delivered me from sin and death unto eternal life." Wesley now *knew* what the Scripture says, "These things I have written to you . . . that you may know that you have eternal life" (1 John 5:13).

THE NEW BIRTH—THE PREREQUISITE TO A NEW BIRTH OF FREEDOM

The young pilot and Wesley knew what we need to know today. I believe that if we are ever going to experience a new birth of freedom in America, it must begin with the new birth. Period. Unbelievers didn't settle America and frame its government and institutions. And unbelievers won't get America back on track.

Not that we can't use help from all willing quarters. I welcome cobelligerents, if you will, in the fight against abortion or pornography. But to change American culture completely, we need to change a majority of Americans—from within.

Only the gospel of Jesus Christ can do that.

The gospel is a term bandied about so often that churchgoers think they know what it means. I'm not so sure. In this chapter, I want to clarify this all-important subject of what the gospel is. I begin with the assumption that a new birth of freedom begins with the new birth.

"YOU MUST BE BORN AGAIN"

The new birth was preached over and over during the Great Awakening—that incredible spiritual revival that swept up and down the Atlantic coast during the mid-eighteenth century and helped unify the colonies a generation before the British attacks solidified that unity.

The movement began through the diligent preaching of Jonathan Edwards in Northampton, Massachusetts. Then God used British evangelist George Whitefield—incidentally, a colleague of John and Charles Wesley—to spread the Great Awakening throughout the colonies.

Whitefield's favorite text was John 3, which begins with the story of Christ telling Nicodemus that he must be born again. Whitefield preached often on the new birth. He was once asked, "Why do you preach so often that you must be born again?" His response was, "Because you must."[3]

THE NEED TO "GET LOST"

The problem today is not getting people "saved," but getting them to realize they are "lost." Most Americans see no need for God or His salvation because they have a false picture of Him. We have fashioned a politically correct god who loves everybody, who will do all in his somewhat questionable power to get people to heaven. This god accepts and tolerates everything—and isn't mad at anyone. The picture is far from the one Jonathan Edwards painted in his sermon "Sinners in the Hands of an Angry God." Modern man may chafe or sneer at this classic sermon, but surely its sober message is closer to what the Bible says than our politically correct god.

In Edwards's message, we meet an all-powerful God who has the right to cast people to eternal judgment. We are but pitiful little spiders held over the pit of hell, totally dependent upon God's mercy. When people get a true picture of God as the unchangeable, sovereign, almighty ruler of the universe, when they see a holy God who is angry at the wicked every day, a God who demands perfection and tolerates no sin, then people will cry out as they have done from the beginning of the church, "What must we do to be saved?" Only a person who is close to the light of God recognizes his own filthiness.

If sin were not so serious and such an affront to God, Jesus would not have needed to go to the cross. Once we recoil from the hideousness of sin and decide to follow God's commandments, we have repented. But sorrow over our sins is not conversion. Only as we turn to the Lord Jesus and ask for forgiveness can that miracle happen. To understand this more fully, we need a fuller understanding of the crucifixion.

THE DEEPER MEANING OF THE CROSS

Consider the cross of Christ, the central symbol of our faith and the central fact of our redemption. Indeed, it is a rather incongruous symbol since it is really the symbol of a gallows, an electric chair, a guillotine—an instrument of torture, punishment, and death. And yet for us it has been transmuted into something entirely different: the symbol of peace with God, a symbol of hope and forgiveness and joy.

We are so familiar with the image of the cross that it has lost much of its horror. Imagine if someone wore jewelry with a symbol of an electric chair. Yet the cross in Jesus' day was that utterly horrific. Crucifixion was reserved only for slaves and criminals; Rome would not crucify its own citizens—it was too horrible.

Historian Dr. Edwin Yamauchi, professor of ancient history at Miami University, Ohio, points out that the early church generally did not paint the crucifixion or depict it in any form of art. Not until four or five centuries later, in the Byzantine era, did Christians depict Jesus on the cross. The cross was a scandal of sorts to the followers of Jesus.

AT THE CROSS, JESUS DEFEATED SATAN

If you were to talk to the apostolic fathers, they would tell you that the cross of Jesus Christ related primarily to Satan. Would you have come up with that answer? Perhaps not, but this, sometimes called the patristic view, was the view of Cyril, Gregory of Nyssa, Gregory of Nazianzus, Basil, Ambrose, Augustine, and numerous other early fathers. They saw humankind as having been taken hostage by Satan, and Christ having come to redeem man or ransom him from this ignominious position. The early fathers said that man, having willfully sinned and renounced God's sovereignty, gave himself over to the dominion of Satan, who had a just rule over him and a just and proper right to hold him as hostage and demand a ransom.

Jesus not only came to pay this ransom, but also to enter into mortal conflict with Satan, the prince of the kingdom of darkness, and destroy his dominion. John said that Jesus came to destroy the works of the devil (1 John 3:8). In His death, Christ extinguished the power and dominion of Satan forever. Having spoiled principalities and powers, Jesus stripped them of their majesty and power by His cross. *So point number one, Jesus came to batter down and destroy the kingdom and bulwarks of Satan.*

Secondly, the cross of Jesus Christ expiates our sin. The atonement of Christ not only destroys the work of the devil, it also contains an element of *expiation*. This word means to wipe out, to rub away, to cleanse. The Scripture says that though our sins be as scarlet, they shall be as white as snow; that our Lord will take away our sins and remove them as far from us as the east is from the west, never to remember them anymore (Ps. 103:12, 16).

Jesus Himself declared that He came to die for our sins (Matt. 26:28). "Christ died for our sin," said Paul, as he set forth the basic premises of the gospel of Jesus Christ (1 Cor. 15:3). But it should be evident that if we are to have a proper estimation of the cross, we must have a proper estimation of sin, as discussed previously. Those cults that deny the reality of sin most certainly diminish the cross of Jesus Christ. So do many in our culture, who see us more as mired down with psychological sickness than with willful rebellion (not that there isn't a place for Christ-centered therapy). If we would see sin as God sees it, we would hate it for what it is. And we would see the cross for what it is.

A victim mentality is one of the symptoms of our current

culture. Turn on a daytime TV talk show and watch the parade of victims who don't acknowledge their responsibility for their abhorrent and dysfunctional behavior. It's their mother's fault or their third-grade teacher's fault. Everybody is to blame but themselves. This is not the Christian view. While others may be guilty of having wounded us, the reality is that we're all guilty before God.

However righteous you may suppose yourself to be, my friend, if you have offended in one point of the law (and who hasn't?), the Bible says you are a transgressor and unacceptable to God, who dwells in light unapproachable. God says in His Word that our sins are a stench in His nostrils. He can neither look upon us nor endure the odor of sin (Hab. 1:13).

In the Evangelism Explosion program I developed, which is now implemented in churches in every nation throughout the world, we use an analogy that drives this point home. Suppose you are making an omelet. You crack open one egg, then another, until you have about five good eggs sizzling in the pan. Then you crack a sixth egg and pour it in with the mix. But lo and behold, it is rotten. What does that do to the rest of the omelet? It makes it unacceptable. In the same way, we may have many good works (the five good eggs), but we have all sinned, and those sins are like the rotten egg. Before a holy God, they make us unacceptable.

The reason so many people in America don't think they are lost is because they think that God will grade on a curve. "Boys will be boys," says this god of our own making. Not so the God of the universe, who has revealed Himself in the pages of holy Writ.

As the Puritans put it when they taught their children the alphabet in the *New England Primer*, "A. In Adam's Fall, we sinned all."[4] We are born with original sin, and even before we have committed one sin, we are sinners and unfit for heaven. When we become "born-again," God gives us a new nature. This new life will grow through sanctification until we get to heaven. Only then will we be sinless. But the whole process starts with the new birth at the foot of the cross.

Thirdly, we see that through the cross of Christ God is propitiated. Webster's Ninth New Collegiate Dictionary defines this word as "to gain or regain the favor or goodwill of, to appease." Most of us have heard John 3:16 so often that we virtually take it for granted, but think about this Scripture with me now. God so loved us that He gave His only begotten Son in order to reconcile the demands of His own nature. This great truth is called *propitiation,* where God becomes pleased with the guilty sinner, and his wrath toward the sinner is directed at His own Son.

Here, I think, we enter into the deeper mystery of the cross. The theologians of the church began to realize that the real impediment to man's salvation did not lie with Satan, or even with man's sin, or with the hardness of his rebellious heart. The great impediment to the salvation of any man lies in God Himself, in His inexorable and immutable justice. "The soul that sinneth, it shall die," says the Lord (Ezek. 18:4 KJV).

Scripture plainly reveals that God is both just and merciful. Justice is satisfied when sin is punished, and mercy is revealed when God gives up His only Son to spare us. Unless the justice and righteousness and holiness of God are in some way satisfied, no man can avoid the descent of that just punishment.

So we see that through the Cross:

- the kingdom of darkness is destroyed;

- sin is expiated; and

- God is propitiated.

Man in his willful rebellion has thrown off the filial cords of love and has left his Father's home and gone off into the far country to sow his wild oats. His heart of adamantine steel is set against God. He wants nothing to do with God. "Don't talk to me about your God, and your fanatical religion. I don't want to hear about it. I've got big doings Saturday night, so get lost, buddy."

What will be done to the heart of such a one as that? Nothing but the cross of Jesus Christ can change the stony heart of man and draw him back to his Father.

What a reconciling influence flows from the cross. I clearly remember, as though it were just yesterday, that day when that influence, that river of love, overwhelmed my soul, and I discovered for the first time in my life that God was not simply some great dictator in the sky, telling me what to do and what not to do. Instead, He was a loving Father who had given His own Son up to death. I saw this One lifted up as if His cross were right there in my apartment. I knew for the first time that He was dying for me. I could feel this hard heart melting within me. I slipped onto my knees for the first time in my adult life and said, "Oh God, forgive me. Lord, I'm so sorry. I didn't know. Have mercy on me." And Christ came into my life and set up that cross in my soul. I knew that my sins were forgiven, and I knew that I had been reconciled to my Father. I knew that I was on my way to heaven. And that created a love in my heart for Jesus Christ that has grown year by year for half of a century.

When that happens, we find our old nature beginning to wither under the spikes of the cross. The pomp and glory of the world, which once caused our hearts to pant after them, now seem dull and empty and meaningless because Christ is in our hearts.

Unfortunately, a major misunderstanding often overshadows what Christ accomplished on the cross.

FAITH AND GOOD WORKS

Some people think that our salvation comes about by our good works, which is the first view of salvation. Similarly, many others think it will come about by some sort of combination of faith and good works, the second view of salvation.

Why will neither of these theologies work? I think an illustration may suffice: Suppose that you faced a great chasm five thousand feet deep, with a cliff on either side, and you must go from one side to the other. You say, "Well, I have a stout rope that could hold up an elephant. It is two inches thick. There's just one problem: my rope is only fifty feet long and the chasm is a hundred feet across."

Then I answer, "Fear not. The problem is solved because I have a spool of thread in my pocket. Now we will tie my thread to your rope and then we may go across easily."

You do not look thrilled at the idea. Do you not trust the rope?

"Oh, yes," you say. You trust the rope completely—but the thread bothers you.

"Oh, I see. Well, let's change the story and make it seventy-five feet of rope and only twenty-five feet of thread. Now, don't you feel much better?"

No, you do not.

"Okay, ninety feet of rope. That should do it—and only ten feet of thread."

You still look very skeptical.

"Let's make it ninety-nine feet, eleven inches of rope and just one inch of my very fine thread."

You still do not look very happy.

"One little inch of thread would not hurt, would it?" No, the inch of thread would not hurt at all. But those rocks five thousand feet below would hurt. And anybody who has half a brain knows that one inch of thread is going to make the whole contraption no safer than if we had a hundred feet of thread.

Christ provides the rope. He provides us a sacrifice that is quite sufficient. But if we try to add the thread of our own good works to that sacrifice, we will inevitably foul it all up.

Charles Spurgeon said that if we have to put one stitch in the garment of our salvation, we will ruin the whole thing. The great hymn "I Hear the Savior Say" reminds us, "Jesus paid it all. All to Him I owe."[5]

The third view of salvation says that our hope is built entirely upon what Jesus Christ, the Son of God, has done for us. He lived a perfect life. He died an atoning death, and we must place our trust completely in Him. This, of course, is the view of evangelical Christianity throughout the world—that Jesus paid it all—all to Him I owe. That means salvation is offered to me as a *gift*, and it is received by faith.

THE CLEANSING OF OUR SIN

If you have never asked Jesus Christ to come into your heart, if you have never received Him as the Savior and Master of your life, I would urge you to do so right now. Please say this prayer (or paraphrase it in your own words):

> Father, I confess that I have never had the cross set up within my heart. I confess that I have been trusting in my own goodness. I confess that I have proclaimed that I am not so bad. I confess that I am indeed a sinner who deserves nothing but Your wrath. Thank You so much, Jesus, that You died for me, on my behalf. You paid a debt You didn't owe, a debt so great that I could never repay it. Please come into my heart. Come and set up Your cross in my heart this day. With nothing in my hands, I place my trust in You and take hold of Your cross. In Jesus' name. Amen.

If you said that prayer from your heart, let me be the first to congratulate you! You have just begun a new journey in a new, wonderful life.

I recommend that you take a few immediate steps. First of all, get a Bible and begin to read it for yourself. This is the greatest book in the world. I look at it as food. What happens if you don't eat for a few days? You go hungry. How about indefinitely? You starve to death. Spiritually, God's Word is food. We should consume a portion every single day. It makes a huge difference in our lives.[6]

I also recommend you find a Bible-believing, Christ-centered church where fellow believers can encourage you in your new-found faith. You may find that some of your old friends abandon you. That's okay. A whole world of Christians from virtually every country and every culture are now family to you. The Church of Jesus Christ in its many different forms is the largest institution in the world. If you sincerely said that prayer and placed your trust in Christ, you are now part of this worldwide congregation.

Be sure to tell others about Jesus Christ. This is one of the great privileges that God has entrusted to Christians—that we can actually lead loved ones, friends, neighbors, strangers, to faith in Jesus Christ.

I spoke earlier about how we are not saved by good works or by a combination of faith and good works. Now I want to add one more element to that point. True faith *will* result in good works. If it does not, it is not true faith.

When we have come to Christ for forgiveness and have experienced the new life, there are consequences. We do good works because we are saved and we want to follow God and walk in His ways. Within Christianity good works are a result of our new life. In all other religions, people do good works to appease God and to earn salvation.

Unless this new birth is experienced by far more Americans, our nation will continue its downward spiral. On the other hand, if more and more Christians winsomely share their faith so that more and more people become committed believers, they will personally experience the new birth and we as a nation will experience a new birth of freedom.

★ ★ ★ ★ ★

FOURTEEN

ONE NATION UNDER GOD?

"He has shown you, O man, what is good;
And what does the LORD *require of you*
But to do justly,
To love mercy,
And to walk humbly with your God?"
— MICAH 6:8

IN THE SUMMER OF 2002, AMERICANS WERE SHOCKED
when two circuit court judges took it upon themselves to declare
the phrase "under God" in our Pledge of Allegiance unconstitutional. I think this decision was a wake-up call to millions of
Americans. President George W. Bush called the decision "ridiculous"[1] and said it was out of step with our traditions, including
the Declaration of Independence, which acknowledges God.
Politicians, even the more liberal ones, were falling all over themselves to see who could get to a microphone first to decry the decision. They raced to the television cameras to be seen saying the
Pledge of Allegiance, including the banned phrase "under God."
Here's what some of the politicians had to say immediately after
the decision became known:

• Sen. Christopher Bond, (R) Missouri: "Our founding fathers
  must be spinning in their graves. This is the worst kind of political correctness run amok."[2]

- Tom Daschle, (D) South Dakota, senate leader at the time, said the decision was "just plain nuts."[3]

- Dennis Hastert, (R) Illinois, the speaker of the House, remarked: "Obviously, the liberal court in San Francisco has gotten this one wrong."[4]

The reaction startled the chief judge in the decision, who chose to put his own ruling on hold the very next day.

The fallout from the decision probably startled even many liberals. In some ways, as obnoxious as the decision was, it didn't surprise me. Why not? Because this decision was the natural outworking of the faulty view of "the separation of church and state," which liberal judges have been holding for years. Decades, in fact. If America is to ever become a Christian nation again, we must get back to the historical interpretation of the First Amendment, which does not strike down as unconstitutional any mention of God in public places.

THE MISUNDERSTANDING OF "SEPARATION OF CHURCH AND STATE"

There is probably no area with more confusion in our society than the whole matter of "separation of church and state," which began with very liberal courts and has now filtered down to ridiculous decisions.

For example, just this month I heard about a case in rural Byron, Illinois, about two hours west of Chicago, where there was an egregious violation of a Christian's civil liberties because the young man was allegedly violating "the separation of church and state."

Joshua Hendrickson, a junior in a public high school, is blind. While silently reading his braille Bible in the lunchroom, some friends asked him to read aloud. He happened to be reading in the Old Testament book of Isaiah. When he did, the principal found out, and suspended the boy for three days, putting this on the boy's permanent record. Thankfully, the Christian Law Association of Seminole, Florida, successfully got involved to show the school how wrong this principal was. This provides an excellent illustration of the fact that the assault against Christians has even reached Main Street, small-town America.

Suppose the boy wasn't blind, and he was turning the pages of *Playboy* or some other pornographic magazine. Would he be suspended for three days and have it on his permanent record? It's almost as if the Bible is X-rated in our public schools.

The tragedy is that this story typifies the great misunderstanding of the "separation of church and state" in our society today. Is this what the founders intended? Absolutely not. Did the founding fathers give us any kind of clue as to what they envisioned for America and the relationship between public expression of religion (specifically Christianity) and the state?

I believe the answer is "Yes." And it's not at all hard to find. It's a matter of public record. In this chapter, I propose to demonstrate that the founders did not intend us to have "state-sanctioned atheism," which seems to be the goal of the American Civil Liberties Union (ACLU), the so-called People for the American Way (their views differ sharply from those of the majority of Americans), the Americans United for the Separation of Church and State, and all the other legal groups that are suing to completely remove our Christian heritage. I also want to address the liberal judges they have managed to persuade.

Our history is rich with examples proving that the modern-day purge of Christianity from the public square is not at all what the founders intended.

AMERICA—"A CHRISTIAN NATION"
The documentary evidence of the Christian origin of this nation is voluminous; it would take hours even to quote it. The Supreme

Court of the United States thoroughly studied this issue, and in 1892 gave us what is known as the Trinity Decision. In that decision, the Supreme Court declared, "These, and many other matters which might be noticed, add a volume of unofficial declarations to the mass of organic utterances that this is a Christian nation."[5] That is where this nation began.

"ONE INDISSOLUBLE BOND"

John Quincy Adams, the sixth president of the United States, said, "The highest glory of the American Revolution was____" Can you guess what he cited? That the revolution secured our independence from England? Or that it got rid of the Stamp Tax? Or the Tea Tax? Or that the Revolution dissolved our bonds with parliament and the king? No. What was the highest glory of the American Revolution, according to this president? Listen well. John Quincy Adams said, "The highest glory of the American Revolution was this: it connected in one indissoluble bond, the principles of civil government with the principles of Christianity."[6]

"One indissoluble bond." Government and Christianity. Well, today there are those who have come with their solvents of unbelief, skepticism, atheism, Marxism, humanism, and secularism and are doing everything in their power to totally dissolve that indissoluble bond. Some will say, "Yes, but doesn't the First Amendment say there should be a wall of separation between church and state?" I wonder how many still believe that. If you do, let me remind you of something: The First Amendment never mentions "a wall," it never mentions "separation," it never mentions the "church," and it never mentions the "state." The First Amendment says, "Congress shall make no law respecting an establishment of religion, or prohibiting the free exercise thereof . . ."

As we saw in an earlier chapter, Thomas Jefferson, in a *private* letter to the Danbury Baptists, used the phrase "a wall of separation between Church and State." Yet a wall inhibits people equally on both sides; the First Amendment inhibits only the Congress: "*Congress* shall make no law respecting an establishment of religion . . . *Congress* shall make no law forbidding the free exercise thereof." The First Amendment says absolutely nothing about what Christians or people adhering to any religion, ministers, or churches may or may not do.

Furthermore, Mr. Jefferson, though one of our most noteworthy founding fathers, was thousands of miles away in France when both the Constitution and the Bill of Rights were written. Modern courts have mistakenly made him *the* authority on the matter, and misquoted him at that. David Barton asks, "Where are their quotations from George Washington, James Madison, Alexander Hamilton, and Gouverneur Morris—the founding father who spoke the most times at the Constitutional Convention—to settle the matter?" What's happened in American jurisprudence in the last several decades has been very dishonest.

INDIFFERENCE TO RELIGION?

Most people don't realize the Christian makeup of our country in its earliest days. Even as late as 1775—150 years after the Pilgrims landed—the makeup of America was 98.4 percent Protestant, 1.4 percent Catholic, and .2 percent Jewish.[7]

That is why Charles Hodge, probably the greatest theologian America ever produced, who was sometimes called the glory and jewel and crown of Princeton Theological Seminary, said, "The proposition that the United States of America is a Christian and Protestant nation, is not so much the assertion of a principle, as the statement of a fact."[8]

HARMFUL TO GOOD GOVERNMENT?

Today, people seem to think that in some way religion in general, and Christianity in particular, is inimical to good government and that the purpose of the government is to keep religion away from the governors of our land. This is a very different view from that held by George Washington, who said, "True religion offers to government its surest support."[9]

In fact, Washington said that without a humble imitation of Christ we could never hope to be a happy nation.[10] Perhaps that is why we have found that our Congress cannot even produce a budget, and that it is becoming increasingly impossible to govern this nation, much less to do so happily.

Nineteenth-century American statesman Robert C. Winthrop, who served as Speaker of the House of Representatives, said, "It may do for other countries, and other governments to talk about the state supporting religion. Here, under our own free institutions, it is religion which must support the State."[11]

Samuel Adams, who was called the firebrand of the American Revolution, said, "Let divines and philosophers, statesmen and patriots, unite their endeavors to renovate the age, by impressing the minds of men with the importance of educating their little boys and girls, of inculcating in the minds of youth the fear and love of Deity."[12]

No National Church—Period

The phrase *separation of church and state* is an unfortunate choice of words, because it contains a kernel of truth. America's founding fathers did not want a national church, but they did allow states to have their own state-churches. These eventually died out, but they were never declared unconstitutional. It was only at the federal level that there was to be no national denomination.

Why not? Because the United States was comprised of Anglicans, Congregationalists, Presbyterians, Quakers, Huguenots, Catholics, a few Baptists, a few Methodists, and so on. Yet the founders were definitely Christian for the most part. At least 90 to 95 percent of them were practicing, Trinitarian Christians. You can go to Christ Church in Philadelphia today, where George Washington and several others from the Constitutional Convention worshiped that long, hot summer of 1787. John Adams, normally a Congregationalist, also worshiped that summer at the Presbyterian Church.

Years earlier, during the very first day of the Continental Congress, September 6, 1774, the members held a discussion on whether they should open in prayer. One of the most committed Christians, John Jay, later our first chief justice of the Supreme Court, said he didn't think it wise because of the plethora of denominations represented in the assembly.

But Samuel Adams, a Congregationalist from Massachusetts, stood up and persuaded them to hold prayer. Here's what happened that day, according to eyewitness John Adams: "Mr. Samuel Adams arose and said that he was no bigot, and could hear a Prayer from any gentleman of Piety and virtue, who was at the same time a friend to his Country. He was a stranger in Philadelphia, but had heard that Mr. Duché deserved that character and therefore he moved that Mr. Duché, an Episcopal clergyman, might be desired to read Prayers to Congress tomorrow morning."[13]

So the next day, Rev. Jacob Duché led the whole group in prayer in a service that lasted three hours. It was a very moving service, wherein he read Psalm 35, the reading for that particular day in the Anglican "pontificals." It just so happened to be what the Congressmen needed to hear.

In Psalm 35, David, who was being unjustly persecuted, poured out his heart to God, and he asked to be vindicated: "Plead my cause, O LORD, with those who strive with me; fight against those who fight against me. Take hold of shield and buckler, and stand up for my help."

Even as these words were read, some of the delegates from Massachusetts understood that British troops were attacking their homes and farms. John Adams wrote his wife, Abigail, about the impact of this psalm and the three-hour prayer meeting that followed:

I never saw a greater effect upon an audience. It seemed as if heaven had ordained that Psalm to be read on that morning. After this, Mr. Duché, unexpectedly to every body, struck out into an extemporary prayer, which filled the bosom of every man present. I must confess, I never heard a better prayer, or one so well pronounced . . . It has had an excellent effect upon everybody here. I must beg you to read that Psalm.[14]

At the very beginning of Congress, the representatives opened in prayer. And they have been praying ever since. How does this square with the supposed "separation of church and state" the liberals try to shove in our faces?

So here's a memo to all the liberal judges who write decisions like the one banning the phrase *under God* in the Pledge of Allegiance. This is a memo to the ACLU and others like them as to how wrong they are in their reading of the Constitution.

TWENTY-FIVE REASONS STATE-SANCTIONED ATHEISM IS OUT OF STEP WITH OUR HISTORY

Here are twenty-five reasons why the decision to ban the words *under God* in the Pledge of Allegiance and every ruling like it is out of step with our history and the intent of the founders as seen in their writings, sayings, and actions. There are probably many more I could muster, but this will suffice to make the point:

1. *Our nation's birth certificate, the Declaration of Independence, mentions God four times—and not in any minor way.* He is the source of our rights, according to this document. The Declaration also argues that the British king is guilty of trying to take away something that God has given us; therefore, King George III ought not to be obeyed. If the ACLU interpretation of strict "separation of church and state" (really, the separation

of God and state) were correct, then the Declaration would be unconstitutional (even though the founders said the Constitution is predicated on the Declaration as its foundation). Children would not be allowed to read it in school.

2. *The forerunner to the Constitution was the Articles of Confederation, adopted in 1777, which also mentions God.* In fact, the Constitutional Convention initially met in order to revise the Articles, not to create a totally new document. The Articles say of God, "And whereas it has pleased the Great Governor of the World to incline the hearts of the Legislatures we respectively represent in Congress, to approve of, and to authorize us to ratify the said Articles of Confederation and perpetual union . . ."[15]

3. *The Constitution is explicitly signed "in the year of our Lord."* Not only does the Constitution mention God, but it affirms the deity of Jesus Christ, our Lord. Take the Pledge and similar rulings to their logical conclusion, and we would have to declare the Constitution unconstitutional.

It's funny how things that are clearly constitutional, like freedom of religion and the right to bear arms, are often ruled "unconstitutional," while things like the right to abort your unborn child are "constitutional." Of course, you can read the Constitution and all of its amendments repeatedly and never find a hint about abortion, or even about "the right to privacy," the premise upon which the abortion decision was based.

Furthermore, the U.S. Constitution is a direct outworking of the hundred or so Puritan covenants, charters, and frames of government that had been developed in America beginning with the Mayflower Compact. Political science professor Dr. Donald S. Lutz, author of *The Origins of American*

Constitutionalism, writes, "The American constitutional tradition derives in much of its form and content from the Judeo-
Christian tradition as interpreted by the radical Protestant
sects to which belonged so many of the original European settlers in British North America."[16] We must never forget that
Christianity gave birth to the U.S. Constitution.

4. *When the Constitution was finally ratified in 1789, the
Congress was so thankful that they requested that President
George Washington call for a national day of thanksgiving to
honor the event.*[17] These were the very same men who wrote
the First Amendment ("Congress shall make no law respecting
an establishment of religion . . ."). Are we supposed to believe
that modern secularists know what the First Amendment
means better than the very men who wrote it? I think not.

5. *The same men who gave us the First Amendment also wrote
the Northwest Ordinance in 1787 and then adopted it again
in 1789.* This was one of our nation's four most important
founding documents, along with the Declaration, the
Constitution, and the Articles of Confederation. The founders'
goal was that they would retain a certain degree of uniformity
as new states were being added to the new nation. Article III
of the Northwest Ordinance states, "Religion, morality, and
knowledge being necessary to good government and the happiness of mankind, schools and the means of education shall
be forever encouraged."[18] Religion and morality, according to
our founders, were to be driving forces in school; they were
not to be systematically censored as they are so often today.

6. *The Treaty of Paris of 1783, negotiated by Ben Franklin, John
Adams, and John Jay, acknowledged the Trinity as it made
official our separation from Great Britain.* This was the peace

treaty that formally ended the Revolutionary War, which had ended unofficially at the Battle of Yorktown two years earlier. How does it begin? "In the name of the Most Holy and Undivided Trinity."[19]

7. *Chaplains have been in the public payroll from the very beginning.* Though the ACLU has unsuccessfully challenged chaplains, our government allocated public funding for congressional and military chaplains before we were even a nation. The entire chaplain system absolutely violates the current, popular, and totally wrong ACLU interpretation of strict "separation of church and state."

8. *The Constitutions of all fifty states mention God in one way or other.* Every single one of them, usually in the preamble. For instance:

- "We, the people of the State of Alabama . . . invoking the favor and guidance of Almighty God . . ."[20]

- "Preamble. We, the people of Hawaii, Grateful for Divine Guidance . . ."[21]

- "Preamble. We, the people of Montana, grateful to Almighty God for the blessings of liberty . . ."[22]

- Vermont's Constitution refers to the "blessings which the Author of existence has bestowed on man."[23] And it declares, "That all men have a natural and Unalienable right to worship Almighty God according to the dictates of their own consciences . . ."[24]

Each of these constitutions would be unconstitutional according to the ACLU's logic. So would the other forty-six.

9. *The Liberty Bell has a Bible verse engraved on it:* "Proclaim liberty throughout the land, to all the inhabitants thereof" (Lev. 25:10 KJV). This is one of our great symbols of national liberty.

   This reminds me of a true story involving a group of youngsters from our church. A few years ago, our choir director and his wife took our youth choir on their annual tours. They went to Philadelphia, ministering in churches throughout the area. Upon returning home, one of the girls said the trip was fine, except she had this complaint: "I couldn't believe it. One time, we were real close to the second-largest mall in the country, and instead we had to go see some stupid bell with a crack in it!" Well, I guess we have our work cut out for us to get even our Christian young people to appreciate our heritage.

10. *Our national anthem ("The Star-Spangled Banner") mentions God, specifically in the fourth stanza.* "And this be our motto: In God is our Trust!"[25] I have heard some say that they would prefer Irving Berlin's "God Bless America" to take its place. But that wouldn't pass constitutional muster either if the ACLU is the group deciding what is and is not constitutional.

11. *Every president, from George Washington to President George W. Bush, has been sworn in on the Bible, saying the words, "So help me God."* This custom is not spelled out in the Constitution, but George Washington started the practice because that had been the common way to take an oath in the West for centuries. All presidents have followed suit.

12. *Prayers have been said at the swearing in of each president.* Yet the same atheist who sued to get the phrase *under God*

in the Pledge of Allegiance banned also sued President George W. Bush, unsuccessfully, because he had the audacity to let Rev. Franklin Graham officiate in prayer at his inauguration, something presidents have done from the beginning.

George Washington even stooped over and kissed the Bible when he was sworn in as president. Then he led everyone present down the street (in New York City, our capital in 1789) to a two-hour prayer service at St. Paul's Church, which still stands a block from where the World Trade Center once stood. Miraculously, St. Paul's survived 9/11 while other buildings around it didn't.

13. *Virtually every president has called for national days of prayer, of fasting, of thanksgiving.* James Madison, Abraham Lincoln, Ronald Reagan. This, too, is a long-standing practice in the United States—from the very beginning. Before the birth of the nation, the settlers of the colonies called for hundreds of prayer days, fasting days, and days of thanksgiving in their individual colonies.

14. *Every president that has given an inaugural address has mentioned God in that speech. Several of them quoted the Bible.* Consider a small sampling:

- On March 4, 1841, William Henry Harrison, our ninth president, expressed "a profound reverence for the Christian religion and a thorough conviction that sound morals, religious liberty, and a just sense of religious responsibility are essentially connected with all true and lasting happiness."[26]

- On March 4, 1905, Teddy Roosevelt, the twenty-sixth president, said, "My fellow-citizens, no people on earth have more cause to be thankful than ours, and this is said reverently, in no spirit of boastfulness in our own strength, but with gratitude to the Giver of Good who has blessed us with the conditions which have enabled us to achieve so large a measure of well-being and of happiness."[27]

- On January 20, 1977, Jimmy Carter, the thirty-ninth president, declared, "Here before me is the Bible used in the inauguration of our first President, in 1789, and I have just taken the oath of office on the Bible my mother gave me a few years ago, opened to a timeless admonition from the ancient prophet Micah: 'He hath showed thee, O man, what is good; and what doth the LORD require of thee, but to do justly, and to love mercy, and to walk humbly with thy God'" (Mic. 6:8).[28]

15. *The founding fathers often quoted the Bible in their writings.* Two professors of political science conducted a major study on more than fifteen thousand books, monographs, pamphlets, articles, and so on from 1750 to 1805, the founding era. They discovered that 34 percent of the quotations came from the Bible, far more than any other single source.[29] According to the current, popular understanding of "the separation of church and state," many of the writings of the founding fathers could not be legally studied in school. The writings of James Madison, the so-called father of our Constitution, could conceivably be no longer acceptable in school—"violation of the separation of church and state."

16. *Oaths in courtrooms have invoked God from the beginning.* Up until recently the belief was that one might lie before men, but would hesitate to lie before God almighty. The

Bible can still be found in some courtrooms. It is disappearing in others. And that's a shame. Our heritage is slipping away in our own time at an unprecedented level.

17. *As a nation, we have celebrated Christmas to commemorate the Savior's birth for centuries.* To adhere to state-sanctioned atheism, Christmas would have to go. The term *holiday* would also have to be replaced since it is the contraction of *holy* and *day*. Already Christmas break is called "winter break" in some places. In one public school someone wished someone else, "Merry Unmentionable!"

18. *Thanksgiving has been an unofficial holiday since the Pilgrims' time.* George Washington proclaimed it a national observance. President Lincoln made it an official, annual holiday. As I said earlier, Thanksgiving is a built-in, annual reminder of our nation's Christian heritage.

19. *God is mentioned in stone all over Washington, D.C., on its monuments and buildings.* Many of these were constructed in the 1930s. If they had been built earlier, there would probably be even more references to God. Meanwhile, if the ACLU were right, it would be time to take a sandblaster to the Washington Monument (where "Praise be to God" is written at the top and numerous Bible verses are quoted beneath). They would also have to chisel away the words at the Lincoln Memorial, the Jefferson Memorial, the Library of Congress, and so on.

20. *The Supreme Court building, also built in the 1930s, has carvings of Moses and of the Ten Commandments.* Alabama Attorney General Bill Pryor—long-time defender of the "Ten Commandments judge" (Alabama Supreme Court Chief

Justice Roy S. Moore)—says there are more than twenty artistic depictions of Moses or the Ten Commandments throughout the Supreme Court building. Time to reach for the chisel and hammer!

21. *Emblazoned over the Speaker of the House in the U.S. Capitol are the words* In God We Trust. This has been our official national motto for some fifty years and our unofficial motto for more than a hundred years before that. If state-sanctioned atheism becomes the norm, these words would have to be removed from both the House *and* from all our money. ("In God We Trust" has been placed on American coins since the days of President Abraham Lincoln and on the currency since President Dwight D. Eisenhower.)

22. *The deistic, atheistic founding fathers represented a small portion of the total picture.* David Barton, author of *Original Intent*, points out that approximately 250 men could be called America's founding fathers. They served on the Continental Congresses and gave us the Declaration of Independence, the Articles of Confederation, the Constitution, the Bill of Rights, and the Northwest Ordinance. Of these 250 men, about a dozen, fewer than 5 percent of the total, were not orthodox Christians. These include Jefferson (as we've seen), Ben Franklin, Thomas Paine, and Ethan Allen. But even these men were pro-Bible and had somewhat of a Christian worldview. (Later, Paine completely rejected such a worldview, but when he wrote *Common Sense* in 1776, he referred positively to the Bible.[30])

Jefferson and Franklin were by no means anti-Christian.

Modern secularists often quote this handful of men *as if they represent the total picture.* This is misleading and dishonest. The exception proves the rule, but the exception is not the rule. This is a shell game of the worst kind, yet unfortunately, millions of Americans today are exposed to this type of shell game; and they never hear the other side.

23. *Early commentaries on the Constitution showed that the founders did not intend a secular government that would silence any Christian presence in public.* So, for example, Supreme Court Justice Joseph Story, who lived through the formation of this government, wrote a massive commentary on the Constitution of the United States in 1828. He said this concerning the First Amendment: "Any attempt to level all religions [most notably, Christianity] and to make it a matter of state policy to hold all in utter indifference, would have created universal disapprobation, if not universal indignation . . ."[31]

24. *The Freedom Shrine exhibits tell the story of American liberty, and God is mentioned in many, if not most, of these documents on public display.* Funded by the Exchange Club, the Freedom Shrine exhibits can be found throughout the country in libraries, court buildings, public schools, and even the John Wayne Airport in Orange County, California. These exhibits contain plastic replicas of documents important to American history, usually spread out in some public place on a large wall. There for anyone to read is the Mayflower Compact, the Declaration of Independence, the Constitution, the epitaph Benjamin Franklin wrote for himself, the Northwest Ordinance, the Gettysburg Address, and so on.

25. *Reforms have often been informed and motivated by Christian beliefs.* This was true from the very beginning of the new nation to the present day.

If state-sanctioned atheism was what our founders intended, many societal reforms would have been declared unconstitutional and might not have happened. Notice how so many reforms of one sort or another began largely in the church. I won't say that 100 percent of the following have always been correct, but most of them have been. In any event, these were by and large Christian-inspired movements:

- The church was instrumental in banning the practice of dueling around the turn of the nineteenth century.

- The abolition of slavery was largely a Christian movement. Most of those fighting the slave trade were Christians, as were the conductors of the Underground Railroad. Evangelicals in England, notably William Wilberforce, helped pave the way for the abolition of slavery there. Even unchurched men and women (Abraham Lincoln when he began to serve as president) found their biggest impetus against the "peculiar institution" in the pages of the Bible.

- The prohibition movement began with women who were tired of the ravages of alcohol. Cary Nation lived in nine-teenth-century (and early twentieth-century) Kansas, where alcohol was theoretically illegal. Yet because of a technical-ity, it was flowing freely and consequently wreaking havoc in the lives of men and their families. Cary went into saloons with her customary hatchet in one hand and a Bible in the other. She destroyed every liquor bottle she could find. The men would quake in fear when she came in. Meanwhile, a national movement arose to amend our Constitution. For good or bad, prohibition was a reform born in the church.

- The activists of the civil rights movement used the churches as the base for their work. People sometimes forget that Dr.

Martin Luther King, Jr. was the *Reverend* Dr. King, a Baptist minister. Dr. King headed the Southern *Christian* Leadership Conference. His speeches abound with references to Jesus Christ.

Could a student read these in school today without worrying about ACLU persecution? Probably, but only because Dr. King is so politically correct. Does this mean that God, or even Jesus or the Bible, can be quoted when the statement leads to a liberal outcome? Meanwhile, I challenge a Christian young person in one of our public schools to write a report on Dr. King in his own words—yes, including even the *J* word (Jesus).

• The controversial Operation Rescue clearly had its inspiration in Scripture. Although their tactics may be questionable (and may have alienated some undecided Americans on the abortion issue), they had a marvelous track record of nonviolence. They are not to be confused with the radical fringe of the pro-life movement that has taken God's law into their own hands by shooting abortionists. That is not a pro-life act.

As society has wrangled with these types of issues—and Christians can sometimes be found on both sides of the gray ones—there is no question that Christianity has often played a significant role—and still does—in informing the conscience of many Americans.

It was like that in the very beginning of the country. One group that did so much to help further the cause of American liberty was the New England ministers who preached independence and liberty. Rev. Jonathan Mayhew of Boston preached that when King George did all the things he did in contradiction to the will of God that he "unkinged" himself.[32] Mayhew said this in 1750, twenty-six years before Thomas Jefferson articulated a similar argument in the Declaration of Independence.

To sum up this point, if today's version of the "separation of church and state" were correct, there essentially would never have been the abolition movement, prohibition, civil rights, the pro-life movement, and so on. But in light of the fact that the founders quoted Scripture in many of their *political* arguments, it is unreasonable to think they would only approve secular reasoning in the marketplace of ideas.

CONCLUSION

If American is ever to become a Christian nation again, it's time to stop the ACLU in their tracks with the facts and in the courts. It's time to rediscover the rich Judeo-Christian heritage that made this nation into the greatest, freest country in the history of the world. It's time to say, "Enough!" to the forces of godlessness who would send us to the back of the bus—or force us off the bus.

In the spring of 1999, Michelle Shocks, a pregnant woman, was riding a bus in Seattle, Washington. She struck up a conversation with a fellow passenger, and they began to discuss church. She told him about her church, and he was quite receptive to it. The bus driver overheard the conversation and asked them both to come forward. The driver told them to stop talking about God in this public setting. If they didn't, she would have to kick them off.

Michelle was shocked at this and returned to her seat. The gentleman next to her asked a quick question about what they had been discussing before since they weren't finished with it. The bus driver then declared, "That's it. At the next stop, you two are off my bus!"

Even though she was pregnant, it was pouring rain, and the next bus would not come for quite a while, even though religious liberty (not to mention free speech) is protected by the Constitution, and even though this took place on Good Friday, Michelle got kicked off the bus for talking about God with a fellow passenger. She walked at least a mile in the rain, on the side of the highway, and felt like a drowned rat when she finally got home.

So it's "Get off the bus" for Christians in modern America. Virtually every one of the founding fathers would have also been thrown off that bus, because they mentioned God and quoted the Bible in public in all sorts of settings.

★ ★ ★ ★ ★

FIFTEEN

"IF MY PEOPLE . . ."

"If My people who are called by My name
will humble themselves and pray and seek My face,
and turn from their wicked ways,
then I will hear from heaven,
and will forgive their sin and heal their land."
—2 CHRONICLES 7:14

DID YOU HEAR ABOUT THE OPEN PRAYER SESSIONS IN
a public high school? Probably not. Several students and even
teachers huddled together in a room at this school. Someone asked
if there was anyone religious in the room who might be able to
lead them in prayer. One of the students volunteered, and they held
prayer there at school during normal school hours. What happened next? An ACLU lawsuit?

Not exactly. These students and teachers were fleeing the
bloodshed at Columbine High School on April 20, 1999, in
Littleton, Colorado, the day of the massacre of twelve students and
one teacher, and the double suicides of the two murderers. Oh,
prayer came to the public school in America on that day—only it
came too late.

Ours is a nation in need of prayer, in need of a spiritual revival.
How greatly we're in need of revival was encapsulated in a politi-
cally incorrect prayer delivered by a Wichita minister before the
Kansas state legislature in 1996:

Heavenly Father, we come before you today to ask Your forgiveness and to seek Your direction and guidance.

We know Your Word says, "Woe to those who call evil good," but that is exactly what we have done. We have lost our spiritual equilibrium and inverted our values.

We confess that we have ridiculed the absolute truth of Your Word in the name of moral pluralism.

We have worshiped other gods and called it "multi-culturalism."

We have endorsed perversion and called it an "alternative lifestyle."

We have exploited the poor and called it "a lottery."

We have neglected the needy and called it "self-preservation."

We have rewarded laziness and called it "welfare."

In the name of "choice," we have killed our unborn.

In the name of "right to life," we have killed abortionists . . .

Search us, O God, and know our hearts today. Try us, and show us [if there be] any wicked way in us. Cleanse us from every sin, and set us free . . . [1]

A Renewed Vision

If America is truly to be renewed, it will not be through the political process, as important as that is. I believe we need a renewed vision, for "where there is no vision, the people perish." God can do the impossible, so we can experience a renewal in this land. And a genuine revival is what we need most if there is to be a new birth of freedom in America.

The most appropriate of all Bible verses that spells out the remedy for a nation that has lost its way is 2 Chronicles 7:14: "If My people who are called by My name will humble themselves and pray and seek My face, and turn from their wicked ways, then I will hear from heaven, and will forgive their sin and heal their land."

Let's look carefully at this verse so we can apply it to our land today.

"If My People . . ."

First of all, God said these things to His people in ancient Israel, in the context of the one and only true theocracy in history. America is not a theocracy. There has been no true theocracy on earth since the days of ancient Israel. Nonetheless, I believe we can glean general principles from this verse.

God spoke these words after Solomon completed the temple in Jerusalem, perhaps the most glorious building ever constructed by man, which would today cost between four and five billion dollars to reproduce. The temple was, indeed, a wonder to behold. At the worship service that opened the temple, fire came down from heaven, and the Shekinah glory of God filled the temple with such brightness and brilliance that the people fell upon their faces and worshiped in awe. The priest could not go into the temple because of the brightness of that Shekinah glory.

What exactly is the Shekinah glory of God? Actually the word *Shekinah* in Hebrew simply means "dwelling." It was the glory of the fact that God was dwelling in that "house"—a visible token of His presence. Those present in the temple on the day of Solomon's dedication could not have endured a longer exposure to God's glory, so the glory remained in a milder form in the Holy of Holies, where the blood was sprinkled upon the mercy seat.

After Solomon had completed his prayer, God audibly spoke the words of 2 Chronicles 7:14. If you haven't memorized this verse, you should engrave it upon the walls of your mind that you might remember it always.

Certainly the Israelites needed to repent and turn to God. But that is not what the verse says. It says *we* need to repent. It says *we* need to turn from our wicked ways, and then God will heal our land. God indicates His proprietary interest in His own. We are His own peculiar people who belong to Him ("who are called by My name").

These words are a great command from God to repent. There is no doubt that the United States needs to repent of its wickedness. We are overrun with pornography and blasphemy and ungodliness and immorality—perversion of every sort.

We are called by the name of the second person of the Triune Godhead, Jesus Christ. We are Christians—a name first applied to us as a word that was meant to be an insult. Yet we consider it a noble title to be called after the name of Him who loved us even unto death. We are His people. We are the ones who are commanded to repent, to turn from our wicked ways. Then and only then will God heal our land. Judgment begins at the house of God.

"If My People . . . Will Humble Themselves . . ."

President Abraham Lincoln warned Americans about the sin of pride. He said:

> We have been the recipients of the choicest bounties of Heaven. We have been preserved these many years in peace and prosperity. We have grown in numbers and power as no other nation has ever grown, but we have forgotten God. We have forgotten the gracious hand which preserved us in peace, and multiplied and enriched and strengthened us; and we have vainly imagined, in the deceitfulness of our hearts, that all these blessings were produced by some superior wisdom and virtue of our own. Intoxicated with unbroken success, we have become too self-sufficient to feel the necessity of redeeming and preserving grace, too proud to pray to the God that made us. It behooves us, then, to humble ourselves before the offended Power, to confess our national sins, and to pray for clemency and forgiveness.[2]

The sin of pride is where it all begins. Pride turned Lucifer, the angel of light, into Satan, the demon of darkness. And pride goes before destruction and a fall. The Bible is very clear that many other sins that most people take to be far more serious are peccadilloes compared to the spiritual sin of pride. Pride makes devils.[3]

Think of the Pharisees. What was the sin that blinded them to the reality of the Son of God and caused them to deliver Jesus up to be crucified? Envy—fueled by their pride. So pride nailed Christ to the cross.

The warnings in Scripture against pride are numerous. For example:

- "The LORD will destroy the house of the proud,
  but He will establish the boundary of the widow" (Prov. 15:25).

- "The one who has a haughty look and a proud heart, him I will not endure" (Ps. 101:5).

- "Let nothing be done through selfish ambition or conceit, but in lowliness of mind let each esteem others better than himself" (Phil. 2:3).

- "God resists the proud, but gives grace to the humble" (James 4:6b).

We Christians need to humble ourselves, to acknowledge our sins, to confess our unworthiness. We need to ask God to grant us humility of spirit so we may be able to pray in a way that is acceptable and pleasing to Him. Until we have first confessed our sins and our unworthiness, our prayers will bounce off heaven. If we humble ourselves and confess our sins, God will hear from heaven, answer our prayers, and forgive our sins.

"IF MY PEOPLE . . . WILL PRAY AND SEEK MY FACE . . ."
Many Christians pray for themselves, their families, their children, their businesses, and their health. But how many of us regularly pray for our native land to experience revival? I am afraid many Christians do not. We have a land desperately in need of God, and

we should pray for that land. We should ask God to heal it, to bring our country to Himself, to restore it to godliness and make it once again a "city set upon a hill."

One day in nineteenth-century New York City, a man put up a poster advertising a prayer meeting in that place (it was just a rented room) on a certain day at noon. The following week he came to the place at the appointed time, and nobody was there, so he started praying. A half an hour later, somebody else came. Before the hour was over six people were there. The next week there were fifty people, and a hundred the week after that. And then prayer meetings were started all over New York City, and suddenly, a quarter of a million people were swept into the kingdom of God. At that time a million was an enormous proportion of the people in that great city. God can act to build up as quickly as He can tear down.

". . . AND TURN FROM THEIR WICKED WAYS"

We live in a world where the ungodly are so plunged into the mire of wickedness that it is difficult for many of us to even be able to recognize wicked ways in ourselves. But if we will bend our knees, bow our hearts and minds before God, and ask the Holy Spirit to show us those things in our lives that are displeasing to Him, we will find that, alas, there are more wicked ways in us than we may have imagined, and we need to confess them.

Long ago Abraham Lincoln called our nation to renewal when he said:

> It is the duty of nations as well as of men, to own their dependence upon the overriding power of God, to confess their sins and transgressions in humble sorrow, yet with the assured hope that genuine repentance will lead to mercy and pardon; and to recognize the sublime truth, announced in the Holy Scriptures and proven by all history that those nations only are blessed whose God is the Lord.[4]

Jesus Christ came into Galilee proclaiming that the kingdom of God was at hand. Then He issued the first words to those who would be His followers—the words He had thought about for countless millennia. What were those words? "Repent, for the kingdom of heaven is at hand" (Matt. 4:17). Christ began His ministry with repentance, and He continued it with repentance when He said, "Unless you repent you will all likewise perish" (Luke 13:3). Repentance means turning from all of your sins and turning unto God. Have you repented?

I recall a story about a rather humble Christian, not too well educated, who ran across a sophisticated and highly educated skeptic. The Christian shared the gospel of God's love in Christ with this unbeliever, who rejected it scornfully, bringing up some rather obtuse objections that the Christian could not answer.

The humble believer answered, "Yes, that may be so, but Christ said, 'Except ye repent, ye shall all likewise perish.'"

The skeptic brought up another objection, which the believer couldn't answer, but he said, "Well, yes, but Jesus Christ said, 'Except ye repent, ye shall all likewise perish.'"

Yet another objection of a rather esoteric sort was brought up, and this Christian replied, "Well, I'm not sure about that, but this I know: Christ said, 'Except ye repent, ye shall all likewise perish.'"

Then they went their separate ways.

At three o'clock the next morning there was a knocking at the Christian's door, and when he answered it, there stood that skeptic, very distraught. He said to him, "I cannot sleep. I cannot think of anything except those words, 'Except ye repent, ye shall all likewise perish.' What shall I do?"

The Christian had the privilege of kneeling with this skeptic and leading him in repentance and faith as he accepted Christ as his Savior. Those words had been etched in his conscience and his mind: "Except ye repent, ye shall all likewise perish."

Christ began His ministry with that demand. He continued with that demand; He ended with it. In the seven letters to the seven churches in Revelation, Jesus told them to repent eight different times. When Peter gave the first sermon of the Christian era at Pentecost (Acts 2), the people were pricked in their hearts and they said, "Men and brethren, what shall we do?" and Peter said, "Repent." Paul said that Christ came that repentance and faith might be preached unto the Gentiles (Acts 26:17–18). Repent. Repent. Repent.

We live in nation that is awash in sin of every kind. We sorely need to repent. Even many "Christians" in America need to repent.

- Some need to get rid of a few of their cable channels. (Oooh, I hit a nerve.)

- Some need to cancel a few magazine subscriptions. Christ said, "Whoever looks at a woman to lust for her has already committed adultery with her in his heart" (Matt. 5:28).

- Some may be addicted to drugs. Repent.

- Some may be addicted to alcohol. Repent.

- Some Christians are thieves. "Thieves in church? Why, the very idea!" you might say. Yet some Christians pull off a heist every Sunday morning. They rob God week after week. God said to Israel, "You have robbed Me, even this whole nation" (Mal. 3:9). And they said, "In what way have we robbed You?" God's response: "In tithes and offerings" (3:8).

- Some Christians are guilty of anger and animosity toward another person. They need to repent of that sin.

Paul said he would not be brought into bondage to anything (1 Cor. 9:27). Are you in bondage? Then turn from those chains if you would be saved. We cannot live in sin on earth and expect to live in heaven above. I don't know what your sin is, but I do know this: Whatever it is, God knows it, and you know it, and right now He is speaking to you about it. Repent, for "Unless you repent you will all likewise perish."

"... I WILL HEAR FROM HEAVEN ... AND HEAL THEIR LAND"

Are you a man or woman of prayer? Have you truly humbled yourself before God? It has often been said that we seek God's hand, but seldom His face. Are you seeking His face? Do you pursue a *personal relationship* with God? What place does adoration—praising God for who He is, a marvelous, holy, wise, gracious, and good God—play in your prayers?

Pockets of revival are breaking out in this nation in various places.

- The Concerts of Prayer organization is mobilizing believers all over the country in various citywide prayer rallies. In their literature, they state, "Following the pattern of Great Awakenings over the past 250 years, a nation-wide and world-wide movement of prayer is emerging today, joining Christians in eager pursuit of God for spiritual awakening and world evangelization."[5]

- Luis Palau has been holding two-day family festivals that draw incredible crowds exposed to the gospel—including attendance of 140,000 in Portland, Oregon, 200,000 in Connecticut, 150,000 in Seattle, Washington, and 300,000 in Ft. Lauderdale, Florida (Beachfest 2003). People are hungry for God and are finding Him in such events. Denominational barriers have come down, as virtually all the ministers of Ft. Lauderdale had worked together for Beachfest 2003 in our city.

- Many Christians report God at work in various places, both in America and abroad. The Web site www.revivaltoday.com reports on such pockets of revival from a charismatic perspective.

- The Prayer Breakfast Network reports that citywide prayer breakfasts are a great way to spread the gospel and that nearly one quarter of our nation's cities hold annual prayer breakfasts so far.

- Consider the incredible evangelistic and influential parachurch movement in our time. Two or three generations ago, there was no Evangelism Explosion, no Focus on the Family, no Campus Crusade for Christ, no InterVarsity Christian Fellowship, no Reformed Student Fellowship. Christian media was virtually in its infancy or was marginal at best. But all of these movements, and many others combined, have brought untold multitudes into the kingdom. They have equipped the saints and encouraged involvement in the culture. These national ministries go across denominational barriers and shine the light of the gospel in dark places. At the 2003 National Religious Broadcasters Convention, President Bush told the delegates that Christian broadcasting now reaches an audience of 141 million a week.[6]

As bad as things are now, we would be much worse off without these organizations. They are evidence that God is at work in our time.

If we turn from our wicked ways, God will bless and heal our land. May God do that. May it start with you and me, and may it be right now.

SIXTEEN

WHAT IF AMERICA WERE A CHRISTIAN NATION AGAIN?

*"Who knows whether you have come
to the kingdom for such a time as this?"*
—ESTHER 4:14

WHEN I THINK OF "AMERICA: A CHRISTIAN NATION," I realize that this concept has been so systematically blotted from the collective memory of this country that it sounds like an alien philosophy, an intrusion of religion into the tranquillity of a secular nation.

You and I were born in a Christian nation. I am afraid our children and grandchildren might well be born in an atheistic one. Amazingly, America's move toward atheism has been taking place at a time when most of the atheistic states of Communism around the world have been crumbling, and people there are clamoring for the Word of God. I think of an incident at a book fair in Moscow about a decade ago, just as the Iron Curtain was dismantling. Traffic was stopped in every direction as people desperately tried to get their hands on one of the fifty thousand Bibles being given away. Just when the rest of the world is realizing the folly of unbelief and the fatal results in the lives of people, America continues apace down the foolish path toward godlessness and secularism.

Liberty First

Patrick Henry, a Christian patriot, the golden-tongued orator of the Revolutionary period, said in his will, "I have now disposed of all my property to my family. There is one thing more that I wish I could give to them. That is the Christian religion. If they had that and I had not given them one shilling, they would have been rich; and if they had not that and I had given them the world, they would be poor."[1]

Knowing the foundations of liberty, knowing the bedrock of Scripture and the Christian foundations of this nation, Henry was willing to sacrifice even his life to defend it. In March 1775, a month before the shot heard round the world ignited the Revolutionary War, Henry said these words in his celebrated speech: "The battle, Sir, is not to the strong alone; it is to the vigilant, the active, the brave . . . Why stand we here idle? What is it that gentlemen wish? What would they have? Is life so dear, or peace so sweet, as to be purchased at the price of chains and slavery? Forbid it, Almighty God! I know not what course others may take, but as for me, give me liberty or give me death!"[2]

So said the Christian patriot and one of the founders of our nation. Thankfully, there are yet those in recent times with similar sentiments.

Either a "Spiritual Awakening" or a "Progressive Deterioration"

One of the greatest military geniuses America ever produced was General Douglas MacArthur. For fifty years he devoted his life to this country. Do you remember what he said after he conquered the empire of Japan? Was it "What is needed now are tax collectors to collect the taxes for the conquerors"? No. He said that what was needed now was ten thousand missionaries for Japan. But they didn't come. Now we see how right he was.

Douglas MacArthur once made another very astute observation that shows the importance of morality to our nation: "History fails to record a single precedent in which nations subject to moral decay have not passed into political and economic decline. There has been either a spiritual awakening to overcome the moral lapse, or a progressive deterioration leading to ultimate national disaster."[3]

This is precisely where we are—in need of a spiritual awakening, lest we experience complete societal collapse.

A New Birth of Freedom

America, a Christian nation, demands an equal sacrifice from each of us. Did you ever consider the fact that birth itself involves a great sacrifice?

If you're a mother, you know all about birth. All the rest of us should listen carefully. A birth is a process of all-consuming pain. Babies come into this world in a bloody mess that brings intense pain and suffering for the mother. As the child begins to grow, the mother forgets what she went through in the birthing process. So, too, has America forgotten what it took to bring forth this nation.

Even when President Abraham Lincoln uttered the phrase "a new birth of freedom," the ground surrounding him was saturated with blood, and tears were flowing throughout the land. There was a new birth of sorts after the Civil War. The Union was safe, and slowly the nation healed.

Today, if we ask for a new birth of freedom, is it not possible that people again will have to suffer? (I don't mean by any type of extremist acts; I simply mean people suffering for doing that which is right.) Is it not likely that some of us will again be called to mutually pledge "our lives, our fortunes, and our sacred honor"?

If "freedom's holy light" is to keep shining on our land, are enough Christians willing to pay the price?

The Judeo-Christian heritage that made this nation great in the first place has been sifting through our fingers like sand because too many Christians are "engaged simply in personal peace and prosperity," as Dr. Francis Schaeffer used to say.

We are losing the cultural war, because of what those on the other side say and do, and what we *don't* say and do. Those, of course, are called sins of "omission," and I believe that in the long run, what we don't do or say may be the things that create the greatest amount of evil in our world. I'm reminded of the famous quote from Saint Ambrose: "Not only for every idle world must man give an account, but for every idle silence."[4]

We have been commanded to proclaim the gospel of Jesus Christ to every creature. All we have to do to disobey is nothing. Say nothing, do nothing, and we are guilty. And we are the ones who have indirectly brought a flood of unbelief and wickedness upon our land.

FOR SUCH A TIME AS THIS

Do you remember when all the Jews of Persia and beyond were sentenced to death? By the grace of God one woman was able to prevent this: Queen Esther.

Haman, a fifth-century B.C. version of Adolf Hitler, was incensed because Mordecai the Jew would not bow down to him. So he concocted a plan to destroy all the Jews in Persia and the surrounding areas. He managed to talk Persian King Xerxes into this plan. The date was set. The plan was in motion, and thousands upon thousands of Jews would die. Nothing but God's active intervention could stop this demonic plan.

But God delivered His people, and, as He so often does, He used a person to do it. Queen Esther. Unbeknownst to Xerxes, his beautiful wife and queen was Jewish. In those days the king's power was so great that she risked her life just coming into his presence to request a hearing.

So initially Esther was not happy with the notion of approaching the king. But Mordecai, her fellow Jew (except he was out of the closet, so to speak), told her, "For if you remain completely silent at this time, relief and deliverance will arise for the Jews from another place; but you and your father's house will perish. Yet who knows whether you have come to the kingdom for such a time as this?" (Esther 4:14)

If Esther held her peace, would the result have been that all of the Jews would have been killed? No. Read it again: "Relief and deliverance will arise for the Jews from another place."

One of my professors in seminary, Dr. Manford George Gutzke, made this point very forcefully fifty years ago. This very famous preacher was not too tall, but was very broad and thick; he was a former heavyweight boxing champion of the Canadian army. He had a hand like a ham, and all he had to do was just drop it—BOOOOM! And if he dropped it on your head, you would be lying on the ground. But he had the spirit of a cherub and of a little, sweet child.

I remember this Presbyterian pastor and professor saying, "It may be that the Presbyterian Church will fail to obey the Great Commission. If it does, God will raise up others, instead, to do it. For example," he said, "the Pentecostals." Back then, hardly anyone had heard of a Pentecostal; there just weren't many of them. But you know what happened. At large, the Presbyterian Church failed to fulfill the Great Commission. Now the Pentecostals (charismatics) are everywhere throughout the world—exactly as Dr. Gutzke said.

Help, deliverance, shall come from another source. Now, there are some who will say, "Oh, well, that's good. I can sit back and forget about it. I don't have to worry anymore. God, just check me out. I'm not going to be involved."

Well, before you vote yourself out of the game, remember another part of Mordecai's comment to Esther: "But you and your father's house will perish." In short, if we don't get involved, we will suffer loss. Let me make one thing clear: Every sin we commit, whether of commission or omission, will inevitably involve our suffering loss.

If we could see things aright, we would realize that it is a great privilege to be a part of what God is doing in our world today, just as it was a privilege for Queen Esther to take a stand for her people. Haman's evil plot backfired. The Jews were spared, and he was hanged on the very gallows he had created for Mordecai to swing on.

I believe that you and I were called to live in America and serve in America at this very time, "for such a time as this."

You ask, "Do you really mean that Christianity and faith make a difference?" In Part Two of this book we saw that in one area after another, unbelief has a huge price tag. Now let's look at the effect faith can have upon our culture. Let me give you an example.

THE EFFECTS OF FAITH

Around the turn of this century, a remarkable revival took place in the Hebrides Islands near Scotland. This began in a church where a revival was already going on. The Spirit of God began to work, and hundreds of people were converted. The movement spread to other churches in the community, and soon the entire Hebrides were involved in a tremendous spiritual revival. The power of God was so at work that people walking down the street would suddenly be convulsed and found writhing along the side of the road. They were not sick—they were simply under the conviction of their sin and were seeking to find peace with God.

The result: virtually the entire population of the Hebrides was converted to Jesus Christ. What happened next? The police were fired. The jails were closed. The courts closed. The bars closed themselves. There were no murders, no thefts, no burglaries. People didn't have to lock their doors at night. There were no rapes, no kidnappings, no drunkenness, no drug addiction. There was, however, the "terrible problem" of prayer and Bible reading in schools and prayer and Bible study in the homes and churches.

My friends, weigh the difference that faith makes. I hope that when you consider the cost of secularism and humanism and unbelief, you will begin to say, "Enough. We have had enough of this. This is an alien, godless view and we want no more of it foisted on our children. We don't want them or ourselves having to pay the consequences now and in the years to come." If you think it is bad now, what will happen when the millions of young people who are indoctrinated with this view in our schools reach maturity and get to the graduate school of unbelief?

FREEDOM FOR ALL

When committed Christians play a decisive role in our nation, generally everybody benefits. But frankly, it's hard to get secularists or non-Christians to realize that fact. One man who does realize this is Rabbi Daniel Lapin, whom we heard from earlier. We interviewed Rabbi Lapin for our national television broadcast, "What If Jesus Had Never Been Born?"[5] and we were impressed with how much insight he has on the cultural struggle in America. The rabbi cut to the heart of conflict in modern America when he said:

> We Jews need to recognize that the struggle in America is not a struggle between Jew and Christian. It's not a struggle between blacks and whites. It is not a struggle between rich and poor. And, it's not a struggle between men and women. There is a cultural struggle in America today. It is between those who are comfortable with God's divine blueprint for society and that includes serious devoted Christians and Orthodox Jews. And on the other side, those who are fanatic extremists, who are determined to rip every element of traditional Judeo-Christian faith out of the Village Square.[6]

Rabbi Lapin points out that the United States of America has protected the Jewish faith: "No country in the last two thousand years has provided the same haven of tranquillity and prosperity for Jews as has the United States of America. And, this is not in spite of Americans being Christian; it is because of it. You might say that America's Bible belt is the Jewish communities' safety belt."[7]

Therefore, says the rabbi, the very safety of Jews (and others) is put at risk when the Christian faith is undermined in America: "Jews need to understand that our safety and security in the United States is dependent upon the health and vitality of American Christianity."[8] Would to God that more Jews and other non-Christians in our country were as insightful as Rabbi Lapin.

GET INVOLVED

The pastor of a little church attended one of Coral Ridge Ministries' Reclaiming America for Christ conferences, where he picked up the booklet *101 Ways to Reclaim America*.[9] The pastor went back to his town and put up an unusual, large flag (with red-and-white stripes and the blue field, but no stars). Each time a person committed to doing one of the activities to help reclaim America, the pastor put up a star. Week by week, they would put new stars up as laypeople in the church completed various activities to help reclaim their community. Before the pastor even came to the conference, the members of the church had taken so many action steps that they had exceeded fifty stars. In fact, they had put *fifty-seven* stars on that flag.

I may not be able to do everything, but I can do something, and what I can do, I will do. The sin of doing nothing at all—that is the great sin of the Christian church at this present time. "Who knows whether thou art come to the kingdom for such a time as this?"

HOW CAN AMERICA BE RECLAIMED?

If we are going to reclaim America, how are we going to do it? I think the Scriptures are very explicit. Two things need to be done. Interestingly, they are the first and the last commandments God gave us. The first one, called the Cultural Mandate, is found in Genesis 1:28, where we are told to "be fruitful, and multiply, and replenish the earth" (KJV), and that we are to have dominion over all things. The last commandment is the Great Commission to spread His Word into all the world (Matt. 28:18–20).

The famous hymn declares, "This is my Father's world."[10] As the regents of God, we are to bring His teaching to every sphere of society—not only to the individual, but to the family, the parents, the schools, the government, the arts, and every subject God has spoken about. If we don't, society will take another avenue, and that is the problem we are in today, because we failed to fulfill the Cultural Mandate.

About thirty years ago one study showed that 50 percent of evangelical Christians weren't even registered to vote. I am optimistic and hopeful that this is not the case today. Certainly every Christian should be registered, become informed, and vote.

Jesus Christ tells us, "Render therefore to Caesar the things that are Caesar's, and to God the things that are God's" (Matt. 22:21). For a secular American citizen to fail to register and vote is a failure to fulfill a patriotic civic duty. For a Christian American citizen to do so is not only to fail in that way, but also to sin against God. You ask, "Did he say what I thought he said?" Yes, I'll say it again: For you as a Christian American citizen to fail to register and vote is a sin against God.

How do I know that? Because sin is any failure to do that which God has commanded us to do; the other side of the coin is committing any act that He commanded us not to do. God commanded us to render to Caesar the things that are Caesar's, which, at the least in a democratic republic, means that we exercise our franchise—we register and vote.

Do you remember how close the election was in 2000, between Bush and Gore? For more than thirty days, the nation suffered a great deal of anxiety as to who would be the next president. The contest was finally decided in the courts. Former U.S. representative Helen Chenoweth-Hage from Idaho reminds us of just how close the contest was: "The electorate was split 49-51 and the presidency was decided by 537 votes. At least one congressional district was decided by 33 votes."[11] Indirectly many Christians contributed to this problem. It's estimated that about four million *Christian* voters sat out that election.[12] Even a fraction of those four million could have made a huge difference in that cliffhanger of an election.

Furthermore, in the elections of 1996, millions more Christians (and other Americans) indirectly determined Bill Clinton's reelection as president. The Associated Press noted, "More than half [of] America's eligible voters stayed home on Election Day, producing the lowest turnout since 1824, when only slightly more than a fourth went to the polls."[13] This would mean that millions of Christian voters neglected their duty to vote—even when such critical issues as abortion were at stake.

So, dear friend, if you are not registered and you haven't been voting, you need to repent. Get registered, get informed, and vote. I hope you will become active in our society—not only involved in voting, but that you will become involved in our libraries, in our schools, in our parental associations, and in all phases of the culture in which we live. Otherwise, views antithetical to that which God has taught us in His Word will prevail as they do today, not only in education, the media, and entertainment, but also in government.

It is interesting that some people like to hurl epithets at Christians who get involved. Unbelievers who scorn God's commandments, who want to do their own humanistic, godless thing, are not happy with us. So they call us "radicals."

Gary Bauer, one-time presidential candidate and former president of the Family Research Council, serves as the president of American Values in Washington, D.C. He has spoken at our Reclaiming America conferences. One time, he was being interviewed by CBS's Dan Rather, who got a little flustered with Bauer and said to him, "What do you want for America?" Gary paused for a moment of reflection and answered in this way:

> I want to see an America . . . where I don't have to worry about date rape when my daughter goes out for the first time at college. I want an America where, when a young man pledges to love and cherish and honor her for the rest of their lives, there's a good chance he means it. I want a country where children come first again and where virtue is honored; a place where values matter and the American dream is still real. I want a country where families no longer have to hide behind barred windows, where criminals do real time and aren't released on a whim or a technicality. I want a place where children can play in public parks again without fear, and where adults can walk across those parks at night.

What Gary Bauer is asking for is quite reasonable. Do you realize that there are capital cities in this world with huge populations—in the Orient, in Europe, in Africa—where you can go out at ten o'clock at night, ladies, and walk around the public park with no fear for your life or person? It was once that way in America.

Bauer continued:

> Families would spend more time being real families, not watching artificial ones on television.

I hope for a land where love of country is seen as a virtue again.

Where the young are taught the unique blessing they have received just to have been born in such a place.

In my America, the schools would work once more. Political correctness would be thrown out, and the goal of education would once again be to teach our children to have "knowing heads and loving hearts."

In this land, racism, quotas, and special rights would be rejected, and all our children would be taught to judge their fellow citizens by the content of their character, not the color of their skin. I see a country that respects life again, where drive-by shootings and one and a half million aborted babies each year are seen as disasters. Here responsibilities would be as important as rights, and a handshake would be something [once again] to rely on. In my country, working men and women would be praised, not penalized by ever-growing government. The truly poor would get a hand up, not a handout.[14]

This is the kind of country we in the Christian movement want. Is that radical? If it is, count me in. How about you? Is that the kind of country you would like to see in America? I believe that it is.

THE ANSWER

The second thing that must be done is evangelization. Christ's last commandment to His disciples was "Go ye into all the world and preach the gospel to every creature" (Matt. 28:16–20). If all of the Christians in America simply led one person to Christ this year, this nation would once again be overwhelmingly Christian, and most all of the problems of society would vanish like snow before the rising sun. If Christians would become involved in our culture and proclaim the gospel of Jesus Christ, this nation and this world would be transformed almost overnight. It would be *glorious*. Will you do it?

Dear friend, Christ commanded, "Follow me and I will make you fishers of men" (Matt. 4:19–20). Are you living in silent rebellion to that, day after day, year after year? The problems of this country are due to that rebellion. Judgment must begin at the house of God.

Please join me in a prayer for America:

> Dear Father, make us salt as well as light. Help us to render unto Caesar and unto You, O God, those things which are respectively yours. Use us, we pray, in our generation to help transform this nation and reclaim it, O Christ, for You, and in that glorious reclamation, the people will rejoice. In Jesus' name we pray. Amen.

Soli Deo Gloria.

★ ★ ★ ★ ★

NOTES

INTRODUCTION

[1] Transcript from an interview with Jeremiah Denton, CRM-TV, on location in Mobile, Ala., September 1991.

[2] [Abraham] Lincoln's Address at Gettysburg, 1863, *World Almanac 2001* (Mahwah, N.J.: World Almanac Books, 2001), 468.

[3] Remarks from Lynn Buzzard, founding director of the Christian Legal Society, in D. James Kennedy, *The Constitution in Crisis,* Ft. Lauderdale: Coral Ridge Ministries, September 1987, a videotape.

CHAPTER 1—GOD'S PROVIDENTIAL HAND ON AMERICA

[1] *Compton's Pictured Encyclopedia and Fact Index* (Chicago et al: F. E. Compton Co., 1965), Vol. 15, 192.

[2] William Cowper, "God Moves in a Mysterious Way," 1774, Donald P. Hustad, ed., *Hymns for the Living Church* (Carol Stream, Ill.: Hope Publishing Company, 1974/1984), Hymn #47.

[3] For some of the concepts in this chapter, I am in debt to Sir Edward Shepherd Creasy (1812–1878), author of *Fifteen Decisive Battles of the World* (Marathon, Syracuse, Arebela, Metaurus, Teutoburger Wald, Chalons, Tours, Hastings, Orleans, Spanish Armada, Blenheim, Poltava, Saratoga, Valmy, and Waterloo). I am also indebted to George Bancroft (1800–1891), America's first major historian, author of the multivolume *History of the United States of America, from the Discovery of the Continent* (author's final revision, 1890). Bancroft's history of our country was the standard for at least half a century. However, Bancroft is not as widely read today in part because he is politically incorrect.

[4] For example, in the New England Confederation of 1643, the Pilgrims and Puritans proclaimed, "[W]e all came into these parts of America, with one

and the same end and aim, namely, to advance the Kingdom of our Lord Jesus Christ." David Barton, *Original Intent* (Aledo, Tex.: WallBuilder Press, 1996), 79.

[5] Quoted in Paul Little, *Know What You Believe* (Wheaton, Ill.: Victor Books, 1987), 124.

[6] George Washington letter to Thomas Nelson, 20 August 1778. John C. Fitzpatrick, ed., *The Writings of Washington* (Washington, D.C.: U.S. Government Printing Office, 1932), Vol. XII, 343.

[7] Benjamin Hart, "The Wall That Protestantism Built: The Religious Reasons for the Separation of Church and State," *Policy Review* (Washington, D.C.: Heritage Foundation, Fall 1988), 44.

[8] Cowper, "God Moves in a Mysterious Way."

[9] John Winthrop, "A Model of Christian Charity," 1630, *The Annals of America* (Chicago et al: Encyclopedia Britannica, Inc., 1976), Vol. 1, 115.

[10] George Washington, letter to his brother, 18 July 1755, quoted in George Bancroft, *History of the United States From the Discovery of the American Continent* (Boston: Little, Brown and Company, 1854), Vol. IV, 190.

[11] David Barton, *The Bulletproof George Washington* (Aledo, Tex.: Wallbuilders, 1990).

[12] George Washington letter to Thomas Nelson, 20 August 1778.

[13] Alexander Hamilton, *The Royal Danish-American Gazette*, 3 October 1772. Norman Cousins, ed., *In God We Trust: The Religious Beliefs and Ideas of the American Founding Fathers* (New York: Harper & Brothers, 1958), 330.

CHAPTER 2—THE PILGRIM ADVENTURE

[1] William Bradford, *Of Plymouth Plantation*, 1650, Harold Paget, ed., *Bradford's History of the Plymouth Settlement 1608–1650* (San Antonio: Mantle Ministries, 1988. Paget's original version published 1909), 21.

[2] William Bradford, Samuel Eliot Morison, ed., *Of Plymouth Plantation 1620–1647*, updated (New York: Alfred Knopf, 1952, 2001), 3.

[3] Winston S. Churchill, *The New World; Volume II of A History of the English-Speaking World* (New York: Dodd, Mead & Company, 1956), 106.

[4] Robert Merrill Bartlett, *The Pilgrim Way* (Philadelphia: A Pilgrim Press Book, 1971), 54.

[5] Transcript from an interview with Dr. Robert Bartlett, on location in Plymouth, Mass., Coral Ridge Ministries-TV, Ft. Lauderdale, August 1989.

[6] Robert Linder, entry on Geneva Bible, in J. D. Douglas, gen. ed., *The New International Dictionary of the Christian Church* (Grand Rapids: Zondervan, 1974, 1978), 405.

[7] Kenneth L. Woodward with David Gates, "How the Bible Made America: Since the Puritans and the Pioneers, Through Wars and Social Conflicts, a Sense of Biblical Mission Has United Us, Divided Us and Shaped Our National Destiny," *Newsweek*, 27 December 1982, 44.

[8] Bradford, Morison, ed., *Of Plymouth Plantation*, 11.

[9] Ibid., 17.

[10] Ibid., 23–24.

[11] Jordan D. Fiore, ed., *Mourt's Relation: A Journal of the Pilgrims of Plymouth* (Plymouth, Mass: Plymouth Rock Foundation, 1985), 9.

[12] Bradford, Morison, ed., *Of Plymouth Plantation*, 58.

[13] Ibid., 61.

[14] The Mayflower Compact, 1620, *The Annals of America*, vol. 1, 64.

[15] Churchill, *The New World*, 170.

[16] Paul Johnson, *A History of the American People* (New York: HarperCollinsPublishers, 1997), 28.

[17] Bancroft, *History of the United States of America*, Vol. I, 207.

[18] Bradford, Morison, ed., *Of Plymouth Plantation*, 78.

[19] Ibid., 236.

Chapter 3—"Our Lives, Our Fortunes, Our Sacred Honor"

[1] Declaration of Independence, 4 July 1776, *The World Almanac and Book of Facts: 1998* (Mahwah, N.J.: World Almanac Books), 512–13.

[2] Transcript from a Coral Ridge Ministries TV interview with Dr. M. E. Bradford conducted on location at the University of Dallas (17 June 1992).

[3] Johnson, *A History of the American People*, 204.

[4] Samuel Adams, "The Rights of the Colonists," 1772, *The Annals of America*, Vol. 2, 218–19.

[5] John Adams, letter to Thomas Jefferson, 25 December 1813, *Correspondence*, II, 412, quoted in Harnsberger, ed., *Treasury of Presidential Quotations*, 20.

[6] Thomas Jefferson to the Virginia delegates to Congress, August 1774, *Writings* I, 211. Quoted in Ibid., 116.

[7] William Livingston quoted in Vincent Wilson Jr., *The Book of the Founding Fathers* (Brookeville, Md.: American History Research Associates, 1974), 44.

[8] Benjamin Rush, *Essays, Literary, Moral, and Philosophical* (1798, 2nd edition, 1806) quoted in Stephen Abbott Northrop, *A Cloud of Witnesses* (Portland, Ore.: American Heritage Ministries, 1987), 388.

[9] Declaration of Independence, *The World Almanac and Book of Facts: 1998*, 512–13.

[10] See Chief Justice Roy S. Moore, *Our Legal Heritage* (Montgomery, Ala.: The Administrative Office of Courts, June 2001).

[11] Johnson, *A History of the American People*, 172.

[12] Interview with Dr. M. E. Bradford (17 June 1992).

[13] Benjamin Franklin, *The Autobiography of Benjamin Franklin: Poor Richard's Almanac and Other Papers* (Reading, Penn.: The Spencer Press, 1936), 146.

[14] Bancroft, *History of the United States of America*, Vol. IV, 43–44.

[15] Ibid., 54.

[16] Massachusetts Provincial Congress quoted in Ibid., 121.

[17] Quoted in Ibid., 45–46.

[18] Quoted in Ibid., 35.

[19] George Washington quoted in Ibid., 199.

[20] Russell T. Hitt, ed., *Heroic Colonial Christians* (Philadelphia: Lippincott, 1966), 228–29.

[21] Benjamin Franklin quoted in Gorton Carruth and Eugene Ehrlich, *The Harper Book of American Quotations* (New York et al.: Harper & Row, Publishers, 1988), 59.

[22] David Gibbs Jr., *Minuteman Alert*, (Seminole, Fla.: Christian Law Association, July 1996), 1.

[23] Declaration of Independence, *The World Almanac*, 513.

[24] For further details on this subject, see Paul Harvey, *Our Lives, Our Fortunes, Our Sacred Honor* (Waco, Tex.: Word Books, 1976).

[25] Count Heinrich Coudenhove Kalergi, *Anti-Semitism Throughout the Ages*, edited and brought up to date by Count Richard Coudenhove Kalergi, trans. by Dr. Angelo S. Rappoport (London: Hutchinson & Co., 1935), 223.

[26] Richard Stockton quoted in William J. Federer, *America's God and Country: Encyclopedia of Quotations* (St. Louis, Mo.: Amerisearch, 2000), 573.

[27] Benjamin Rush, *The Annals of America*, vol. 4, 29.

[28] William J. Federer, "American Quotations," in William J. Federer, ed., *Library of Classics* (St. Louis, Mo.: Amerisearch, Inc., 2002), a CD-ROM, based on George Washington, 9 July 1776, quoted in *American Army Chaplaincy—A Brief History* (Office of the Chief of Chaplains,1946), 6.

[29] George Washington quoted in Jared Sparks, ed., *The Writings of George Washington,* 12 vols. (Boston: American Stationer's Company, 1837; NY: F. Andrew's, 1834–1847), Vol. III, 456.

[30] George Washington, "First Inaugural Address," 30 April 1789, *The Annals of America,* Vol. 3, 345.

[31] George Washington, "Farewell Address," 19 September 1796, in ibid., 612.

CHAPTER 4—THE REAL THOMAS JEFFERSON

[1] Page Smith, *The Shaping of America: A People's History of the Young Republic* (New York, et al.: McGraw-Hill Book Company, 1980), Vol. 3, 800. [Emphasis mine].

[2] For example, see Paul Johnson, *A History of the American People* (New York: HarperCollinsPublishers, 1997).

[3] For example, see William J. Federer, *America's God and Country: Encyclopedia of Quotations* (St. Louis, Mo.: Amerisearch, Inc., 1994/2000).

[4] For example, see David Barton, *Original Intent* (Aledo, Tex.: WallBuilder Press, 1996).

[5] Mark A. Beliles's Introduction to an updated version of *Thomas Jefferson's Abridgement of the Words of Jesus of Nazareth* (Charlottesville, Va.: The Providence Foundation, 1993).

[6] Ibid., 7.

[7] Walter Grab, *The French Revolution: The Beginning of Modern Democracy* (London: Bracken Books, 1989), 165. Cited in Gary DeMar, *America's Christian History: The Untold Story* (Atlanta: American Vision Publishers, 1993), 89, 91.

[8] Thomas Jefferson to William Canby, 18 September 1813, *Writings*, XIII:377. Quoted in Harnsberger, ed., *Treasury of Presidential Quotations*, 194.

[9] Theologically, that's flawed (to try to teach only the ethics and teachings of Jesus by removing the miracles). Nonetheless, Jefferson's approach was a far cry from the skeptical, anti-Christian tract that skeptics make the Jefferson Bible out to be.

[10] Charles E. Rice, *The Supreme Court and Public Prayer* (New York: Fordham University Press, 1964), 64.

[11] Federer, *America's God and Country*, 326.

[12] Here is Thomas Jefferson's letter to the Danbury Baptist Association, January 1, 1802:

> Gentlemen,— The affectionate sentiments of esteem and approbation which you are so good as to express towards me, on behalf of the Danbury Baptists Association, give me the highest satisfaction.
>
> My duties dictate a faithful and zealous pursuit of my constituents, and in proportion as they are persuaded of my fidelity to those duties, the discharge of them becomes more and more pleasing.
>
> Believing with you that religion is a matter which lies solely between man and his God, that he owes account to none other for faith or his worship, that the legislative powers of government reach actions only, and not opinions, I contemplate with solemn reverence that act of the whole American people which declared that their legislature should "make no law respecting an establishment of religion, or prohibiting the free exercise thereof," thus building a wall of separation between Church and State.
>
> Adhering to this expression of the supreme will of the nation in behalf of the rights of conscience, I shall see with sincere satisfaction the progress of those sentiments which tend to restore man to all his natural rights, convinced he has no natural right in opposition to his social duties.
>
> I reciprocate your kind prayers for the protection and blessing of the common Father and Creator of man, and tender you for yourselves and your religious association, assurances of my high respect and esteem.
>
> Source: Bruce Frohnen, *The American Republic: Primary Sources* (Indianapolis: Liberty Fund, 2002), 88.

[13] Gaillard Hunt, ed., *Writings of James Madison*, 9 vols. (N.Y.: G. P. Putnam's Sons, 1900–1910), Vol. 5, 132, 176.

[14] *Everson vs. Board of Education of Ewing*, 330 US 1 (1947) <http://www.supremecourtus.gov/opinions>

[15] Frohnen, ed., *The American Republic*, 349.

[16] William Rehnquist's dissent in the 1985 decision, *Wallace v. Jaffre*. Reprinted as a Special Supplement to *The Journal of the American Center for Law and Justice*, Virginia Beach, Va.

[17] Beliles's Introduction to an updated version of *Thomas Jefferson's Abridgement of the Words of Jesus of Nazareth*, 11.

CHAPTER 5—LIBERTY OR LICENSE?

[1] Billy Graham, "The Hope for America," upon receipt of the U.S. Congressional Gold Medal, 2 May 1996, in Federer, "American Quotations," in Federer, *Library of Classics*.

[2] Charles Hummel, *Becoming Free* (Downers Grove, Ill.: IVP, 1973), 10. A booklet.

[3] John Adams, "To the Officers of the First Brigade of the Third Division of the Militia of Massachusetts," 11 October 1798, quoted in William J. Bennett, ed., *Our Sacred Honor: Words of Advice from the Founders in Stories, Letters, Poems, and Speeches* (Nashville, Tenn.: Broadman & Holman Publishers, 1997), 370.

[4] James Madison, Virginia Ratifying Convention, 1788, quoted in Os Guinness, *The Great Experiment* (Colorado Springs: NavPress, 2001), 152.

[5] George Washington, "Farewell Address," 1796, *The Annals of America*, Vol. 3, 612.

[6] Michael Kammen, ed., *The Origins of the American Constitution: A Documentary History* (New York: Penguin Books, 1986), ix.

[7] Donald S. Lutz, *The Origins of American Constitutionalism* (Baton Rouge: Louisiana State University Press, 1988), 85. [Emphasis his].

[8] Ibid., 86.

[9] DeMar, *America's Christian History*, 1993 version, 58.

[10] Hummel, *Becoming Free*, 8.

[11] Ibid., 21.

[12] Gene Edward Veith, "Sweden's Shame: Liberal Sweden, Supposedly a Land of Tolerance, Is About to Make Criticism of Homosexuality a Crime," *World*, 10 August 2002, 12.

[13] John Train, "The Lonely Voice of Alexander Solzhenitsyn," *Wall Street Journal*, 23 June 1983, in Franky Schaeffer, *Bad News for Modern Man: An Agenda for Christian Activism* (Westchester, Ill.: Crossway Books, 1984), Appendix 1, 148.

[14] Paul Kurtz, ed., *Humanist Manifestos I & II* (Buffalo, N.Y.: Prometheus Books, 1981).

15 "Update," *Signs of the Times* (Nampa, Idaho: Pacific Press), January 1987, 6.
16 Ibid.
17 Please note that if you or anyone you know or love is trapped in the vice of addiction to pornography of any kind, we suggest you contact Focus on the Family (719) 531-3400, or Esther Ministries (662) 342-1112, for anonymous, Christ-centered counseling.
18 Cheryl Wetzstein, "Abortion Decline Seen Through 1999," *The Washington Times,* 4 December 2002.
19 Federer, *America's God and Country,* 15.

CHAPTER 6—WHOSE VERSION OF TOLERANCE?

1 Mortimer J. Adler, ed., *The Great Ideas: A Syntopicon of Great Books of the Western World* (Chicago et al: Encyclopedia Britannica, Inc., 1952), Vol. 1, 543. Note: Robert Maynard Hutchins was the editor-in-chief of *The Great Books of the Western World,* for which *The Great Ideas* served as the introduction.
2 George W. Cornell, "Rules of Religion Changing, at Least for Some Americans," *Sun-Sentinel,* 21 September 1991, 7D.
3 Paul Johnson, *Modern Times: From the Twenties to the Nineties* (New York: HarperCollins, 1991), 4.
4 Quoted in Haven Bradford Gow, "Moral Relativism," *Populist Observer,* January 1993, 14.
5 Media Research Center Cybertalert, 2:00 P.M. EST, Wednesday 31 October 2001 (Vol. Six; No. 171): <http://www.mediaresearch.org/mainsearch/search.html>
6 Kathryn Jean Lopez, "Bloomberg's Gift: Mandatory Abortion Training Arrives in NYC Public Hospitals," *National Review Online,* 1 July 2002, 1:00 P.M.
7 Josh McDowell and Bob Hostetler, *The New Tolerance* (Wheaton, Ill.: Tyndale House Publishers, Inc., 1998), 27.
8 Ibid., 26–27.
9 Ibid., 32.
10 If you would like information on how to be freed from homosexuality and lesbianism through the power of Jesus Christ, please call (407) 599-6872 or visit www.exodusnorthamerica.org.
11 Reggie Rivers, "Self-Centered, Self-Righteous? Lions Might Fix That," *RockyTalk,* Denver, Co., 4 August 1998.

CHAPTER 7—AS THE FAMILY GOES...

1 Daniel Webster, remarks upon completion of the Bunker Hill Monument, 17 June 1843, Carruth and Ehrlich, eds., *The Harper Book of American Quotations,* 586.

[2] Betty Friedan, *The Feminine Mystique* (New York: Dell Publishing Co., Inc., 1963/1977), 325.

[3] Ibid., 294.

[4] Ibid., 325.

[5] Joan Beck, "Women Can't Have It All Until Workplaces Adjust," *Fort Lauderdale News,* 6 August 1986.

[6] Betty Friedan quoted in *Fort Lauderdale News,* 17 November 1985.

[7] William Ross Wallace, "The Hand That Rocks the Cradle," quoted in Carruth and Ehrlich, eds. *The Harper Book of American Quotations,* 606.

[8] William J. Johnson, *Abraham Lincoln the Christian* (New York et al: The Abingdon Press, 1913), 24.

[9] Paul Lee Tan, *Encyclopedia of 7,700 Illustrations: Signs of the Times* (Rockville, Md.: Assurance Publishers, 1984), 845.

[10] Paraphrase of Enrico Caruso in the movie, *The Great Caruso* (MGM, 1951).

[11] Mitchell Landsberg and John L. Mitchell, "In Gang's Territory, a Weary Hope," *Los Angeles Times,* 5 December 2002 <http://www.streetgangs.com/topics/2002/120502territory.html>

[12] Wade Horn and Andrew Bush, "Fathers, Marriage, and Welfare Reform," Hudson Institute Executive Briefing <http://patriot.net/~crouch/adr/kids.html>

[13] Transcript from a Coral Ridge Ministries TV interview with Anthony Falzarano, a former homosexual, on location in Washington, D.C., 19 August 1998. See also "Health Implications Associated with Homosexuality" from the Medical Institute for Sexual Health, Austin, Tex..

[14] *Ben Franklin's Wit & Wisdom* (based on *Poor Richard's Almanack*), (Mount Vernon, N.Y.: Peter Pauper Press, undated), 48.

CHAPTER 8—LIFE: AN INALIENABLE RIGHT

[1] Transcript from a Coral Ridge Ministries TV interview with Carol Everett on location in Dallas, Tex., 2 April 1992.

[2] Ibid.

[3] Frohnen, *The American Republic,* 189.

[4] Dr. Malcolm Watts, "A New Ethic for Medicine and Society," *California Medicine* 113 (September 1970), 67–68. Quoted in William Brennan, *The Abortion Holocaust: Today's Final Solution* (St. Louis, Mo.: Landmark Press, 1983), 106–107.

[5] Bernard N. Nathanson quoted in Ibid., 13.

[6] For example, see Amy Sobie and David C. Reardon, Ph.D., "Who's Making the Choice? Women's Heightened Vulnerability During a Crisis Pregnancy" <http://www.afterabortion.org/PAR/V8/n1/crisistheory.html>

[7] Dr. Phillip G. Ney, "Infant Abortion and Child Abuse: Cause and Effect," in *The Psychological Aspects of Abortion,* 1979, cited by Diane Dew in an

article called "The Myth of Abuse of Unwanted Children," in *The Standard*, 1992, available online at: <http://dianedew.com/myth.htm>

8 Jerry Seper, "FBI Report Shows Rise in Crime Rate," *Washington Times, National Weekly Edition*, 4–10 November 2002, 11.

9 Ibid.

10 Mother Teresa, "Whatsoever You Do . . .", Speech to the National Prayer Breakfast, Washington, D.C., 3 February 1994, <http:www.priestsforlife.org/brochures/mtspeech.html>

11 Norma McCorvey with Gary Thomas, *Won by Love* (Nashville: Thomas Nelson, Inc., 1997), 52.

12 Ibid., 78.

13 Ibid., 79.

14 Ibid., 83.

15 Ibid., 113.

16 Transcript from a Coral Ridge Ministries TV interview with George Gallup Jr., on location in Princeton, N.J., 5 August 1999.

17 Carol Everett with Jack Shaw, *Blood Money: Getting Rich off a Woman's Right to Choose* (Sisters, Oreg.: Multnomah Press, 1992), 209–210.

CHAPTER 9—THE DUMBING DOWN OF AMERICA

1 "Robert Ressler: The Man Who Lives With Monsters," *Mugshots*, Court TV, 29 January 2001.

2 John J. Dunphy, "A Religion for a New Age," *The Humanist* (January/February 1983), 26.

3 Tucker Carlson, "That's Outrageous: Reading, Cheating and 'Rithmetic" *Reader's Digest*, July 2002, 39.

4 Ibid.

5 Dr. David C. Gibbs Jr., *The Legal Alert* (Seminole, Fla.: Christian Law Association, December 2002).

6 "Education Briefs," *Education Reporter* (Washington, D.C.: Eagle Forum, September 2002).

7 Ibid., November 2002.

8 Ibid.

9 Ellen Sorkin, "NEA Delivers History Lesson," *The Washington Times*, 9 September 2002.

10 "Education Briefs," *Education Reporter*, November 2002.

11 Ibid.

12 Allen Quist, *Fed Ed: The New Federal Curriculum and How It's Being Enforced* (St. Paul, Minn.: The Maple River Education Coalition, 2002), 19.

13 The book of standards can be purchased for $12 plus 10 percent for postage and handling from Center for Civic Education, 5146 Douglas Fir Road, Calabasas, Calif. 61302-1467.

[14] Lisa Kozleski, "New Math Program a Cause for Complaint," *Morning Call*, Allentown, Pa., 2002.

[15] Quist, *Fed Ed*, 15.

[16] Ibid., 43.

[17] Ibid., 68.

[18] Ibid., 69.

[19] Ibid., 27.

[20] Julie M. Quist, "Perverting the SAT," Maple River Education Coalition, 5 July 2002.

[21] "Education Briefs," *Education Reporter*, October 2002.

[22] "Average test scores at Christian schools show students at all grade levels are at least one year and eight months above national norms, according to Stanford Achievement Tests, which administers the national Scholastic Aptitude Tests." Source: David J. Dent, "African-Americans Turning to Christian Academies," *New York Times* Magazine, 4 August 1996. Also, *Time* Magazine reports: "We know the average SAT score for home schoolers in 2000 was 1100, compared with 1019 for the general population. And a large study by University of Maryland education researcher Lawrence Rudner showed that the average home schooler scored in the 75th percentile on the Iowa Test of Basic Skills; the 50th percentile marked the national average." Steve Barenes et al, "Home Sweet School," *Time*, 21 August 2001.

CHAPTER 10—IS GAMBLING A SIN?

[1] Transcript from a Coral Ridge Ministries TV interview with a security guard from a major Atlantic City casino, conducted with the guest's identity hidden, on location in nearby Ocean City, N.J., 4 February 1995.

[2] Dr. James Dobson, Focus on the Family Newsletter, Colorado Springs, Colo., July 1999.

[3] John Piper, "Wages from Sin," *World*, Vol. 18, No. 1, 11 January 2003.

[4] Stuart Winston and Harriet Harris, *Nation of Gamblers: America's Billion-Dollar-a-Day Habit* (Englewood Cliffs, N.J.: Prentice-Hall, Inc., 1984), 105.

[5] Tom Heymann, *The Unofficial U.S. Census* (New York: Fawcett Columbine, 1991), 69.

[6] "Gambling on a Way to Trim Taxes," *Time*, 28 May 1984, 42.

[7] Ovid Demaris, "Casino Gambling Is a Bad Bet," *Parade*, 11 May 1986.

[8] Ibid.

[9] Ibid.

[10] William Webster quoted in John Eidsmoe, *Legalized Gambling: America's Bad Bet* (Lafayette, La.: Huntington House Publishers, 1994), 102–103.

[11] Transcript from a Coral Ridge Ministries TV interview with John Kindt, 20 February 1995.

12 Ron Reno, "Guess Who Stopped the Gambling Juggernaut?" *Citizen*, 1999, 2. <<http://www/family.org/cforum/citizenmag/features/a0008685.html]>

13 "Alabama Rejects Governor's Plan for a Lottery," Associated Press, 13 October, 1999.

14 Reno, "Guess Who Stopped the Gambling Juggernaut?," 1.

15 Tom Grey remark on "Easy Money," *Frontline*, PBS <http://www.pbs.org/wgbh/pages/frontline/shows/gamble/interviews/grey.html>

CHAPTER 11—CHRISTIANITY AND THE MEDIA

1 Michael Novak, "The Revolt Against Our Public Culture," *National Review*, 4 May 1984, 48.

2 "Living in Truly Tasteless Times," *Ladies' Home Journal*, November 1984, 130, 184.

3 Laurie Goodstein, "As Attacks' Impact Recedes, a Return to Religion as Usual," *New York Times*, 26 November 2001. <http://www/nytimes.com/2001/11/26/national/26FAIT.html?ex=10074420 00&en=9b85baa5fd0bbff5&ei=5040&partner=MOREOVER> cited at: http://www.religioustolerance.org/rel_rate.htm>

4 Barbara Reynolds, "Religion Is Greatest Story Ever Missed," *USA Today*, 16 March 1990, 13.

5 Richard N. Ostling, "In So Many Gods We Trust," *Time*, 30 January 1995, 72.

6 Greg Hoadley, "Fewer Homosexuals on Prime Time This New TV Season," <http://www.recolaimamerica.org/PAGES/NEWS/newspage.asp?story=1023> based on "GLAAD: Gay Presence on Network TV Down," *Reuters News Service*, 17 September 2002.

7 Robert T. Michael, John H. Gagnon, Edward O. Laumann, and Gina Kolata, *Sex in America: A Definitive Survey* (Boston et al.: Little, Brown and Company, 1994), 176.

8 Bernard Goldberg, *Bias: A CBS Insider Exposes How the Media Distort the News* (Washington, D.C.: Regnery Publishing, Inc., 2002), 215. (The original guest editorial by Bernard Goldberg appeared in the *Wall Street Journal*, 13 February 1996.)

9 Ibid., 27.

10 Ibid., 28.

11 S. Robert Lichter, Linda S. Lichter, and Stanley Rothman, with the assistance of Daniel Amundson, *Prime Time: How TV Portrays American Culture* (Washington, D.C.: Regnery Publishing, Inc., 1994), 422–424.

12 Goodstein, "As Attacks' Impact Recedes, a Return to Religion as Usual."

13 Max Frankel quoted in "For the Record," *National Review*, 21 February 2000.

14 Goldberg, *Bias*, 123.

15 Frank Lallie, "Face to Face with Peter Jennings, Newsman on the Heartland," *Reader's Digest*, October 2002, 101.

[16] Ibid., 104–105.
[17] Goldberg, *Bias*, 3.
[18] Segment on Jesse Dirkheising, *The Coral Ridge Hour*, 12 March 2000.
[19] *The British Medical Journal* as quoted in *The Pastor's Weekly Briefing* (Colorado Springs, Colo.: Focus on the Family, 9 September 2002).
[20] Press Release from the Family Research Council, Washington D.C., 28 February 2002.
[21] A national survey taken by the Independent Sector, a nonprofit coalition as quoted in *The Pastor's Weekly Briefing* (Colorado Springs, Colo.: Focus on the Family, 9 November 2001).
[22] Ibid., 16 November 2001.
[23] Ibid., 5 October 2002.
[24] Goldberg, *Bias*, 13.
[25] Ibid., 57.
[26] Syndicated columnist Mary McGrory, *Washington Post*, 22 April 1999.
[27] Marvin Olasky, "Watch Out, Left, Here Comes Political Multiculturalism: The Legs of Journalistic Spectrumoloists—Those Who Classify Candidates As 'Left' or 'Right'—Are Getting Shaky," *World* 18 May 02, 7.
[28] Jake Tapper, <http://www.salon.com>, 24 January 2000.
[29] Mike Licona, *Cross-Examined* (Virginia Beach, Va.: TruthQuest Publishers, 1998).
[30] Finalist Award with the New York Festivals (Film & Television), 2001, Angel Award 2001, Gold Award from the Aurora Awards 2002. "Who Is This Jesus?" featured Dean Jones as the co-host.
[31] Richard N. Ostling, AP Religion Writer, "Conservatives Tackle New Testament Debate," Associated Press, 2 January 2002, 11:26 EST.
[32] See P. Cameron, W. Playfair, and S. Wellum, "The Longevity of Homosexuals: Before and After the AIDS Epidemic," *Omega Journal of Death and Dying*, 29 (3), 1994, 249–272. This one studied obituaries of men in gay papers and found the average death from AIDS was at age 39 and from all causes, 42.
[33] Robert H. Knight, quoted in a review of his book, *The Age of Consent*. Robert Stacy McCain, "Author Throws the Book at Insidious Evils of Relativism," *The Washington Times, National Weekly Edition*, 20–26 July 1998, 25.
[34] "Follow the Money: Moviegoers Favor Movies with Strong Moral Content; New Trend May Mean the End to Hollywood Sleaze." *Movieguide* September B/October A, 2002, 5.
[35] Quoted in Jack Nelson, *Terror in the Night: The Klan's Campaign Against the Jews* (New York et al.: Simon & Schuster, 1993), 9.
[36] Michelle Malkin, "The Rise of Religious Radio" (Los Angeles: Creators Syndicate, Inc., 9 October 2002).

CHAPTER 12—"THE FASTEST-GROWING RELIGION IN AMERICA?"

[1] Shaikh Muhammad as-Saleh Al-'Uthaimin, translated by Dr. Maneh Al-Johani, *The Muslim's Belief* (North Riyadh, Saudi Arabia: The Cooperative Office for Call, Guidance and Edification of Expatriates, 1998), 22.

[2] Bancroft, *History of the United States of America*, Vol. I, 178.

[3] Remarks of Rabbi Daniel Lapin in D. James Kennedy, "What If Jesus Had Never Been Born?" (Ft. Lauderdale, Fla.: Coral Ridge Ministries TV, 25 December 2002), a television special.

[4] Volume 1, page 22, as cited in Robert Morey's "An Analysis of the Hadith," The Hadith, published by Faith Defenders, P.O. Box 7447, Orange, Calif. 92863.

[5] Vol. 1, p. l., as cited in Morey's "An Analysis of the Hadith."

[6] Thomas Arnold, *Sermons on the Christian Life: Its Hopes, Its Fears, Its Close*, sixth edition (London: T. Fellowes, 1859), 324.

[7] Jerry Seper, "'Advance Man' Got Cash from Saudis," *Washington Times, National Weekly Edition*, 2–8 December 2002, 1.

[8] Transcript from a Coral Ridge Ministries TV interview with Eric Reeves on location in Northampton, Mass., 10 April 2002.

[9] Don Feder, *Who's Afraid of the Religious Right?* (Washington, D.C.: Regnery Publishing, Inc., 1996), 222–225.

[10] For example, see "Maluku Church Sends Christmas SOS to Kofi Annan," Agence France-Presse, 23 December 2000. Haris Syamaun, "Reports: Armed Muslim gangs forcing Christians to convert," Associated Press, 22 December 2000. "Governor admits forced Islamization in Indonesia's Maluku islands," Agence France-Presse, 21 December 2000. For more details and other examples, please see http://www.freedomnow.com.

[11] Transcript from a Coral Ridge Ministries TV interview with Nina Shea, 25 September 1997.

[12] Transcript of a Coral Ridge Ministries TV interview with Nina Shea on location in Washington, D.C., 16 January 1996.

[13] Palestinian Media Watch Bulletin, 14 April 2002. <http://www.pmw.org.il>

[14] Betsy Pisik, "Suicide Bombers Say They Are Obeying 'a Holy Duty' to Kill" *Washington Times, National Weekly Edition*, 27 May–2 June 2002, 25.

[15] Bill O'Reilly, "Pray for Peace but Polish the Weapons," *Washington Times: National Weekly Edition*, 22–28 April 2002, 35.

[16] *Truths That Transform* broadcast, 11 December 2002 (Coral Ridge Ministries Radio).

[17] Kathleen Parker, "Yo, Muhammad, It Was a Joke!" <http:www.townhall.com/columnists/kathleenparker/kp20030108.shtml>

[18] Michael Elliott, "Islam's Prophet Motive" *Time*, 23 December 2002.

[19] Daniel Pipes, "Become a Muslim Warrior," *Jerusalem Post*, 2 July 2002. See also Ellen Sorokin, "California School Sued over Islamic Drills," *Washington Times*, 10 July 2002.

CHAPTER 13—RELIGION WITHOUT REGENERATION?

[1] Horatio G. Spafford, "It Is Well with My Soul," 1873, *Hymns for the Living Church*, hymn 401.

[2] The Journal of John Wesley, 14 May 14, 1738 entry: <http://www.everyday-counselor.com/archives/sh/wesley6.htm.>

[3] <http://www/kprbc.org.sg/cw/CW_Nov12_2000.html.> (January 2003).

[4] "New England ABC," *New England Primer*, quoted in *The Annals of America*, Vol. 1, 276.

[5] *Hymns for the Living Church*, hymn# 232.

[6] One book I highly recommend to help you study the Bible for yourself is Alan M. Stibbs, ed., *Search the Scriptures* (Downers Grove, Ill.: IVP, 1949, 1974).

CHAPTER 14—ONE NATION UNDER GOD?

[1] "Lawmakers Blast Pledge Ruling," 27 June 2002, Posted: 1:11 PM EDT, <http://www.cnn.com/LAW CENTER>

[2] Ibid.

[3] Ibid.

[4] Ibid.

[5] *Holy Trinity Church v. United States*, 1892, quoted in Rice, *The Supreme Court and Public Prayer*, 58.

[6] John Quincy Adams, quoted in Verna Hall, ed., *The Christian History of the Constitution of the United States of America* (San Francisco: Foundation for American Christian Education, 1960/1993), 372.

[7] Benjamin Hart, "The Wall That Protestantism Built: The Religious Reasons for the Separation of Church and State," *Policy Review* (Washington, D.C.: Heritage Foundation, Fall 1988), 44.

[8] Charles Hodge, *Systematic Theology*, 1871 (reprinted Grand Rapids, Mich.: Wm. B. Eerdmans Publishing Co., 1975), 343.

[9] George Washington to the General Assembly of the Presbyterian Church, 1789, quoted in Guinness, *The Great Experiment*, 130.

[10] George Washington wrote, "I now make it my earnest prayer that God would have you, and the State over which you preside, in His holy protection . . . that He would most graciously be pleased to dispose us all to do justice, to love mercy, and to demean ourselves with that charity, humility, and pacific temper of mind, which were the characteristics of the Divine Author of our blessed religion, and without an humble imitation of whose example in these things, we can never hope to be a happy nation." Quoted in Federer, *America's God and Country*, 646.

[11] Robert C. Winthrop quoted in Gary DeMar, *America's Christian History*, 58.

[12] Samuel Adams, letter to his cousin, Vice President John Adams, 4 October 1790, quoted in Hall, ed., *Christian History of the Constitution of the United States of America*, IV.

[13] John Adams, letter to wife, Abigail, 7 September 1774, quoted in Gary DeMar, *God and Government: A Biblical and Historical Study* (Atlanta, Ga.: American Vision Press, 1982), Vol. I, 108.

[14] John Adams, letter to wife, Abigail, 7 September 1774, from Charles Francis Adams, ed., *Letters of John Adams: Addressed to His Wife* (Boston: Charles C. Little and James Brown, 1841), Vol. I, pp. 23–24, quoted in Federer, *America's God and Country*, 7.

[15] "Articles of Confederation" quoted in Frohnen, ed., *The American Republic*, 204.

[16] Donald S. Lutz, *The Origins of American Constitutionalism* (Baton Rouge: Louisiana State University Press, 1988), 7.

[17] *Annals of the Congress of the United States: First Congress* (Washington, D.C.: Gales & Seaton, 1834), Vol. I, 729, 731.

[18] Northwest Ordinance, Article III in *The Annals of America*, Vol. 3, 194–195.

[19] Treaty of Paris, 1783, quoted in Gary DeMar, *America's Christian History*, 83.

[20] Rice, *The Supreme Court and Public Prayer*, 167.

[21] Ibid., 169.

[22] Ibid., 172.

[23] The Constitution of Vermont, 1777, in *The Annals of America*, Vol. 2, 483.

[24] The Constitution of Vermont, 1793, in Rice, *The Supreme Court and Public Prayer*, 175.

[25] Federer, *America's God and Country*, 351.

[26] J. Michael Sharman, ed., *Faith of the Fathers: Religion and Matters of Faith Contained in the Presidents' Inaugural Addresses from George Washington to Bill Clinton* (Culpeper, Va.: Victory Publishing, 1995), 44.

[27] Ibid., 82.

[28] Ibid., 121.

[29] John Eidsmoe, *Christianity and the Constitution: The Faith of our Founding Fathers* (Grand Rapids, Mich.: Baker Book House, 1987), 51.

[30] Please read Thomas Paine's *Common Sense* for yourself to see the biblical allusions. See Frohnen, *The American Republic*, 179–188. For example, here are a few sentences from it: "But where, say some, is the king of America? I'll tell you, friend, he reigns above, and doth not make havoc of mankind like the royal brute of Great Britain. Yet that we may not appear to be defective even in earthly honors, let a day be solemnly set apart for proclaiming the charter; let it be brought forth placed on the divine law, the Word of God; let a crown be placed thereon, by which the world may know, that so far as we approve of monarchy, that in America the law is king." (Frohnen, *The American Republic*, 188.).

[31] Rice, *The Supreme Court and Public Prayer*, 48.

[32] Federer, *America's God and Country*, 436.

CHAPTER 15—"IF MY PEOPLE..."

1 Paul Harvey, "Does God Ever Know!," Paul Harvey Products, Inc., Distributed by Creators Syndicate, Inc., Los Angeles, 1996.
2 Marion Mills Miller, ed., *Life and Works of Abraham Lincoln,* Centenary Edition. In Nine Volumes (New York: The Current Literature Publishing Co., 1907), Vol. 6, 156–157.
3 C. S. Lewis, *Mere Christianity* (New York: MacMillan, 1960), 109.
4 Miller, ed., *Life and Works of Abraham Lincoln,* Vol. VI, 156.
5 "A Movement Has Begun," Brochure from the Concerts of Prayer International, Minneapolis, Minn., undated.
6 Tom Raum, "Bush Asks Faith-Broadcasters for Help," Associated Press, 10 February 2003, Posted 2:33 P.M.

CHAPTER 16—WHAT IF AMERICA WERE A CHRISTIAN NATION AGAIN?

1 William Wirt Henry, ed., *Patrick Henry: Life, Correspondence and Speeches* (New York: Charles Scribner's Sons, 1891), Vol. II, 631.
2 *The Annals of America,* Vol. 2, 323.
3 John Eidsmoe, *God and Caesar: Biblical Faith and Political Action* (Westchester, Ill.: Crossway Books, 1984), 68.
4 Henry Hyde, *For Every Idle Silence* (Ann Arbor, Mich.: Servant Books, 1985), 46.
5 D. James Kennedy, "What If Jesus Had Never Been Born?" television special.
6 Transcript of a Coral Ridge Ministries TV interview with Rabbi Daniel Lapin, 17 May 2001.
7 Ibid.
8 Ibid.
9 For your complimentary copy of *101 Ways to Reclaim America* (Ft. Lauderdale: Center for Reclaiming America, Coral Ridge Ministries, 2000), simply write to me: D. James Kennedy, Box 40, Ft. Lauderdale, FL 33302.
10 *Hymns for the Living Church,* hymn #58.
11 *Washington Times: National Weekly Edition,* 21–27 October 2002, 6.
12 That number comes from J. Thomas Smith, president of America 21, whose goal is to turn out Christian voters, and is cited in Ibid.
13 Harry F. Rosenthal, Associated Press, 7 November 1996, 1:16 EST.
14 Gary L. Bauer, *Our Hopes, Our Dreams* (Colorado Springs, Colo.: Focus on the Family Publishing, 1996), 3–5.

★ ★ ★ ★ ★

INDEX

DATE DUE

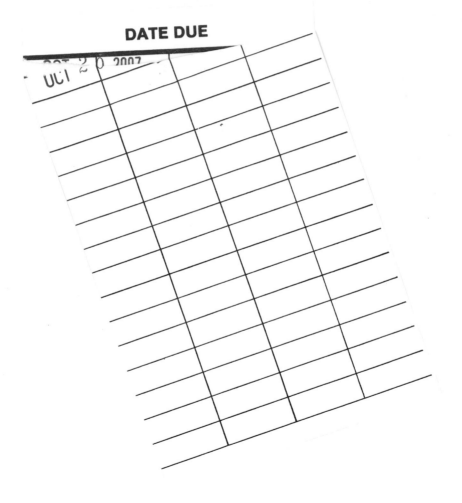

OCT 2 0 2007